To Hubert Gray
who is largely responsible
for this book

READ THIS!

It's frightening how some people, though adept at walking and scrambling, have none of the mountain sense usually learned through decades of mountain wandering, problem solving and familiarity with mountains in all weather.

Learn to read topo maps and be able to find a grid reference. Turn back if it looks too hard for you, if you can't handle loose rock, if the river is too high, if you can't hack a 10-hour day, or if the routefinding is out of your league. Turn back from a summit or ridge if a thunderstorm is approaching or if conditions are made dangerous by rain, snow and ice. At *all times use your own judgement.* The author and publisher are not responsible if you have a horrible day or you get yourself into a fix.

Gillean Daffern's

KANANASKIS
COUNTRY trail guide

Third Edition   Volume 1

Canadian Cataloguing in Publication Data

Daffern, Gillean, 1938-
  Kananaskis Country trail guide

  Previous ed. has title: Kananaskis Country: a guide to
  hiking, skiing, equestrian & bike trails.
  Includes index.
  ISBN 0-921102-31-3 (v.1)

  1. Hiking--Alberta--Kananaskis Country--Guidebooks. 2.
Trails--Alberta--Kananaskis Country--Guidebooks. 3.
Kananaskis Country (Alta.)--Guidebooks. I.Title. II. Title:
Kananaskis Country: a guide to hiking.
GV199.44.C22K36 1995   917.123'32043   C95-910504-2

ISBN 0-921102-31-3

The publisher gratefully acknowledges the
assistance provided by the Alberta
Foundation for the Arts and by the federal
Department of Canadian Heritage.

COMMITTED TO THE DEVELOPMENT OF CULTURE AND THE ARTS

Copyright © 1996 Gillean Daffern
4th printing 2000

**Published by
Rocky Mountain Books
#4 Spruce Centre SW
RMB Calgary, Alberta T3C 3B3**

CONTENTS

ACKNOWLEDGEMENTS

The following people have been extremely helpful and supportive: Don Cockerton (as always), Brooke Melchin, Harry Connolly, Eric Kuhn, Brian Godwin, Len Wilton, Roger Myer, Bill Baxter, Bob Johnson, Jack Paterson, Terry Beck, Richard & Louise Guy, Brian Carter, Dan Verall, Ken Pawson. All photos are by the author unless credited otherwise. Thank you Clive Cordery, Ruthie Oltmann and especially Alf Skrastins, who gives me free rein with his extensive photo collection in the effort to get the best photos possible.

Thanks also to all the readers who write in with suggestions and to our long suffering friends Pete and Gill Ford, and Norm and Fran Dymond.

Guides to Kananaskis Country

Kananaskis Country Ski Trails
by Gillean Daffern

Canmore & Kananaskis Country [#1 in series Short Walks for Inquiring Minds]
by Gillean Daffern

Scrambles in the Canadian Rockies
by Alan Kane

Backcountry Biking in the Canadian Rockies by Doug Eastcott & Gerhardt Lepp

PHOTO CAPTIONS
Front cover: Second Memorial Lake (#49).

Page 1: Good friends.

Title Page: Northover Ridge (#107). Looking back along the ridge to Mt. Northover (left page, top centre). The treacherous false ridge can be seen heading out of the photo at top left. To far right is the white fang of Mt. Joffre rising above Warrior Mountain. Photo Alf Skrastins.

Contents page: Descending from North Kananaskis Pass to Maude Lake (#101). In the background is Beatty Glacier. Photo Alf Skrastins.

Opposite: Upper Headwall Lake (#84). At the head of the valley is The Fortress, showing the ascent route up the left-hand ridge (#85).

Back cover: Northover Ridge (#107). Photo Alf Skrastins.

PREFACE TO THIRD EDITION

Two big changes. First, all ski trails are out and in a book of their own "Kananaskis Country Ski Trails". If you want to walk the ski trails I suggest you use the maps from that book. Likewise, all interpretive trails and very short walks can be found in "Short Walks for Inquiring Minds #1, Canmore and Kananaskis Country". This is to make way for a spate of new hikes, including a further sampling of ridge walks and easy ascents available to hikers.

Second, the guide has been split into two volumes. Volume 1 covers Canmore and the Bow Valley, Kananaskis Valley, Spray/Smith-Dorrien and Peter Lougheed Provincial Park. Also included is the adjoining area of The Ghost and the core area of Elk Lakes Provincial Park in B.C. which is usually accessed from Peter Lougheed Provincial Park. Volume 2 takes in the rest: the Highwood, the upper Oldman and Livingstone, the Sheep River, the Elbow and the Jumpingpound areas.

Between editions, 'Kananaskis Provincial Park' has become Peter Lougheed Provincial Park, a controversial name change instigated by Don Getty's government. Kananaskis Village has been finished, highways have been rebuilt, new parking lots put in, some day-use areas removed. Many trails have been refined, even completely realigned. Special mention should be made of the 100-year flood in the spring of 1995, which wiped out trails and bridges and rearranged creekbeds. As we go to press, repairs are still underway.

In the last few years sections of equestrian-hiker trails have reached the proportion of mud baths. This mainly affects trails described in Volume 2. In these days of severe cutbacks, Kananaskis Country is asking for the public's help through either donations or through their 'Adopt a Trail Program', which gives groups and clubs a chance to look after their favourite trail. For more details contact Ron Chamney (403-678-5508) at the Head Office in Canmore.

KANANASKIS COUNTRY

THE NAME

It's kind of fun listening to Japanese tourists pronounce the name 'Kananaskis'. The strange name dates back to 1858 when explorer John Palliser named the pass he was about to cross 'Kananaskis', "after the name of an Indian, of whom there is a legend, giving an account of his most wonderful recovery from the blow of an axe which had stunned but had failed to kill him, and the river which flows through this gorge also bears his name". Possibly the Indian in question was the great Cree Koominakoos who lost an eye and part of his scalp in a battle with the Blackfoot in the Willow Creek area, but made a miraculous recovery and showed up at Fort Edmonton some weeks later "ready to take to the warpath again".

THE CONCEPT

Today, the Kananaskis Passes, Kananaskis Lakes and the Kananaskis River form the heart of Kananaskis Country (or K Country as it is more commonly called), a provincial recreation area established October 7th, 1977 to "alleviate congestion in National Parks, and to provide greater recreation opportunities for Albertans".

Although former Alberta Premier Peter Lougheed certainly deserves credit, it was actually Clarence Copithorne, rancher and MLA for Banff-Cochrane and Minister of Highways, who got the ball rolling with the reconstruction of Highway 40—the future Kananaskis Trail. Copithorne's vision for the Kananaskis Valley was one of strenuous physical outdoor activity accessible from a good road but with minimal services. As we all know, that simple idea turned into grand plan called Kananaskis Country, encompassing a lot more country (over 4000 square hectares) and a lot more development. Namely: interpretive centres, picnic areas, campgrounds, one alpine village, two Olympic venues, golf courses, riverbeds refashioned for competition and trails built for every conceivable sport.

LOCATION

K Country is located on the eastern slopes of the Canadian Rockies, west and south of the Olympic city of Calgary, Alberta. From the city outskirts the eastern boundary is only a 20-minute drive away.

The west boundary adjoins Banff National Park, then runs down the Continental Divide. The northern boundary is delineated by the Trans-Canada Highway and the fringe communities of Exshaw, Dead Man Flat and Canmore. The eastern boundary coincides neatly with the Bow-Crow Forest reserve boundary, while the southern boundary is marked by Highway 732 (Johnson Creek Trail).

GETTING THERE

Calgary is served by major airlines, several bus companies and by train from the east. Greyhound buses run west along the Trans-Canada Highway to Canmore, but stops are infrequent. That's it as far as public transportation goes. You need a car.

The core area, Kananaskis Valley and Peter Lougheed Provincial Park, is usually accessed from the Trans-Canada Highway via Highway 40. The Elbow, Sheep, Highwood, Livingstone and Oldman areas are reached from the east via the border towns of Bragg Creek, Turner Valley and Longview.

SEASONAL ROAD CLOSURES AFFECTING VOLUME 1

December 1 to June 15. Kananaskis Trail (Hwy. 40) is closed between Kananaskis Lakes Trail and Highwood Junction. Biking is allowed and cyclists can enjoy the traffic-free road once the snow has melted.

December 1 to April 30. Powderface Trail south of Dawson day-use area.

KANANASKIS COUNTRY

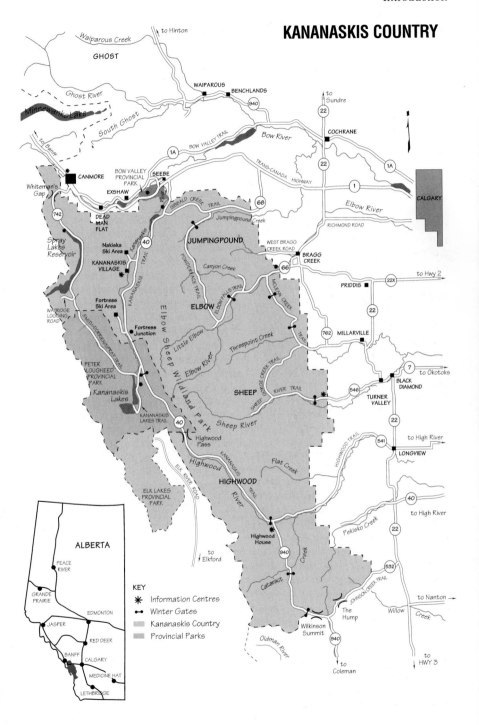

KEY

* Information Centres
• Winter Gates
▓ Kananaskis Country
▓ Provincial Parks

WHAT TO EXPECT

The photo on the title page gives you a clue. The fact is, all you people carrying on into Banff Park and paying outrageous entrance fees, the trails in the Parks are nowhere near as exciting as the trails in K Country.

In the west the scenery is much the same: high peaks (up to 3449 m), glaciers, waterfalls, alpine meadows, blue-green lakes, boisterous streams, densely-forested valley bottoms. Trails may not be clear of snow until mid July.

Conversely, the friendly eastern foothills are a mosaic of forest and meadow navigable for most of the year. Apart from a few trails in The Ghost, the east is covered in Volume 2, so I'll move on to the third scenery type: the in-between ranges that make up a large area of Volume 1.

The Front Ranges may be lower (up to 3218 m), but rock peaks like the Opals can be spectacular and so are the canyons. Being a rain shadow area, valleys are often arid which makes for easier going. It's mainly here where you'll find easy peaks to climb and grassy ridges to wander over, the Mt. Allan traverse being a prime example.

WEATHER TRENDS

Hiking season starts as early as April in the Bow Valley and The Ghost, and generally ends (in the same areas) by November.

Snow can fall in any month of the year. In the rotten summer of 1992, for instance, snow fell on three consecutive weekends through late July into mid August. Conversely, the summer of 1994 was consistently brilliant with few thunderstorms. For two months the temperature stayed in the mid 30s, leaving me and others who suffer from heat as limp as a dish rag despite the low humidity. Generally, low cloud is not the problem it is in other wetter ranges of the world and navigating by compass is an unusual event. Rain often comes as a good downpour and is often associated with late afternoon thunderstorms that have accounted for a number of fatalities in K Country. If climbing a big peak start early and aim to be off high ground before the afternoon clouds start rolling in. Indian summers (should they occur) through September and October are glorious, bringing sunny stable weather with no thunderstorms, no flies and no flowers, but then you can't have everything.

NATURAL HISTORY IN A NUTSHELL

I urge you to buy the appropriate field guides or Ben Gadd's all-in-one *"Handbook of the Canadian Rockies"*.

Mammals Most commonly seen: elk, moose, Mule deer, Bighorn sheep, coyotes. Less common: wolves, goats, lynx, bobcats, cougars, wolverines. Black bears are found everywhere, while grizzlies are more prevalent along the Continental Divide. Having said that, grizzly sightings regularly close down the Kananaskis Valley bike path. Then there's the usual bevy of beavers, porcupines, ground squirrels, tree squirrels, chipmunks, picas, marmots, muskrats, fishers, martens, ermine and mink. In The Ghost, spotting wild horses is a thrill.

Birds Most common: Whiskey Jacks (the ones that gather around when you stop to eat), Clark's nutcracker, hummingbirds (wear red), bluebirds, ravens, crows, Golden eagles, chickadees, kinglets, warblers, woodpeckers, grouse, ptarmigan, assorted ducks, numerous hawks and falcons (including the Peregrine), dippers in fast running creeks, Great Grey owls.

Fish Trout (Cutthroat, Rainbow, Brown, Bull), Arctic grayling and whitefish. Some lakes are stocked.

Vegetation In the area covered by this book, trees range through fire succession Lodgepole pine and aspen to spruce and fir, with larch at treeline. Balsam poplar grows in arid valley bottoms and is associated with Dryas flats. Nibble on strawberries, raspberries and blackcurrants.

Alpine meadows are sandwiched between forest and rock and coat many ridges constructed of Kootenay strata. For too brief a time they are crammed with flowers.

Overseas visitors will be intoxicated by the gaudy colours of North America's Indian Paintbrush. In windy places, look for Alpine poppies, Golden and Woolly fleabanes and Townsendias. Glacier lilies cover glades near treeline, while a large number of orchids and wintergreens brighten up the forest floor.

HAZARDS & NUISANCES

River crossings Generally, larger creeks and rivers are impassable during spring runoff and after prolonged heavy rain. Schedule river-crossing trips for mid summer on. Caribbean water it is not. If cold water makes you feel sick to your stomach wear neoprene socks.

Bears and other beasts At all times be aware of bears, but particularly in early spring and late fall. A fall coupled with bad weather and a scanty berry crop drives grizzlies to the valley bottoms in search of easier pickings. Should a bear hibernate hungry, be extremely wary the next spring. It's a good idea to phone ahead and find out if there have been any sightings in the area you are going to. Often K Country will close a trail until a bear has moved out of the area. This is where Troy Hurtubise's grizzly suit would come in handy. Weighing in at 68 kg, I'm not sure how one's supposed to walk in it. Made of chain mail, galvanized steel, titanium and high-tech plastic, it comes equipped with TV monitor, air bag, and sensors to monitor your racing heart rate and record stress. Lacking 100,000 dollars, buying a bear repellent is clearly more viable.

In the paranoia over bears we often forget that elk and moose should be given a wide berth, especially in spring when with young and in fall during the mating season when males get very ornery. In the nuisance category, porcupines snack on anything salty like boots and waist straps on packs, so keep them out of reach when camping.

Hunters and Bears Hunting is allowed everywhere except in Peter Lougheed Provincial Park and the Ghost River Wilderness area. September to November is the time to dress in psychedelic shades of orange and pink. Supposedly, Sunday is a safe-day, but I wouldn't bet on it. Apart from the danger of being mistaken for an elk (hunters occasionally kill each other), the other danger occurs when hunters shoot an animal late in the day and after dressing it out leave it lying overnight with the intention of coming back the next day for the meat. Often a grizzly gets there first and woe betide any innocent hiker happening along. K Country grizzlies, apparently, have learned to associate a rifle shot with an easy meal.

Although you may not agree with hunting, it's sometimes useful to chat with hunters who can tell you, for instance, that three grizzlies have been doing a five-day circuit through the hunter's camp and that they left that morning up the same valley you were going up.

Ticks Between about March and mid June ticks are abroad and are found mainly in areas where there is a lot of sheep, such as Teahouse Ridge on Lady MacDonald and in all the valleys on the north side of the Bow Valley. It's a fallacy that ticks wash off in the shower; search yourself thoroughly. While mosquitoes and horse flies can be a darn nuisance they don't give you quite the same creeps.

Loose rock In Calgary an insurance company's ad on a billboard once read "As firm as the Rockies", which made me laugh aloud. The Rotten Rockies aren't called that for nothing, the sedimentary limestone being subject to extremes of heat and cold. Of course there *is* firm limestone, but it's safer to expect the worse. On scrambling pitches develop the technique for pushing handholds back into place. Be careful of rockfall in gullies, especially if a party is ahead of you. On routes you'll run into scree—lots of it. Utilize game trails where the scree is more stabilized.

Helicopters While I've nothing against helicopters used for legitimate purposes, I draw the line at heli-hiking and heli-sightseeing. Call me selfish if you like, but I like the mountains quiet. In the Bow Valley, particularly, the constant whirr is irritating.

PRACTICALITIES

BUYING MAPS

The perfect map does not exist. 1:50000 government topo maps are in imperial, which means you have problems converting everything from metric. Contour lines at 100-foot intervals can't be relied upon. Occasionally, features like small lakes, streams and glaciers are omitted, which leads to exciting discoveries. Trails, if marked at all, are often wrong, a mistake from 20 years back not corrected over several editions.

1:50000 recreation maps by Map Town Publishing show up-to-date road alignments, main power lines, official trails and a few of the more popular unofficial trails. Looking good, you might think. However, contour lines are still in imperial and in the latest edition drawn at 200-foot intervals, which is no good at all for off-trail wanderers.

Provincial Resource Base Maps from Alberta Energy and Natural Resources are updated fairly regularly and show what the other maps don't: cutlines, all powerlines, exploration and logging roads and some trails. Unfortunately, the reality is sometimes nothing like what is shown on the map. Sigh....

A FEW RULES TO KNOW ABOUT

K Country is nowhere near as bureaucratic at the National Parks.

• No registration is necessary for overnight trips. However, for your safety, registration books are available at information centres and at some trailheads.

• Respect trail closures, open fire bans.

• Dogs must be on a leash.

• A few trails are closed to mountain bikers. Read individual trail descriptions or buy a copy of "*Backcountry Biking in the Canadian Rockies*".

• Anglers require an Alberta fishing licence.

• There are some restrictions on camping. Read the next heading....

CAMPING

Official campgrounds by the highways

These fill up quickly in the summer, even walk-in tenting areas and overflow parking pads. Reserve several days ahead if you can; it's galling to find campgrounds full of people watching cable TV and whose idea of exercise is a stroll to the biffy and back. In fall, numbers fall off and some loops are closed.

Camping in the backcountry

In the provincial parks no overnight camping is allowed except in designated sites with picnic tables, portable biffies and bear bars. Contact park rangers for bivouacking information. Elsewhere, camping is allowed almost anywhere as long as you're one kilometre from a road.

The exceptions. No camping at Tombstone Lakes. No camping around Ribbon and Lillian Lakes except at designated sites. No camping within 15 metres of the trails into Ribbon Lake and Lillian Lake. No camping in Marmot Basin, Nakiska Ski Area, Kananaskis Country Golf Course and, surprisingly, on the wedge of land between the Wedge Connector and Hwy. 40.

SUMMER FACILITIES

The Ghost

There are no facilities of any kind at the hamlets of Benchlands and Waiparous Creek. For information try the information kiosk at Ghost Ranger Station. Official campgrounds are Waiparous (one on either side of Hwy. 940), North Ghost and Air Strip group camp.

Canmore, Bow Valley

Canmore, the location of K Country's head office, has everything for all budgets: hotels (with convention facilities), motels, inns, B&Bs, campgrounds, restaurants, pubs and fast food outlets, grocery stores, bookstores, sportshops and bike rentals. The Information Centre is located on Hwy. 1A. Up the hill is the Canmore Nordic Centre (cafeteria) with over 60 km of ski trails lacking interest to hikers. Further east, Dead Man Flat has a motel, future hotel, B&Bs, one or two eating places and gas station/grocery stores. Seebe has a gas station/grocery store, Exshaw, a gas station and cafe. Rafter Six and Kananaskis guest ranches offer meals for nonresidents. Not too far away, Nakoda Lodge offers accommodation, a restaurant and gift shop. Campgrounds along Hwy. 1: Bow River, Three Sisters, Lac des Arcs. Willow Rock, Bow Valley and Jamboree group camp are located in Bow Valley Provincial Park, which also has a Visitor Information Centre.

Kananaskis Valley
Information Centres are located at Barrier Lake and at Kananaskis Village Centre. Kananaskis Village features three hotels (bars, restaurants), a grocery store, upscale shops and bike rentals at Peregrine Sports. Down the road is Ribbon Creek youth hostel. For something different try Sundance Lodges (teepees, grocery store). Kananaskis Country Golf Course restaurant is my favourite eatery in the valley. Fortress Junction gas station sells snacks, groceries and guidebooks. Fortress Mountain Chalets (minimum stay two nights) have kitchen facilities and house up to 13 people per chalet. Campgrounds are two: Eau Claire and Mt. Kidd RV & Tent Park (snack bar, groceries, hot tubs). Group camps are located at Canoe Meadows, Porcupine Creek and Stony Creek on Hwy. 68.

Spray Smith-Dorrien
Spray Lakes Ranger Station at Three Sisters Dam gives out information. Right now the only facility is Mt. Engadine Lodge (accommodation, meals). One campground at Spray Lakes West.

Kananaskis Lakes Area
The Park Visitor Centre is a must-see. William Watson Lodge is reserved for seniors and the disabled. Boulton Creek Trading Post has licensed restaurant, grocery store and bike rental. There are a spate of campgrounds along Kananaskis Lakes Trail: Canyon, Elkwood, Lower Lake, Boulton Creek, Mt. Sarrail and Interlakes. Group camps: Lower Lake and Pocaterra.

Elk Lakes Provincial Park
No tourist facilities.

TELEPHONE NUMBERS

Kananaskis Country Head Office,
Canmore 403-678-5508
Calgary Office 403-297-3362

Information Centres
Barrier Lake 403-673-3985
Bow Valley 403-673-3663
Kananaskis Village 403-591-7555
Peter Lougheed Provincial Park 403-591-6344
Canmore 403-678-5277
Spray Lakes Ranger Station 403-591-6344
Ghost Ranger Station 403-932-5668
Ghost Information Booth (summer weekends only) 403-932-4551
B.C. Provincial Parks, Wasa 604-422-3212

Campground reservations
Bow Valley Provincial Park 403-673-2163
Peter Lougheed Provincial Park 403-591-7226
Sundance Lodges 403-591-7122
Mt. Kidd RV Park 403-591-7700

Facilities
Canmore Nordic Centre 403-678-2400
William Watson Lodge 403-591-7227
Lodge at Kananaskis 403-271-0459
Kananaskis (Motor) Inn 403-266-5020
Hotel Kananaskis 403-271-0459
Fortress Junction 403-591-7371
Fortress Mountain Chalets 403-591-7108, 1-800-258-7669
Boulton Trading Post 403-591-7678
Mount Engadine Lodge 403-678-2880
Rafter Six Ranch Resort 403-673-3622
Kananaskis Guest Ranch 403-265-7094
Nakoda Lodge 403-881-3949

Emergency
591-7767

USING THE BOOK

TYPES OF TRAILS

Official Trails maintained by Kananaskis Country and Forest Services are a mix of new and old trails, logging and exploration roads, fire roads and cutlines. Expect parking lots at trailheads, biffies and the occasional picnic table. Junctions are marked with signposts of the "You are here" variety. En route some trails have directional arrows or coloured markers located on trees or posts. Above treeline watch for cairns and paint splodges on rocks. Unless the trail is equestrian (this applies mainly to trails in Vol. 2), expect bridges over creeks.

Unofficial Trails sometimes have no obvious trailhead, are neither signposted nor marked in any way, except, perhaps, for the occasional piece of flagging or cairn. They follow well-established pack trails, game trails, logging and exploration roads and cutlines. Creek crossings are the norm.

Routes Carrying on from the second edition, the third edition introduces more easy climbs and ridge walks ranging from hands in pocket strolls along grassy hogsbacks to gruelling uphill flogs in excess of 1000 m to the top of a mountain. In the upper end of the range you can be sure of scree and possibly a pitch or two of easy scrambling and mild exposure. Hard hats are not necessary and, unless otherwise recommended, neither are ropes *in optimum conditions when the mountain is devoid of snow and the weather is good.* There may be remnant people trails or game trails, but mostly there's no trail at all. Most routes feature some bushwhacking.

RATING DIFFICULTY

No attempt has been made to classify trails. What's difficult for one person is easy for another. It's all relative. Read the description carefully. If you're going off official trails for the first time, start easy and don't go charging off up to Aster Lake. If you're having a horrible time, turn back and try something easier. Just don't burn the guidebook!

RATING TIMES

Times are dependent on too many variables—everybody chugs along at a different rate. Some will be carrying heavy packs, others, like me, make frequent flower stops. And then there are the underfoot conditions to consider, the weather and so on.

Half day means up to 3 hours

Day, up to 6 hours

Long day, up to 10 hours *plus*

Backpack, overnight camping.

Some of the trails are suitable for 'bike 'n' hike' trips, which can cut down the time considerably even if you do have to push up the hills. I've often squeezed a weekend trip into one day.

MAPS

Maps in the back of this book should not be used in place of topo maps. They do, however, attempt to redress a few problems. For instance, they have been redrawn in metric from topo maps, with contours at 100-metre intervals and shading starting at 2500 metres (8,200 ft.). Because we've had to draw between contour lines they can not be considered accurate. We have, however, done our best to mark the following accurately: roads, trails, cutlines, logging and exploration roads. Please write the publisher if you find any discrepancies so we can make corrections.

GRID REFERENCES

Government topo maps have blue grid lines running east-west and north-south. Each line is numbered. The first two numbers indicate the grid line forming the west boundary of the kilometre square in which your point is located, and the third number the estimated number of tenths of a kilometre your point is east of that line. The fourth and fifth numbers indicate the grid line forming the south boundary of the square and the last number the estimated number of tenths of a kilometre your point is north of that line.

#79 Burstall Pass. Mt. Sir Douglas

THE TRAILS

1 AURA CREEK SAND FOREST — map 3

Day hike
Unofficial trails, river crossing via route 2
Distance route 1 via Eau Claire tote
road 7.3 km, route 2 via Ghost Ranger
station 4.2 km
Height gain route 1, 90 m; route 2, 130 m
High point 1465 m
Map 82 O/7 Wildcat Hills

Access: Highway 940.
Route 1 9.1 km north of the forest boundary and just north of Waiparous Creek bridge is a road on the right (east) side. This is the gated road to Whispering Pines Bible Camp at Cow Lake. Park on the shoulder or walk/bike from Waiparous Creek campground south of the bridge. In fall the gate is opened to let the hunters in and at such times you'll be able to drive to the tote road turn-off.
Route 2 1.5 km north of the forest boundary turn right (east) at an information kiosk and drive for almost 1 km to the Ghost Ranger Station. Park just before the station on the left.

I've been back a few times to this seductive area of sand for a sunbathe and a roll down the bank. Include such extras as bikini, suncream, buckets and spades, etc. Two routes lead to Aura Creek. It's a case of Hobson's choice: longer with no river crossing or shorter with river crossing. It boils down to this: Are you up to wading the Waiparous River and do you have a bike?

Route 1 via Eau Claire tote road
Twice as long as the other route but with no river crossing to worry about. Walking is so easy you can bike it.

Follow the Bible Camp road across flats within sound of the ice cream van doing the loops at the campground. After the second side creek crossing the road climbs steeply to a junction with the tote road on the left at a sign 'no motorcycles'. Stay on the road, then, opposite a sign 'Buried pipeline or cable' turn next right onto the tote road.

It's exciting to be walking on the very first Highway 940, which to the uninformed looks like any other OHV road. Built in 1906 by Eau Claire Lumber Company, it started from Cochrane and went past Mount Royal Ranch, over Robinson Creek and—this is where it differed from today's route—took a line up the *east* side of Waiparous Creek. Later, another tote road started west of Morley, and on the line of today's Richards Road gained the Bar C Ranch, after which it followed the route of today's highway and required heavy duty trestle bridges. So as you can see, the present Highway 940 is an amalgamation of both tote roads.

Grassy underfoot, Eau Claire's road climbs along the bank, touches the Bible Camp road briefly, then swings away right downstream, parallelling, though not in sight of, Waiparous Creek. At first it's all downhill. You intersect a cutline and dip steeply to cross Cow Lake's creek at cabin ruins with rusted Edwards Coffee can. Next up is the flat deep section where the road crosses three side creeks on the downside of willowy bogs, where generations of corduroy lie rotting, sinking in the muskeg (you have to remember this road was used mainly in the winter). At one point where the road gets in a muddy groove, follow the trail to the left. It's somewhat of a relief to find the track rising into dry pine forest once more. Wend left (tote road ahead) and arrive at a T-junction with a NE-SW cutline. Turn left. In a short distance route 2 joins in from the right.

Route 2 via Ghost Ranger Station
Although this route is shorter, it involves wading Waiparous Creek.

Walk past the ranger station on land once belonging to the Bar C Ranch. At the time we're talking about it was owned by the irascible George Creighton who had trouble keeping staff and was known for running them off his land with a six-shooter. Anyway, he agreed to lease the Forestry Department some land at Aura Spring for a ranger station under condition that no one was to cut his timber. In all innocence, Forestry sent out a man called Flack to build a cabin, which in those days was done by axing a few nearby trees. Incensed, Creighton promptly razed the cabin and scared the wits out of Flack with his six-shooter. Undeterred, Forestry then sent in Archie Howard to build another cabin. He borrowed Laurie Johnson's 32 revolver, all unknowing that Johnson, who must surely have been hiding behind a tree to watch the fun, had also provided Creighton with black ammunition for his 45, which made a hell of a noise and emitted lots of smoke. The ruse, if that was what it was—no one was ever too sure about Creighton's intentions—worked and no further attempt to build a ranger station was made until after Creighton's death.

At the end of the road a gate leads into a field. Follow the stony track through two more gates to a junction. Keep left, parallelling the valley creek and go through a fourth gate. Jump the valley creek. On the far bank, leave the track (which heads down to the Waiparous and crosses it *far too soon* for our purposes) and neither gaining nor losing height head left across a lumpy grassy terrace. Pass four aspens, one girdled with flagging, and on a developing trail enter forest at a dead tree and blazes.

The easy-to-follow forest trail crosses a side creek close to the Waiparous, then descends into a big meadow where, having successfully bypassed two river crossings, you rejoin the initial track at a T-junction (blazed trees). Follow the track to the left only a short distance before cutting right (no

trail that I could see) to the Waiparous riverbank opposite Aura Creek confluence.

Wade across, aiming for the left bank of Aura Creek where a trail climbs a gravelly rib. Is this the historic Greasy Plains trail to the Red Deer River? Where the trail levels in pine forest cross what is likely the Eau Claire tote road and continue to the NE-SW cutline, gained a little east of route 1 at some blue flagging. Turn right.

To Sand Forest
Regardless of which way you came in, you're now on the NE-SW cutline. At the top of the hill turn left onto a dirt road and when it starts to descend turn left onto a sandy trail giving access to the fabulous sand forest above. It's a huge area covering all three sides of the ridge at GR443902 and features plains, bowls, sand traps and hills to roll down. I can't guarantee your peace won't be shattered by the drone of trailbikers, who as penance should be forced to rake the sand. Surely this special place deserves some kind of protection from dingbats who look upon it as a challenge for their machines rather than as a place of beauty?

GOING FARTHER
Horse Lake (Aura Lake) add 1.6 km one way, extra height gain 10 m.

Return to the dirt road and turn left, continuing to descend to Aura Creek, which was called Lunch Creek in Eau Claire's time. Don't cross, keep left on another OHV road and climb (steeper shortcutting trail available to left) into meadows with dumps of horse dung, where the road is a swath of golf course grass starred with *white* moss gentians. Stay left of the creek and come to a large meadow with standing water and Horse Lake somewhere in the middle.

From here, Greasy Plains travellers, unfazed by bogs being en horse, headed north into the trees, crossing Atkinson Creek, the Little Red Deer and Harold Creek, then riding up Grease Creek to Fallentimber Creek and the Red Deer River valley.

2 MOCKINGBIRD LOOKOUT — map 3

Day hike
Unofficial fire road
Distance 3.2 km
Height gain 355 m
High point 1900 m
Map 82 O/6 Lake Minnewanka

Access: Forestry Trunk Road 940. 13.2 km north of the forest boundary, turn west onto Waiparous Valley Road. Drive for 2.8 km past Camp Mockingbird to a junction. Keep right on the better road. 700 metres after crossing a bridge over a small stream, park at the bottom of the fire road to your right. Or drive up the fire road a short way and park at a gate, but you'd better not block it else the lookout will be after your head.

An easy walk up Mockingbird Hill where you are treated to a panoramic view of The Ghost. Obviously, this trail is very popular because of its short length and proximity to campgrounds and assorted youth camps.

Walk up the fire road. Beyond the gate, you start winding through dense pine forest, intersecting and brushing against assorted cutlines, the rather boring nature of the walk relieved by sampling raspberries, blackcurrants and strawberries growing along the verge. On gaining the south ridge the road levels a little, following the ridge line through a fence to lush summit meadows. This modest hill top, far distant from the Front Ranges, is one stupendous viewpoint in panavision, the kind of place where you expect Brad Pitt to come riding through the meadows to a stirring score by John Barry.

But before sorting out the view in detail, it's obligatory to pay a visit to the lookout. The present one, built in 1973-74, replaced

Opposite:
Top: Aura Creek sand forest messed up by OHV tracks.

Bottom: Mockingbird Lookout. In the background are Devil's Head and Castle Rock.

the old box-like structure that had stood on this spot for over 20 years. In turn, the first Mockingbird Lookout superseded the one on nearby Black Rock Mountain that was abandoned in 1952. Looking southwest across Waiparous Creek you'll spot a solitary mountain closer in than the Front Ranges and about 600 m higher than Mockingbird. This is Black Rock Mountain, and the pimple on top is the old lookout, the thrilling objective of route #7.

To its right, the rock obelisk of Devil's Head is unmistakable and can be used as a reference point. So going clockwise from Devil's Head, pick out Castle Rock, the protruding Sheep Crest and the bare mountains around the head of the Red Deer River just visible to the northwest. Closer in, the eyes travel over forest through which wind the Burnt Timber, Fallen Timber and Little Red Deer rivers and all their OHV roads. A little north of east the eye is stayed by large areas of open ground near the edge of the forest. These are the Greasy Plains, a name with a fine Tolkienesque ring to it. In reality, the Greasy Plains on Grease Creek were named by James Hector, who called them "Pre de Graisse" after the black birch or Grease Wood that grows along the creekbed. They were a well-known feature of the Indian trail between Morley and the Red Deer River, some of which is travelled by route #1. Right of the plains and beyond diminishing waves of forested ridges—Salter, Keystone, Swanson and Wildcat—you can spot a few of Calgary's skyscrapers. Completing the 360 degree panorama is the view to the south. The dominant feature here is Moose Mountain, whose summit is occupied by the next lookout in the chain running south to the U.S. border.

3 WAIPAROUS CREEK — maps 3, 2 & 1

Backpack
Official OHV trail, unofficial trails,
creek crossings
Distance 13.5 km to chasm
Height gain to chasm 305 m
High point 1853 m at chasm
Map 82 O/6 Lake Minnewanka

Access: Forestry Trunk Road 940. 13.2 km north of the forest boundary, turn left (west) onto Waiparous Valley Road. Drive past Camp Mockingbird and camping spots to a junction at 2.8 km. Turn left onto a rougher road (signed Margaret Lake trail), which runs along the north bank of Waiparous Creek. Head west through a mess of camping spots and side roads, cross a NW-SE cutline, splash through Hidden Creek at 3.9 km, pass Camp Howard at 4 km and Camp Chamisall at 4.6 km, after which keep right at all the splits. Intersect two parallel cutlines on the oblique, then cross a really major NW-SE cutline signposted 'Ghost Cross Country' to right, 'Meadow Creek' to left. Shortly after, at the foot of a deeply-trenched uphill turn left into a parking area. At 6.8 km, it's the end of the orange-dashed road as shown on the topo map. Early in the season you may be nervous about crossing Hidden Creek in a sedan with doors below the waterline. But the bottom is firm gravel and who wants to walk another 2.9 km each way?
Also accessible from #8 Ghost River to Waiparous Creek via Johnson Lakes.

Driving farther In OHV country it pays to drive a jeep because not only can you splash through Hidden Creek with impunity, you can bounce another 6.8 km to the Margaret Lake turn-off at the ford (13.6 km), thus saving hours of tedious walking. The scary uphill beyond the normal parking spot is the worst of it with a chance of getting hung up. The descent back down to Waiparous Creek ends with an easy side creek crossing and leads into the braided section where the road twines around a driveable cutline. Follow the yellow OHV and snowmobile signs to the Margaret Lake junction, where the Waiparous road crosses to the south bank.

The north fork of the Ghost River, named Waiparous Creek by James Hector on December 10th, 1858 and which roughly translates to Crow Indian Scalp, is the most accessible of the three Ghost Rivers. An exploration road takes you easily into the head of the valley. Unfortunately, you're in OHV (Off Highway Vehicle) country so you'll be sharing the road with trail bikers, particularly the section to the Margaret Lake turn-off. Don't let this put you off. The rock scenery is superb and it's easy enough to get off the beaten track. Six fords are problematical at runoff, particularly the first one.

From the normal parking area at 6.8 km to Margaret Lake turn-off The road continues up a steep hill. It's a dispiriting climb with a good chance of being mud splattered by a passing OHV. A traverse, then quick descent followed by a side creek paddle to wash off the mud brings you to a four-way intersection. (If you don't fancy the trauma of the road you can scrabble along the riverbank from the parking area and in the trees beyond the side creek crossing, pick up a cutline that leads back to the road at the four-way intersection.)

West of the side creek the road twines around a cutline. I advise following the yellow OHV signs that use a mixture of both, so either turn right onto the cutline or cross the road if you've approached via the riverbank. Shortly after cutline and road join, turn off right for a short road stint. On regaining the cutline turn right and follow it, at the end of the long straight veering left to rejoin the road on the bank of Waiparous Creek. Turn right. Between here and the

Waiparous Creek. Crossing the mouth of the north fork on the return trip.

Margaret Lake turn-off are exciting views of Devil's Head and to its right, the square block of Castle Rock, which was shown as early as 1910 on the map issued by the Department of the Interior showing timber belts. Its last map appearance was in 1930.

Margaret Lake turn-off to the Chasm Arriving at the turn-off after 6.8 kilometres of forest walking, you turn left and wade the Waiparous between riffles. Waiparous Creek road continues and shortly intersects a major NE-SW cutline (route #8 to Johnson Creek and the Ghost River).

The road curves around a river bend, fading out temporarily where the stream from Castle Rock cirque enters the

Waiparous. At the next ford, the road is joined by another road coming in from the NE-SW cutline on your left. Recross the Waiparous and follow the road over a low forested ridge to the third crossing at the confluence of the Waiparous with its spectacular north fork. Except at high water, it's possible to edge along the south bank between the last two fords. Watch for a cairn and survey marker en route.

The north fork is bounded on the west by a 300 metre-high rock prow, frontage for a remarkable line of cliffs extending halfway along the valley, and on the east side by two castle mountains that appear to have been bombarded by rocks slung from a medieval catapult.

21

The chasm marks the usual end of a trip up the Waiparous.

The main valley is no less interesting. You wind past a popular camping spot by the side of a small waterfall, then, reversing the S-bend, travel beneath a long curved wall of grey stones—a perfect example of a former riverbank left high and dry above the river's present shoreline. High above, a cliff rivalling that of the north fork sends forth long shadows. On windy days, water seeping over the edge drifts in a fine spray across black-streaked walls. Cross the creek and

climb steeply over a side ridge below the prow to another creek crossing, the final one. Both crossings can be avoided by an unsuspected traverse along the south bank.

A gloomy stretch of road, often muddy from rills running off the hillside, ends at a viewpoint overlooking a free-falling waterfall across the valley. Zigzag down to the valley floor, cross a major side creek and arrive at a road junction. Either take the road to the left, which wastes no time in climbing to get above the upcoming canyon, or continue along the riverbank to where the road ends at a campsite, then climb a well-trodden trail up the bank to a continuation of the road above. Both routes join above the canyon 200 metres farther on. Clearings in trees to the right indicate the entry point into meadows above the river's plunge into the chasm, a delightful spot that is usually the culmination of a trip up the Waiparous (the road continues for almost another kilometre).

GOING FARTHER

Upper Waiparous Creek 6 km from the chasm, extra height gain 245 m. A more strenuous option.

Continue along the road. Although it can't be seen from road's end, a cutline does in fact carry on into meadows at the very end of the valley. To get to the start of it, descend the bank and wade the river, aiming for the left-hand bank of the side stream sporting a single waterfall called Indian Scalp half glimpsed from the road's end.

The cutline, which climbs high above the river (closeted once more in a gorge), is a grade sixer. Serpentine in nature, it has an annoying habit of traversing steep sidehills on the slant and is additionally clogged with windfall requiring lengthy detours at many points. Two deeply-cut side streams may be difficult to cross during their tumultuous headlong rush to join the Waiparous at runoff. Eventually, the cutline smooths and makes a gradual descent to flat meadows at the valley head.

4 MARGARET LAKE — map 2

Day hike
Official OHV trails
Distance 8.4 km from parking area
Height gain 140 m
High point 1725 m
Map 82 O/6 Lake Minnewanka

Access: Forestry Trunk Road 940. Via Waiparous Creek trail (#3). From the usual parking area below the steep uphill, follow the trail for 6.8 km to the Margaret Lake turn-off.

This gem of a lake has the misfortune to lie smack in the middle of an OHV land use area. Right now, the only route is along roller-coaster cutlines shared with noisy trail bikes. Unfortunately, deadfall in the forest deters shortcutting, otherwise I'd advise you to bash through the trees on a compass setting.

You've followed Waiparous Creek trail to the road junction above the first ford. Walk straight to a major NE-SW cutline and turn right. This cutline is one of the worst kind;

if you're not climbing up or down, then you're pussy-footing around side-to-side puddles gouged out of soft clay. Not far from the junction of road and cutline, a bypass road on the left cuts out the first steep hill.

Many hills later turn second left onto the signposted cutline, and follow it over a hill into a dip. The lake lies on the left-hand side—a sudden blue opening in the pines. All the most spectacular peaks of The Ghost are lined up as backdrop; a grand sight that overpowers your initial repugnance at the mess made by OHVs driving to the water's edge. Quieter spots can be found along the north bank where glades slope down to the lake at sunbathing angle. Fishing is good for Brookies and Rainbow.

Margaret Lake. Looking northwest to the ruined castle mountains enclosing Waiparous Creek's north fork.

5 LESUEUR CREEK TO MEADOW CREEK — map 3

Day hike
Unofficial trail, creek crossings
Distance via start 1, 8 km
Distance via start 2, 8.2 km
Height gain 95 m
High point 1554 m
Map 82 0/6 Lake Minnewanka

Access: Forestry Trunk Road 940. Drive 25.4 km north of Highway 1A to Richards Road (sign). Keep right at this junction, then in 150 metres turn first left (west) onto a gated dirt road that looks like a private road into a field. This is the rough Ghost River Road built by TransAlta Utilities into the forest reserve. Close the gate.

Start 1 Drive along the Ghost River Road for 6.5 km to where there's a fabulous view up the South Ghost. Turn off right onto a wide exploration road that ends at an intersecting cutline and sign riddled with bullet holes. Park here. Down the steep bank is the reclaimed portion of road and Lesueur Creek.

Start 2 Drive along the Ghost River Road for 6.8 km to an intersecting dirt road. Park at the intersection on the right side of the road.

Also accessible from #6 Indian Springs and Enviros Lake.

I have to admit the easy walk to Meadow Creek following an OHV road and horse trail up Lesueur Creek and across 'the great bog' doesn't sound too alluring. "What are you putting it in for?" Because I loved it, the sometimes waterlogged state of the route compensated by marvellous views of the Ghost Mountains. I'd advise taking runners or wellies and enjoy a good splosh. However, don't go just after snow melt or heavy rainfall when the road turns to mud with the consistency of peanut butter. Rather than return the same way, consider a point to point with Indian Springs (#6). Of the starts, 1 is shorter, 2 is easy road.

Start 1 As you can see, the exploration road once carried on to a well on the north side of Lesueur Creek. Nowadays a trail descends the bank from right to left to the stream, which by great good fortune is a string of beaver ponds at this point with convenient dams for crossing. On the north bank pick up the pack trail which has come up the valley from the Bar C, formerly the Le Sueur Ranch. The Le Sueur's (don't forget the first 'u') hailed from the Isle of Guernsey and possibly their only claim to fame is that this is where Ralph Connor wrote *"Black Rock. A Tale of the Selkirks"* in 1896, the first of a hugely successful string of books mixing adventure and religion.

Follow the trail upstream past a beaver devastation area, going either way at a division, and join start 2 at a T-junction with the OHV road. Turn right.

Start 2 The OHV road route is longer, muddier, less interesting, but foolproof for people who get lost in shopping malls. At Lesueur Creek crossing you'll generally find some logs just downstream of the ford. Start 1 comes in from the right. Stay on the road.

Continue along the road which runs high on the northeast bank of Lesueur Creek through the pines and overlooks an incredible number of occupied beaver ponds where you can fish for Brookies. The main road is obvious and has numerous variations where OHVs have made futile attempts to escape the mud. Generally, up to the second side creek crossing use right-hand options. Other things to know: you cross twice as many cutlines as are marked on the topo map, and all side roads heading right are cutline access roads.

The second side creek is bordered with bog—a harbinger of joys to come. Keep left at the split following. The road in its present state ends at a fence with sign 'designated horse trail'—the start of the meadow section.

Keep straight (cutline access road to right) and cross a third side creek, noting Lesueur Creek turning away to the left. In a copse, intersect cutline #4. You emerge in a mammoth bog where there is a wonderful sense of space in every direction, including under the feet. Far off mountains of The Ghost appear as cutout shapes with character: Phantom Crag, Devil's Head and Black Rock Mountain among them, while nearer at hand Lesueur Creek can be traced by the sparkle of beaver ponds. Loose water not gathered in ponds lies around in long grasses punctuated by clumps of dwarf birch and spruce denoting slightly drier islands. To the right of some spruce where the track splits is the largest tarn, worth an extra squelch, where the capillary action of water clinging to the grass makes it appear higher than the surrounding country.

The track crosses a creek, barely distinguishable in the general sogginess, then heads for drier ground below an aspen ridge.

Brewster's Cabin (dating from 1926) in Meadow Creek. Black Rock Mountain in the background.

Next, intersect a cutline and drift fence and cross a meadow bay. At the other side either cut right of a hillock on a trail that leads past the forestry cabin, or stay on the main track that winds left of the hill to a junction with Meadow Creek trail in the beautiful meadows of (Hay) Meadow Creek.

For Indian Springs and Enviros Lake turn left towards the mountains. Beyond the gate is a T-junction with trail #6.

But first I recommend you head right a short distance. Standing well back on the right side in trees is Meadow Creek forestry cabin and a corral. Opposite is Brewster's Cabin where a sign informs you 'Truck eating muskeg' (no kidding) and that no towing is available. I was uncertain whether or not to laugh at another sign 'Never mind the dog, beware of owner' and the drawing of a colt MK IV.

6 INDIAN SPRINGS AND ENVIROS LAKE — maps 3 & 2

Day hike
Unofficial trails, creek crossings
Distance between starts 7.6 km,
whole loop 11.9 km
Height gain 60 m
High point 1600 m
Map 82 O/6 Lake Minnewanka

Above: Enviros Lake backdropped by Devil's Head and Black Rock Mountain. The trail up Black Rock follows the left-hand skyline.

Access: Forestry Trunk Road 940. Drive 25.4 km north of Highway 1A to Richards Road (sign). Keep right at this junction, then in 150 metres turn first left (west) onto a gated dirt road that looks like a private road into a field. This is the rough Ghost River Road built by TransAlta Utilities into the forest reserve. Close the gate.

Start 1 (loop start) Drive for about 12.3 km up the Ghost River Road to a junction on the right with the well-travelled road to Enviros Wilderness School. Either park here or preferably drive the Enviros road for 2.4 km to the gate at an intersecting NE-SW cutline (keep right at the beginning).

Start 2 (loop finish, quick route into Indian Springs) Disregarding all lesser roads and cutlines to left and right, drive for 16.6 km to the top of the steep hill down to the Ghost River. Park on the right side where an exploration road turns off to the right.

Also accessible from the north terminus of Lesueur Creek (#5) at Meadow Creek.

The walking is easy and unexpectedly pleasant if the meadow and pine country of the foothills appeals.

This route can be used in a variety of ways. Undoubtedly, the quickest way into the springs is from start 2. And the quickest way to Enviros Lake is from start 1. However, if you've got two vehicles or a bike (you can bike the whole thing), I strongly recommend beginning at start 1 and taking in Enviros Lake and Indian Springs via Meadow Creek. Travel the loop east to west: never walk with your back to the mountains if you can help it. Another option is to combine this route with Lesueur Creek (#5) to make two point to points of 11.2 and 13.4 km.

If you have two vehicles with good clearance the Enviros road can be driven for 2.4 km to the gate *when the road is dry.*

East to west from start 1
Either walk, bike or drive 2.4 km of winding Enviros Wilderness School access road to the gate at the NE-SW cutline. Beyond the gate stay on the old road, thereafter called a track, and cross Lesueur Creek to a T-junction in a large meadow popular with overwintering dude horses.

DETOUR to Enviros Lake 1.3 km return, height gain 10 m.

Turn left and purely on the good will of Enviros Wilderness School walk through leased land to the lakeshore. You'll be elated. No mud hole like Sibbald Lake (sorry, but Sibbald has never turned me on), Enviros Lake is a pale beauty transposed from the mountains with waters of clearest lime green and turquoise rippling over a marl bottom. The surround of spruce, pine and aspen rises up like a wall on the west side over which peek the mountains of The Ghost.

To Meadow Creek Back at the junction above Lesueur Creek go straight (or right if you've given Enviros Lake a miss) on the track that curves around to the left, and in triplicate runs through a strip of pine forest. You emerge in the bright meadows of Meadow Creek at a T-Junction. (Should you turn right through the gate you'll arrive very shortly at another T-junction where Lesueur Creek trail (#5) turns off to the right.)

The meadows of upper Meadow Creek, looking towards Devil's Gap. The shapely mountain to the right is Phantom Crag.

To Indian Springs Turn left at the T-junction. The track crosses beautiful flat meadow with a vista to the west of ghostly mountains: Orient Point to the left, the peculiar outline of Phantom Crag and Black Rock Mountain to your right. Nearing Meadow Creek and back into trees, you come to a junction. Keep right, then immediately left and into six tiny creek crossings that end you up on the south bank next to a fence. Pass through the densely forested narrows of the watershed. On the right is a camping area and a rickety boardwalk leading to a flume conveying water from a mossy bank. OK, so Indian Springs are not much to look at, but what the heck, it's guaranteed fresh water.

The track continues into the drainage of the Ghost River, wending left and downhill through open pine forest and meadows with spectacular new views of Devil's Gap and Orient Point. En route, two OHV tracks heading right are actually worth following for a rare view of the Ghost River valley dominated by Devil's Head and Black Rock Mountain. The track joins the Ghost River Road (start 2) at the top of the hill down to the Ghost River.

7 BLACK ROCK MOUNTAIN — map 2

Day hike
Official trail with signs
Distance 5.5 km from trailhead, 18 km
return from hill top
Height gain 892 m
High point 2462 m
Map 82 O/6 Lake Minnewanka

Access: Forestry Trunk Road 940. Drive 25.4 km north of Highway 1A to Richards Road (sign). Keep right at this junction, then in 150 metres turn first left (west) onto a gated dirt road that looks like a private road into a field. This is the rough Ghost River Road built by TransAlta Utilities into the forest reserve. Close the gate. Disregarding all side roads and cutlines, drive for 16.6 km to the top of the steep hill winding down to the Ghost River. Stop and check the condition of the hill. In good condition it can be negotiated by sedans with good clearance and determined drivers. If nervous use the parking area at the top and be prepared to walk another 3.5 km (7 km return!) to the trailhead. Try to avoid this and if you can't find a friend with a suitable vehicle, a bicycle might do the trick.

Turn right at the bottom of the hill (sign). Wend left and cross a dry stony creekbed, then head up-valley through trees, ignoring a couple of side roads to right. In a Dryas meadow level with Black Rock Mountain turn right (sign, arrow) onto a side road making a beeline for the mountain. Park at the edge of the stony creekbed.

Although painter Roland Gissing acquainted the name Black Rock with something sinister, when I think 'Black Rock' I see in my mind's eye this big solitary mountain, topped by a lookout, which has provided me with many a good day in the hills. It was Jack Carter's favourite lookout mountain. Understandably. There's nothing boring about this pack trail to the summit. Built in 1928, it takes a daring line up the south slope of the mountain, causing you at many points to wonder where it can possibly go next. Of course, its roughness may not be everybody's cup of tea

*Devil's Head
from the chimney.*

(though I understand it's being improved in 1995) and there's a hint of exposure near the summit. Overall, though, it's still in fair shape after 30 years of neglect.

At the arrow cross the creekbed to the sign 'Black Rock trail' and start up the old road. In a few minutes you're stopped at the linesman's cabin and having a good belly laugh reading the trail register. Fill up the water bottles from the nearby creek and with every expectation of an 'excellent trip', climb further up the road to a junction signed 'Black Rock trail'.

So you turn left here onto the lookout trail which makes a long sweep to the left before winding up to timberline meadows. At every right-hand bend you meet the old telephone line snaking down the hillside. The trail makes one final zig onto the broad south ridge—a good place to stop and look around—then turns straight for the cliffs girdling the mountain.

The defences can be breached at only one spot and judging by the photos of men spread-eagled on precipices, the trail builders had some trouble finding it. Hardly surprising. On screes below the cliff the trail has largely disintegrated

Black Rock Mountain. The traverse before the chimney.

(due for reconstruction), but can be traced zigging left, then far to the right to the cliff base. Traverse left below the cliff on a good built-up section. When it seems some desperate manoeuvre must be made to get higher, a break appears in the cliff and the trail sweeps through the chimney into an uptilted karst basin with wonderful views back to Mt. Aylmer. Who can resist squeezing into slits in the cliffs and throwing rocks into fissures to see how deep they are? Higher up you encounter a line of tripods carrying the telephone wire, which 10 years ago used to drop dizzily down the cliff to the start of the traverse.

The trail climbs out of the basin onto the mountain's most surprising feature. Cliffs you expect, but a plateau? This is truly a 'lost world', several grassy football fields laid end to end, isolated by cliffs on three sides and harbouring a few less common alpines like Townsendia and Dwarf harebell. To the west Devil's Head Mountain sticks up like a thumb above similar tablelands.

The summit pimple is still a long way off and how you approach is up to you; via a new line of cairns or the tripod route on the right side. Starting from two large cairns at the base of the final rise, the trail zigzags up the tapering scree ridge, which high up tapers alarmingly, the distance between the sunny southern cliffs and the gloomy northern precipices lessening to a half-dozen steps in either direction. Pack horses stopped here. Up next is the crux for nervous walkers, a two metre-wide rock ridge that can be crossed in a couple of minutes. Easy, yes, but watch yourself if the wind is blasting.

A few metres of easy ground leads to the summit, a flat square helicopter pad (had there been helicopters in 1929) and in the centre, tethered by wires, the 66 year-old geriatric lookout missing windows and door (scheduled for restoration as an historic building). It took rangers a three-day trip with a string of pack horses to supply the towerman and this was one reason why in 1952 Black Rock was superseded by Mockingbird, which can be driven by pickup.

Below: On the plateau, showing the final ridge to the summit and the lookout.

Johnson Creek trail south of the cutoff to Johnson Canyon. Black Rock Mountain in the background.

8 GHOST RIVER TO WAIPAROUS CREEK VIA JOHNSON LAKES — map 2

Half-day to Johnson Lakes, day hike, backpack
Unofficial trails, creek crossings
Distance 15 km
Height gain 170 m
High point 1815 m
Map 82 O/6 Lake Minnewanka

South access: Forestry Trunk Road 940. Drive 25.4 km north of Highway 1A to Richards Road (sign). Keep right at this junction, then in 150 metres turn first left (west) onto a gated dirt road that looks like a private road into a field. This is the rough Ghost River Road built by TransAlta Utilities into the forest reserve. Close the gate. Disregarding all side roads, drive for 16.6 km to the top of the steep hill winding down to the Ghost River. From here it's another 6.5 km to the trailhead. In good condition, the hill can be negotiated by sedans with high clearance and determined drivers. Turn right at the bottom of the hill (sign), then wend left and cross a dry stony creekbed. Follow the road up-valley, disregarding all minor roads heading right, including the signed road leading to Black Rock Mountain trailhead. Pass TransAlta Utilities buildings, then cross a bridge over the canal. Park at the first ford on the Ghost River.

North access: Via Waiparous Creek (#3). Leave the trail at the NE-SW cutline immediately west of the first creek crossing.

The eclectic selection of trails connecting the two major river systems runs parallel to a tremendous line of cliffs, where the mountains of The Ghost end in abrupt and spectacular fashion. I always find the route enjoyable despite the noisy intrusion by trail bikers, who don't seem too fussy about sticking to official trails. While realizing I'm in an OHV area, I wish they wouldn't mess up the meadows before they've had time to dry out. Most times this trail is used to access the two fishing lakes or best of all, the fabulous Johnson Canyon (#9).

South to north

To Johnson Lakes Wade the Ghost River and pick up the cutline on the north bank. It cuts right to a tributary and climbs up the left bank, where you're treated to an unusual view of Black Rock Mountain showing the final scree ridge bounded on each side by cliffs. Hard to believe there's a trail up there. In spruce forest the cutline flattens, then rises more gently to the watershed, a no-name pass between the Ghost and Johnson drainages. A slight descent brings you to first Johnson Lake on the left, a shallow body of water reflecting the magnificent cliffs of Bastion Wall. The second lake lies a little further on opposite a camping spot and has a reedy surround, meaning anyone fishing for Brookies and Cutthroat should pack waders, even haul in an inflatable. Was Johnson the prankster Laurie Johnson who played both sides in the dispute over the Ghost Ranger Station? No one knows for sure.

To Johnson Creek Continue along the cutline that shortly jogs to the right at a junction (overgrown cutline ahead) and for the next 2 km heads northeast, away from the mountains. "To heck with this". Like others, I've shortcutted from the lakes to Johnson Creek, thereby cutting off a whacking 3 km, and gaining, not time, but a thoroughly bad temper after frequent falls through rotten floorboards sneakily covered in moss. It's something you try only once. So back to the cutline and no grumbling. Shortly after it crosses the overgrown cutline you come to a boggy meadow and a junction. Leave both the cutline and its access road, and cut left across the thin strip of meadow to the other side where, with great joy, you intersect an excellent pack trail. Turn left.

Walking mainly through meadows the rejuvenated hiker heads for the mountains. Pass a pond reflecting an amazing line of cliffs extending north and south as far as the eye can see and at the back of a bowl, the waterfall Sorcerer. Jump a side creek, then descend to Johnson Creek, a nippy little stream crossed seven times in the space of half a kilometre. On the northeast bank, the trail gains height as it traverses grassy hillside, the higher vantage point revealing the splendid isolation of Black Rock Mountain (see photo). Shortly after traversing a scree slope note a side trail descending into Johnson Creek—the route into Johnson Canyon.

To Devil's Head Meadow Your trail now turns away from the creek and runs alongside a tributary past a corral to an area of meadow where another side trail heads off down the tributary bound for Johnson Creek. Ahead is a first view of the mountains above Waiparous Creek. Shortly the grassy avenue you're following opens into Devil's Head Meadow, the tributary's sodden birthplace where feral horses run free under the saturnine eye of Devil's Head and OHVs play merry hell with the grass. There are some places where OHVs should be banned and this is one.

Now you can walk either side of the meadow, but the main trail—mud, courtesy of OHVs—crosses the tributary to the left (west) edge. After passing the mouth of a NE-SW cutline, offering yet another route into Johnson Canyon, the trail continues along a ridge of firm ground between a bright green fen and the tributary trickling lazily out of a seasonal pond, then dekes behind a copse into the north half of the meadow that drains to Waiparous Creek. The multi-track trail follows the left edge to an exploration road. Turn left. (For the curious, the road to right ends shortly on the east side of the meadow.)

To Waiparous Creek The exploration road climbs through pines to your highest point, then swings right and downhill, not too far away from the valley running east from Castle Rock. Here's a chance to explore a new canyon. I never say no. Ultimately the road levels and meets a NE-SW cutline at a T-junction. Turn right and walk down to the Waiparous Creek exploration road within sound of the Waiparous River. For Highway 940 turn right. The first ford is just metres away.

Opposite: looking back down Johnson Canyon.

9 JOHNSON CANYON — map 2

Backpack
Unofficial trail, creek crossings
Distance 3.5 km from trail #8 (12.5 km
from the Ghost River)
Height gain 215 m from Ghost River
High point 1905 m
Map 82 O/6 Lake Minnewanka

Access: Via Ghost River to Waiparous Creek via Johnson Lakes (#8). There are two accesses depending on which direction you are coming from (and one in between).

The quintessential Ghost: canyons, cliffs, waterfalls, mountains shaped like tiaras, is epitomized in the spectacular canyon north of Devil's Head. I count it as one of my favourite destinations, which we've visited as early as the May long weekend, exulting in sunshine and dry rock while our friends were suffering the traditional whiteout on the Columbia Icefield.

Approach from the Waiparous end Use the NE-SW cutline. Near its end watch for where a forest trail cuts across to Johnson Canyon at a cairn.

Approach from the Ghost River The usual way in. After the scree traverse, drop into Johnson Creek on a trail and walk easily up the flat stony creekbed which is constantly being rearranged. No water.

Entering a canyon is always a thrilling moment and here there are sights to make you forget your blistered heels, eh Norm?: vertical walls, overhanging walls, pinnacles, buttresses, towers, culminating in the big daddy of them all, Devil's Head. About halfway along at GR220909 the intermittent trail turns left up a side canyon to an oasis with running stream, an idyllic camp spot backdropped by a string of waterfalls tumbling down a gully.

Devil's Head from the ridge to the east.

STEEP OPTIONS

Ridges to east of Devil's Head high point 2414 m, height gain 510 m. A steep rough climb is prerequisite to an easy ridge walk with spectacular views.

From the oasis in the side canyon clamber up the right side of the waterfalls on a bit of a trail; it's much easier than it looks. At the top cross the creek and gain the upper valley. Keep left of the trees and wending left to avoid rock bands, climb a steepening but straightforward slope (Dryas mats, scree, soil, small unstable rocks) to gain the ridge top some distance left of the low point. Reap your reward by wandering along the wide easy ridge to the southeast over a number of tops for a peek into the fabulous Valley of the Birds, a return distance of 7.6 km (discounting detours) from the oasis.

Devil's Head, seen from close-in and head-on, is breathtaking. "Crowned by ruinous cliffs" is how McConnell described it in 1886 when geologizing. The Indians called it Devil's Nose or Devil's Thumb. The Cree so feared this peak they made offerings to its Manitou in the shape of pipes, tobacco and decorated tomahawks left on certain of its ledges.

Gibson's Ridge. Looking back down on Johnson Canyon (left) and up to Devil's Head, showing its stegosaurus side. To its left you can spot some of the ridge traversed by the first option.

Gibson's Ridge high point 2500 m, height gain 595 m. A more moderate climb to the northwest ridge of Devil's Head ends on the south face of the mountain—the usual ascent route.

Continue up Johnson Canyon (tip of Castle Rock ahead), then follow the valley as it turns to the south and opens up. Devil's Head comes back into view. Forget what I said about tiaras, from this side it's shaped like a stegosaurus. Not too far around the bend, near a waterfall, climb the hillside to the right, choosing the grassy rib to the left of the one topped with pinnacles. Behind your back Johnson Canyon grows in magnificence with every rest stop. After 350 vertical metres of hard work you get to look over the ridge into Claw Creek, which is being looked into by ice climbers.

Travel in the northerly direction is stymied by pinnacles, so head south towards Devil's Head along a wide grassy ridge with rocky outcrops and purple saxifridge. On one smooth facet of rock facing north is a mystery. Printed in yellow paint hard to decipher after all these years are the words

"To the memory of Guy Gibson. Lord of the Ghost. 18?? Ghost River Valley". Gibson, who preceded Tolkien, and really *was* known as 'Lord of the Ghost', lived in Benchlands on Hwy. 940, a skilled axeman who built over 1000 cabins. By all accounts he was one of those eccentrics the west throws up from time to time like Ed Marsden. His own cabin had door hinges made from roots that hooked into one another, and his bedspread was his favourite horse with tail and mane intact. It appears this fabulous ridge was chosen as Gibson's final resting place, but I hate assumptions and I hope some old-timer will set me straight.

Where the ridge rises a game trail appears and takes you up some scree to the left and through a number of little rock bands to the base of Devil's Head. I highly recommend you continue along the trail, traversing steep scree of the west flank to the south face where you get to look up the normal climber's route to the summit, a navigational nightmare. Of more interest is the forest of eroded pinnacles in a saddle to the southeast.

10 GHOST RIVER TO AYLMER PASS — map 2 & 1

Backpack
Unofficial trails, creek crossings
Distance 23 km from Ghost River
Height gain 683 m
High point 2283 m
Map 82 O/6 Lake Minnewanka

Access: Forestry Trunk Road 940. Drive 25.4 km north of Highway 1A to Richards Road (sign). Keep right at this junction, then in 150 metres turn left (west) onto a gated dirt road that looks like a private road into a field. This is the rough Ghost River Road built by TransAlta Utilities into the forest reserve. Close the gate. Disregarding all side roads, drive for 16.6 km to the top of the steep hill winding down to the Ghost River. In good condition, the hill can be negotiated by sedans with good clearance and determined drivers. Turn right at the bottom of the hill (sign). Wend left and cross a dry stony creekbed, then head up-valley, disregarding all minor roads heading right, including the signed road leading to Black Rock Mountain trailhead. Pass TransAlta Utilities buildings. Cross a bridge over the canal and drive to the first ford on the Ghost River. Park.

This is one half of a popular backpack: via the Ghost River and Spectral Creek to Aylmer Pass, and out to Banff via Lake Minnewanka shoreline trail. Naturally, you need two vehicles and many extra hours both before and after the trip to switch vehicles. This horrible logistical problem can be avoided by making the trip a three- or four-day event by returning to your starting point via Devil's Gap. Then, of course, it wouldn't matter if your car was a piece of junk because you'd park at the top of the dreaded hill down to the Ghost River. The downside to all this is that you have to walk an extra 6.7 km right at the start.

The route to the alpine meadows about the pass, while neither difficult nor particularly strenuous, retains an aura of untouched wilderness despite its old roads and cutlines. Numerous river crossings and a preponderance of grizzlies makes it unsuitable for nervous novice backpackers.

Since the 1960s the upper Ghost has been classified as Wilderness Area administered by Alberta Recreation and Parks under statutory authority of the 'Wilderness Areas Ecological Reserves and Natural Areas Act' of 1981, which means, readers, that you're finally free of hunters and trail bikers.

If you want to get off the beaten track there are an amazing number of side canyons and valleys up and down the Ghost to keep you busy for the next 10 years.

To Spectral Creek Ford the Ghost River straight off the bat. A word here on river crossings. For the next 15 km as you travel the alluvial flat, the road crosses back and forth 12 times. Because the river rarely rises above knee height fording is less of a problem than a damn nuisance. By the judicious use of game trails, you can cut the fords down to two. For instance, the first four can be bypassed via the south bank on trails varying from good to crab crawls under deadfall. One kilometre past the fifth crossing, a cliff dipping into the river forces you to wade to the north bank (large pile of stones) and pick up the road just east of Claw Creek at GR200864. Claw Creek issues from Malemute Valley, named by ice climbers "in honour of all northern dogs that love to go on skiing and climbing trips". In keeping with this sentiment, the dozen and more ice climbs have names like Werewolf Waltz and Taiga Trot. "Aha!" Before you go scooting off up the tributary to admire waterfalls, know that most are mere summer seepages. Round about here is the last view you'll have of Devil's Head that for the first half of the route has played peek-a-boo above a succession of walls and box canyons.

Crossing the Ghost River near Claw Creek.
Through the V is Mt. Aylmer.

The Ghost River Wilderness boundary lies a kilometre west of Malemute Valley at the narrows. Again, the next six river crossings can be eliminated by sometimes easy and sometimes frustrating progress along the north bank, where the grass grows unusually long and green below trees charred in the 1970 fire. All through this section, grizzlies have been excavating the riverbank for yummy hedysarum roots.

When you finally pass Mt. Aylmer, which has been in view for many hours, you must ford the Ghost at the crossing upstream of the confluence with Spectral Creek. Fifteen minutes walking through spruce forest brings you to an important junction. Keep left.

Spectral Creek section I'm not overfond of the next section up Spectral Creek, which is marked incorrectly on both the topo map and the Ghost River Wilderness pamphlet. The cutline—for this is what you follow to the forks—intersects all the windings of the creek, about 10 in all, and sometimes *is* the creek. A sopping spruce forest with deadfall puts paid to any idea of circumnavigation. Not only that, you never know what's lurking behind the willow bushes. It's a highway for grizzlies moving down into the Ghost River, having come over a pass into Spectral Creek from Stoney Creek where all the baddies have been banished. Don't plan on setting up camp anywhere along here, not that anybody in their right mind would even want to.

Where fallen trees have blocked a long stretch along the north bank, use a blazed trail on the right that is probably a remnant of original pack trail. Shortly the cutline fords the river one last time, then ends in undergrowth at the river's edge. In between these two points, and well marked by a cairn and flagging, the trail to Aylmer Pass takes off between two blazed trees.

To Aylmer Pass Your new trail rises effortlessly out of the dark spooky forest to timberline, then cuts across a scree slope (views of Apparition Mountain) to the mouth of the pass. Grassy benches on either side of waterfalls provide one or two flat tent sites sheltered from the wind's westerly blast. As you'll discover, Aylmer Pass is long, narrow and endless, a rolling carpet of tough bearberry, juniper and heather mats on which the passage of many feet has made little impression. On the left, Mt. Aylmer has nothing remarkable about it apart from its height of 3163 m. Odds are that somewhere between timberline and the top of the pass, identified by the Banff National Park boundary sign, you are likely to be mobbed by Aylmer's famous Bighorn

sheep, a gregarious bunch who are not after your lunch, but want a lick of your sweaty skin. So make sure the camera's wound on.

OPTIONS
Spectral Wanderings
The various headwaters of Spectral Creek are wonderful walking country if you love meadows. Note I don't suggest starting from the heavily-forested forks (I've never been able to find the trail marked on the Ghost River Wilderness pamphlet anyway). No, start slightly upstream of the aforementioned waterfalls, and find the good game trail on the west bank leading around into the head of the southwest fork, another good camping spot. In early summer, a tarn is edged with alpine buttercups, greening and blooming as the snowbanks melt.

View from Brock's Ridge of Aylmer Pass and Mt. Aylmer. Trail comes in from lower left.

The pass to the north (GR059884, 2460 m) is an easy walk up grass and while up there who can resist wandering along Brock's Ridge (also known as Chocolate Ridge) to a cairn and viewpoint around 2575 m, some 105 m below the summit, where you can look *down* on Aylmer Pass and Spectral Lakes.

From the pass drop into the west fork and nip across to the gap at GR051900 (2454 m), the grizzly route into and out of Stoney Creek (see the *Canadian Rockies Trail Guide* for ongoing routes). Next, head down the west fork and at treeline contour left into the north fork where blue-tinted Spectral Lakes are slung under Apparition and Revenant Mountains. This barren spot must be one of the spookiest places in the Ghost. According to Webster, Revenant means "one that returns after death".

Return the same way to the west fork, and on the south bank find the sheep trail that traverses around the northeast end of Brock's Ridge at treeline into the south fork, gained at about GR075883. From here it's a relatively easy pull up to the Aylmer Pass trail.

If camped near the waterfalls, height gain for all points visited is over 900 m! This ain't no rest day.

Aylmer Pass trail. The waterfalls at the mouth of the pass.

Upper Ghost and Spirit Creek

Leave Aylmer Pass trail at the west bank junction above the Ghost/Spectral confluence. You turn right here and head straight back to the Ghost River. Although a game/packer's trail can be traced along the west bank of the Ghost to a point just north of Spirit Creek, most backpackers elect to use the cutline, river crossings and all, which takes you more or less all the way to the meadows below Mt. Oliver, where you can search for the three tarns not marked on the topo map.

For Spirit Creek valley branch right up a steeply inclined cutline nearly one kilometre south of the confluence at GR103923, just before a river crossing. About the high point, keep left twice and drop to Spirit Creek. The cutline crosses the creek twice, then fades away on the east bank. Continue easily through forest to a large area of meadow around the forks. Attractions include a canyon (below the forks), ongoing meadows, intriguing rock scenery and a chance to wander up the ridge between the forks for a fabulous view back down the valley to Mt. Aylmer.

Paradise Pass 2120 m height gain 325 m.

Although I've never followed it, I'm told that in the vicinity of the tenth overall crossing of the Ghost River, where the valley widens and turns northwest, a bit of a trail heads 6 km south to a boundary marker on the low point of the ridge connecting Mts. Costigan and Aylmer at GR156815. Some wit called it Paradise trail and while I'll admit the view from the ridge of Lake Minnewanka must be fabulous, getting there is apparently purgatory. If bush–whacking and boggy meadows are your thing, by all means go.

Above: Sand dunes before First Ghost Lake.

11 DEVIL'S GAP — map 2

Day, long day hike
Unofficial trails
Distance 6.6 km from boundary
Height gain 20 m
High point 1524 m
Map 82 O/6 Lake Minnewanka

Access: Forestry Trunk Road 940. Drive 25.4 km north of Highway 1A to Richards Road (sign). Keep right at this junction, then in 150 metres turn first left (west) onto a gated dirt road that looks like a private road into a field. This is the rough Ghost River Road built by TransAlta Utilities into the forest reserve. Close the gate. Disregarding all side roads, drive for 16.6 km to the top of the steep hill winding down to the Ghost River. In good condition, the hill can be negotiated by sedans with good clearance and determined drivers. If necessary, use the parking area at the top and be prepared to walk or bike another 3.8 km to the trailhead. My recommendation is to go in your friend's pickup.

At the bottom of the hill turn left on a narrower and rougher road. Almost immediately keep left and drive down valley at the edge of the trees. Turn next right and cross the cobble floodplain. Keep straight and cross up and over the dike at a corner. The driveable road does not run west or south along the dikes, but heads southwest on meadow before swinging west into the trees. Drive as far as you feel able. En route you pass a track to right (camp spot, hiker's shortcut). Most people park before the Banff Park boundary at a left-hand bend below a wall of stones aimed at keeping the Ghost River flowing into Ghost Lakes and ultimately, Lake Minnewanka. You may be able to drive another 400 metres to the boundary at a signboard.

This is an easy walk between the Ghost River and Lake Minnewanka via spectacular Devil's Gap, which oozes with historical significance. If you want to reach the lake, hurry past the sand dunes and intriguing side canyons, which should be left for another day.

While we nowadays use the trail for frivolous pursuits like rock climbing, over 100 years ago it was the major thoroughfare to Canmore and Banff—had they existed at the time—from Morley. Conversely, the gap also brought marauding Kootenai Indians from British Columbia into the Prairies to hunt buffalo. Fierce battles with the Blackfoot who eventually drove the Kootenai back into the mountains, and frequent skirmishes between the warring factions of the Plains Indians are the basis of a legend which tells of a ghost seen going up and down the Ghost River, picking up the skulls of the dead who had been killed by the Cree. In another legend, the restless ghost of a Blackfoot warrior who drowned in the river (considered an ignominious way to die) is seen only after sundown, riding a white horse up and down the river in search of Stonies. It's said he's seated on the horse facing backwards and brandishes a spear. Actually, it's well documented that there are many Indian graves along the riverbank. According to Sir James Hector, the woods atop Deadman Hill in the angle between the Ghost and the Bow rivers were one vast burial ground.

To get in the appropriate mood for this ghostly hike, pick a dull, brooding day in late fall when the wind rattles the dried-up leaves on the poplars and the mountains seem withdrawn from life, waiting patiently shoulder to shoulder for the first snowfall.

Personally, I prefer a fine summer day for lolling about in the sand dunes.

Hiker's shortcut to Banff Park boundary
If it's your misfortune to be parked at the top of the big hill at 16.6 km, read on. If not, skip to the next section. At the bottom of the hill turn left, then almost immediately right on remnants of a road

that crosses the cobble floodplain in a southwesterly direction and gains the driveable road below the dike. Turn right. At the corner of two dikes, continue straight on a track that runs along the top of a dike in a westerly direction. At the next corner it drops off into the stony creekbed of the new-fangled Ghost River, diverted in 1942 from its natural course into Lake Minnewanka. (Conversely, so the geologists tell us, this was the way the Bow River flowed out to the plains pre ice ages.) The track is generally discernable as it winds downstream.

Watch for the obvious gap in the trees on the left side where another road, starting between a dike and the beginning of the wall of stones, takes you through trees to a junction. Keep left (right leads back to the creekbed), pass a camping spot on the left and arrive back on the driveable road. Turn right.

Now you can either follow the road or, much better, the horse trail that weaves about the road. Pick it up on the right just before the junction. Arrive at the Banff Park boundary. Sadly, since the last edition the historic Ghost Lodge, formerly Royal Mounted Police Post No. 7, has been burnt to the ground, so don't bother searching.

Banff Park boundary to First Ghost Lake
Beyond the sign continue into the west, following the wide track (continuation of road) or the smoother trail twining about it (*not* the enticing trail further to the right). Be alert for the junction with Dune option. At this point the main trail sweeps away to the left through trees and willow thickets under a crag bearing an uncanny resemblance to El Capitan at only half the height. Note a trail coming up through the trees from First Ghost Lake. At the talus slope viewpoint overlooking the lake the Dune option joins in. Across the valley rises Phantom Crag, a climber's cliff with route names like Banshee, The Wraith and Rattling Corner. Further to the left the eye is caught by a fall blowing in the wind like a lacy curtain.

Alternate Dune route to First Ghost Lake
Keep straight at the junction on a good wide trail leading down to the creek in a wadi more appropriate to Saudi Arabia. Jump the stream and wallow up and down dunes and along a sand valley, following tracks of desert lions headed for the lake. Peaks covered in snow and the sound of waterfalls thundering down side canyons dispel the illusion, but it's a lot of fun while it lasts. And as I've said, you may not get past this point. It's the wind blasting through the gap that has scattered sand all through the forest and as you'll see, it emanates from First Ghost Lake, which by fall has shrivelled to a puddle in a bed of hexagonal mud plates. On the flats recross the creek and head west along the south shore on a trail. There are two ways to regain the main trail: the trail through the trees and (better) the one up the talus at the southwest corner of the lake.

To Lake Minnewanka Unlike what is shown on the topo map, the trail climbs over the 1500 m contour line and crosses the mouth of a spectacular canyon known as Hoodoo Hall, en route to the south shore of Second Ghost Lake. Cliffs on either side of the gap reach their greatest height in this area. It's awe-inspiring on squally days when mists lift and part momentarily to reveal tantalizing outlines of ridges nearly 1000 metres overhead.

The trail divides at an unmarked junction midway between the second and third Ghost Lakes, an important intersection comparable 100 years ago to the Banff interchange on the Trans-Canada Highway.

The trail to right fords the channel and becomes the north shore trail along Lake Minnewanka to Banff. Strange as it seems, Sir George Simpson, Governor-in-chief of the Hudson Bay Company, passed this way between the 1st and 3rd of August 1841 on the start of his world tour, which is not a route I would have taken myself.

But back to the junction. Straight ahead, the historic Carrot Creek trail edges along the south bank of Third Ghost Lake,

the route taken just a few weeks later by James Sinclair's party. Their guide was the great Cree Mackipictoon of future North Kananaskis Pass fame, a warrior of ungovernable temper, who was so miffed at Simpson for not letting him guide that trip he disregarded instructions to go via Athabasca Pass and took a willing Sinclair over the *southern* route to Oregon: Whiteman's Gap above Canmore and White Man Pass over the Great Divide—all this occurring some years before Father De Smet's famous crossing.

Anyway, if you follow Sinclair's trail past Third Ghost Lake for a further 2 km you come to Minnewanka Reservoir. Why not tell it like is really is? Before the two dams were built in 1912 and 1941, the surface of the lake was lower by 28 m and didn't exist at all in this place. It's had as many names as water levels: Devil's Lake, Cannibal Lake and Wild Cat or Peechee Lake after Simpson's guide Alexis Piche, whose Cree name was Lynx or Wild Cat. Finally in 1888 it was officially designated Lake Minnewanka, 'Lake of the Water Spirit' or 'Where the Spirits Dwell' (Minnee-wah-kah), and the name Peechee transferred to the mountain facing you across the water. The Spirit refers to the resident mermaid.

OPTION
Hoodoo Hall For canyon lovers.
800 m west of First Ghost Lake the trail crosses a creekbed at GR251813. This is Hoodoo Hall, as ice climbers call it, a wide, flat stony valley enclosed between vertical walls. Stream-hop your way past the hoodoos on the right bank to the forks at GR254800. The left-hand fork is a narrow slit sneakily disguised by a few trees and easily missed. Whereas the right-hand fork is regular canyon, the left-hand fork is sensational, a place where you talk in whispers. In breathless anticipation you wind past such features as the yellow wall and 50 metre-high Green Angel waterfall, the entertainment lasting for about a kilometre before the cleft opens out into last forest below Orient Point.

Above: Looking back down the left-hand fork of Hoodoo Hall from where it opens out. Inset: a hoodoo in the main fork.

12 THE SOUTH GHOST — maps 3, 2, 5 & 4

Backpack
Unofficial trails
Distance 24.4 km to pass
Height gain 808 m
High point 2210 m
Maps 82 O/6 Lake Minnewanka,
82 O/3 Canmore

Access: Forestry Trunk Road 940. Drive 25.4 km north of Highway 1A to Richards Road (sign). Keep right at this junction, then in 150 metres turn first left (west) onto a gated dirt road, which looks like a private road, into a field. This is the rough Ghost River Road. Close the gate. Drive for about 7.5 km to an intersecting NW-SE cutline located 700 m beyond #5 Lesueur Creek's start 2. Turn left and park on the bank top.

The South Ghost trail takes you not without some strenuous climbing to the elusive meadows of South Ghost Pass, where options exist to carry on into Carrot Creek or Cougar Canyon. Of course, you can peel off long before then over a pass into Exshaw Creek or poke around several interesting side valleys on the north side.

The most important thing to know about the South Ghost River itself is that there *is* no river. The country is like a sieve, the water generally surfacing in only three spots: a stretch of about 500 m in the meadows below Stenton Lake, which reappears 2.5 km lower down in the vicinity of the hunter's camp, and a long 2 km stretch west of the confluence with the Ghost. In between the confluence and the hunter's camp is 17 km of virtual desert, so don't plan on camping anywhere soon. McConnell was right on when he wrote in his famous report of 1886, "In the latter part of summer, the circuit of the group might be made without crossing a single running stream". Actually, you wonder how can such a small stream cut such a large valley 1000-1200 metres in depth and almost 2 kilometres wide in places.

To the Hunter's Camp From the top of the bank, hike down either the steep cutline or the trail to its left which merges with the cutline just before a T-junction. Turn right and follow the old road down to the Ghost River, which must be waded to the continuation of the road on the other bank. Head downstream then cut across to the South Ghost near the confluence.

Although the going is fast and easy along gravel flats imprinted here and there with remnants of road, nearly half the day will have slipped by before you draw level with the mountains. As you pass by Orient Point to your right, look for the freestanding arch on the ridge of rotten teeth descending towards the creek. At the bottom of this ridge, pick up much longer sections of road on the north bank. The road is well established by the time you enter the inner valley between the portals of End Mountain and a look-alike Devil's Head on the right, which rises sheer from the creekbed. Half a kilometre farther on the road crosses to the south bank.

When the road recrosses to the north bank and ends, the valley undergoes a character change. Gone are the gravel flats. In its place is a narrow V-shaped valley filled with spruce and traversed by a pack trail that crosses back and forth across the creekbed four times before arriving at the hunter's camp at GR228726. Directly opposite, a sheep trail climbs a side valley towards Exshaw Pass (see #28). Cross the river twice in quick succession. By the time you reach the mouth of a large tributary to the north—only 1 km from the camp—the creek is already dry. Another campsite at the confluence is serviced by water five minutes walk away up the tributary.

To South Ghost Pass So far, the route has been flat and easy up what pilots call a 'sucker canyon', because it lulls you into thinking there's an easy way through, only suddenly the ground is rising at a faster rate than what a light aircraft is capable of climbing and the canyon's too narrow to turn round in. Sadly, the forks area was the site of a fatal crash in 1994.

And for the hiker this is where the hard work begins. The trail first gains height up the west bank of the tributary, then settles into a sometimes steeply rising traverse above the gorge of the South Ghost. Levelling off at treeline, it follows the contours of the mountain around a buttress, dips into a shallow cirque, and finally dissipates behind a clump of spruce trees. Cross intervening hillside into a narrow defile that is South Ghost Pass at the Banff Park boundary.

Before disappearing into the defile, you look down into the head of the South Ghost, a chequerboard of meadows and spruce thickets rising gradually to a lake 1.5 km

distant. Rather disappointingly, the spirit of the Ghost was lost when the lake was officially named in 1987 after James Stenton, a Banff Park warden who in 1946 artificially crossed a male Brook trout with a female Lake trout to produce a Splake. Camping just below the lake on flat ground near a small waterfall—source of the distant water music heard from the trail— places you in a good position to cross over into Cougar Canyon and reach Canmore the next afternoon before the bars close.

GOING FARTHER

To Carrot Creek 13 km pass to Hwy. 1, height loss 850 m. The least attractive option with plenty of bushwhacking lower down.

From the pass descend upper Carrot Creek to the vicinity of campsite Ca 9, where you can either descend the canyon trail with its 25 creek crossings to Highway 1, or climb over the timbered pass to Lake Minnewanka and return via Devil's Gap to the Ghost River Road (#11).

From below Stenton Lake looking up at South Ghost Pass (left). The trail crosses meadows from right to left near treeline.

To Cougar Creek

There are two ways to Carrot/Cougar Col (2452 m) at GR186691, but first you have to get to GR195710 on the boundary ridge from wherever you are camped. This is a fabulous viewpoint in its own right.

Valley Route 2 km, height gain 320 m, height loss 280 m. There's a price to pay for taking the easier route.

Descend a little, towards the south fork of Carrot Creek, then veer left onto a good sheep trail that runs along a bench below a talus slope. When the bench gives out, descend at the edge of scree into the valley head. The penalty must now be paid. You've lost 280 metres of height and in the climb to the col you must regain it all plus another 40 on top of it.

Ridge Route 3.3 km, height gain 410 m, height loss 275 m. The Bighorn haute route follows the boundary ridge where the option exists to pick off two summits.

The ridge route to Cougar Creek follows the ridge at centre, then traverses to the col at far right and on up the skyline ridge.

Turn south and walk over a grassy rise with cairn. That was easy, but as you walk down the other side and peruse the next section of ridge, the butterflies start churning. The upcoming step of chossy cliff bands certainly intimidates. Fortunately, it's one of those places that looks harder than it is, and with your nose to the rock you discover the sheep have trodden out such huge indentations in the brown rubble a veritable staircase exists up the right-hand edge where the going is firmer. Sheep have no aspirations on summits (peak GR200693) and from the flat shoulder above the step, the trail traverses the west slope to the col at GR198692. Still the trail continues, climbing red screes towards, then passing to the right of, the highest summit of the day at 2637 m. This is where you and the trail part company. Turn northwest and descend the hogsback to the Carrot/Cougar Col, a welcome return to the feel of soft grass underfoot and the resinous scents of pine wafting up from the valley below.

See route #14 Cougar Creek: Northwest fork to Carrot/Cougar Col.

13 STONEWORKS CANYON — map 4

Half-day hike
Unofficial trail, creek crossings
Distance 2.5 km to end of canyon
Height gain 366 m
High point 1616 m
Map 82 0/3 Canmore

Access:
1. Trans-Canada Highway (Hwy. 1). Take the west Canmore exit and drive back east on a service road that parallels the highway on the northeast side. Park at a gated road on the left 1.3 km from the exit.
2. Canmore. From Bow Valley Trail (Hwy. 1A) turn onto Benchlands Trail. Just after bridging the Trans-Canada Highway turn left at the cemetery onto the same service road as access 1. Park at a gated road on the right 2 km from Benchlands Trail.

This (almost) subterranean climber's canyon is a terrific choice for stinking hot days when you're looking for somewhere cool. While the going is flat and easy routefinding between barbed wire fences, is a trifle complex.

Walk up the short road beyond the gate. Cross the powerline right-of-way and follow red flagging across a meadow to intersect the access road to Johnny's Stables. Turn left, en route crossing the creek, which is hardly recognizable as such. Pass through the gate in the barbed wire fence, then turn right on a good trail. Near a gap in the fence where the trail divides keep left of the fence. Side by side, trail and fence head up a recognizable valley, eventually reaching the stony creekbed. Around the next bend leave the creekbed for a flagged trail on the left bank. Cross the barbed wire fence. The trail is now between the fence on your left and the creek. Just before the fence turns a right-angle and is strung across the creek, descend the right-hand trail to the creekbed and duck under the wire. Finally rid of constraints, the trail crisscrosses the creek. Ahead is a view of Lady MacDonald and to the left

the lower slopes of the Squaw's Tit. I can hear you saying, "tut, tut", but why should I lie when every scrambler living in Canmore knows it by this name?

The first canyon starts without warning, a deliciously cool tunnel of waterworn rock. Emerge momentarily at The Underworld Crag, featuring climbs with off-putting names like Spider in the Tub. The sunlight is blinding. Then it's back into another narrows, emerging a second time into a bay with a cave on the left wall, a cool retreat reverberating with the noise of running water. After a third narrows the valley opens up and you pass Weird Wall on the left. Cairns guide you up a steeper section of creekbed, then head off right to Arcade climbing cliff. At this point the creek turns left, but you've seen the best it has to offer.

Interestingly, a Canmorite had a thriving sideline going in this valley many years ago, collecting flower seeds and selling them all over the world.

14 COUGAR CREEK — map 4

Half-day, day hike, backpack
Unofficial trail, route, creek crossings
Distance 9.5 km to valley head,
11 km to Carrot/Cougar Col
Height gain valley head 640 m,
Carrot/Cougar Col 1082 m
High point valley head 2012 m,
col 2453 m
Map 82 O/3 Canmore

Access:
1. Canmore. From Bow Valley Trail (Hwy. 1A) at the Greenwood Inn turn onto Benchlands Trail and follow it up the hill. A parking lot is located on the left side of the road just before Cougar Creek crossing.
2. Trans-Canada Highway (Hwy. 1). Take the first exit to Canmore. On reaching Bow Valley Trail (Hwy. 1A) turn left. Turn next left onto Elk Run Boulevard and follow to Cougar Creek crossing. The parking lot is on the right side just after the creek crossing.

Peter Sherrington in Cougar Creek.

The best valley I know for producing sore feet! Winding deep into the heart of the Fairholme Range, spectacular, *stony* Cougar Creek offers everything from a half hour's stroll to a weekend's backpack. A trail gradually whittles down to nothing and while there's lots of stream hopping initially, you should be able to keep your feet dry later in the season. The main bed is usually dry past Canadian Forks and the problem then (for backpackers) is to find water without climbing high.

From the parking lot follow the trail up the northwest bank of Cougar Creek which is lined with riprap. If you see lots of people milling around with binoculars they're eagle counters, and the fellow with the aquiline nose is Peter Sherrington who is largely responsible for bringing eagle migration to everyone's notice. Hence the subdivision name 'Eagle Terrace'. Beyond the houses on the opposite bank you can detect two Rundlestone-faced magazines for storing explosives, and Jack Sum-

merhays' Rundlestone quarry. On this side, watch for the teahouse turn-off at a cairn. Carry on to the canyon mouth and cross the creek.

In the next 3 km, the trail crosses and recrosses the stream about 12 times, passing below sport climbing crags with "C" names like Catseye, Catamount and Cosmology. In contrast to its friendly west face (the two caverns apart), the back side of Grotto Mountain is a dramatic scenario of towering cliffs. Animal life seems minimal, but at one time the valley was rife with game. Shamefully, during the 1920s, when the creek was included in Rocky Mountain Park, the policy was to kill all predators, including cougars and eagles, and this is how the creek got its name, from the 18 killed in this valley by predator control officer Ike Mills. Farther on you pass evolving hoodoos and a number of largely inaccessible caves where someone found a projectile point. The long lost rock paintings remain lost, but I'm working on it.

Reach Canadian Forks (GR195633) where two tributaries head off in east and southeast directions. Keep left. The scenery ahead is no less spectacular, with rock ridges winging up to unnamed summits.

The trail has more or less given up, leaving you to stumble along an outrageously rough, stony creekbed. Bypass black boulders on the right side. At GR196645 pass the mouth of a major tributary to left (*not* to be mistaken for the northwest fork, but quite interesting). Another 1.5 km of similar progress brings you to a heap of stones spilling out of a side valley at GR203658. This one leads to Cougar/Carrot Col.

Easier going with the odd boulder step takes you to the narrows where a cliff sweeps down to the creekbed. Around the bend the terrain eases off to the unexpectedly verdant sanctuary of the upper forks where tributaries spin off like the points of a star. Directly east are the Mythic Towers. The main fork makes a right-angled turn to the northwest and ends under ruddy scree slopes crisscrossed with sheep tracks offering a very steep route to the col at GR198692. This is the same col gained more easily, perhaps, by the ridge route from South Ghost Pass (#12).

Cougar Creek between Canadian Forks and tributary GR196645.

Northwest Fork to Carrot/Cougar Col

If you're looking for alpine meadows in a creek where Dryas mats are the norm, this is the place to make for. Unfortunately, heli-sightseeing operators have also cottoned onto this lovely basin under Mt. Charles Stewart.

The valley floor rises gradually to the rockslide which requires the odd detour and scrabble. A prominent rock tower on the right signals water and the beginning of the steeper section. Fight your way through willow bushes arching over the stream to the first waterfall. Turn it on the left side. Before a second fall, it's perhaps easier to switch to the right bank; either way, both routes involve some serious sidehill bashing that make your ankles ache. Gradually you climb into a smooth green bowl curving up to the boundary ridge with Banff National Park which can be crossed almost anywhere into Carrot Creek. The usual route, though, is the Carrot/Cougar Col (GR186691) if going through to the South Ghost. Follow a small stream identified at the confluence in the basin by outcrops of white rock.

Bottom: Lady MacDonald Teahouse. The gazebo where afternoon teas are presently being served.

Top: Cougar Creek. The beautiful meadows under Mt. Charles Stewart at the head of the northwest fork.

15 LADY MACDONALD TEAHOUSE — map 4

Day hike
Unofficial trail
Distance 3.5 km
Height gain 853 m
High point 2225 m
Map 82 0/3 Canmore

Access:
1. Canmore. From Bow Valley Trail (Hwy. 1A) turn onto Benchlands Trail and follow it across the Trans-Canada Highway and up the hill. A parking lot is located on the left side of the road just before Cougar Creek crossing.
2. Trans-Canada Highway (Hwy. 1). If approaching from the east, take the first exit to Canmore. On reaching Bow Valley Trail (Hwy. 1A) turn left. Turn next left onto Elk Run Boulevard and follow it to Cougar Creek crossing. The parking lot is on the right side just after the creek crossing.

Helicopter pilot Bob Johnson built his teahouse on the south ridge of Lady Mac-Donald to succour his clients. Aware that a teahouse acts like a magnet to people on foot, Bob has made his English-style teas available to hikers Friday through Sunday between the hours of 10 am-5 pm. Book 48 hours ahead by phoning Mountain Wings at 403-678-6465. The season runs from July 1st to November 1st, but call anyway on the off chance of helicopter parties flying in earlier. Sometimes the slope's in condition by late April. As of publication, the teahouse is only half built, which means you're eating either in the gazebo or on the breezy roof of the first floor.

Bob relates horror stories of people picnicking on the helipad. And others freaking out at the thought of descending and expecting a free flight out, or staggering in at dusk and expecting free accommodation. I'm sure this doesn't apply to you. Nevertheless, THIS IS NOT the tourist trail to Lake Agnes Teahouse. This is a demanding grunt up a rough steep slope. On a hot day the slope bakes so take plenty of water.

The teahouse as it will look when finished.
Courtesy Bob Johnson.

Follow Cougar Creek trail along the northwest bank of Cougar Creek. Before the valley squeezes in, turn off left at a cairn. The new trail climbs the steep bank, then turns right, running along the top. At a division use the narrower right-hand option, which omits one steep rise. Shortly after the option rejoins the wider trail, you swing left into a traverse across the west face of the mountain. Turn right at a cairn.

The trail wends right to gain the broad south ridge, then turns up the ridge. At the steepening the direct route—multiple intertwining paths at calf-aching gradient up gravel eroded into dust—is a torment. Knowing it takes the helicopter exactly 3.5 minutes from Canmore to the teahouse does not help morale. You can imagine the pilot pointing out gasping red-faced walkers to his passengers and saying things like "they've hardly moved since I was up here four runs ago".

At the halfway point, the trail shifts to the edge of a perpendicular rock band. At two cairns, either cross the band and grovel up the right side on dust and grass, or continue up the edge on rocks until you're forced over to the right side at the next break. In both cases you finish the climb up steep grass. All this trauma comes to an end on a relatively flat shoulder at treeline.

In your likely state of collapse the nearby teahouse is naturally of most interest. Between the building and the helipad a trail drops to the gazebo, perched dramatically above a 100 metre-high cliff (roped off for the security of tourists), which is available as a rain shelter if nothing else is going on there like a wedding.

Entertainment is provided by helicopters unloading and loading as many as 15 times a day, tourists teeing off the ridge with biodegradable golf balls (highest tee & tea in the Rockies), and hang gliders and parapeters floating hither and thither with the eagles. Did I mention the panorama of the Bow Valley is quite magnificent?

Above: Kootenay, a fit 11 year old. On September 30th, 1995, she was likely the first dog to reach the highest summit of Lady MacDonald.

GOING FARTHER
The summit ridge of Lady MacDonald 2499 m extra height gain 274 m.

Upslope of the helipad a large Canadian flag flaps in the breeze next to an Inuit-type cairn called an Inukshuk. The trail continues up the next rise in the ridge to a blue post and a takeoff ramp for the fliers. Still the trail continues, shortly wending right then straight up a mess of scree and slab to the summit ridge of Lady MacDonald. Unless you're a grade 3 scrambler go no further. The vertiginous drop on the east side should do the trick. Or to put it another way, if you have to cross the next section of ridge *à cheval* it doesn't bode well for the difficult pitch below the summit.

Likely the first person to look over the edge was James Hector on August 16, 1859. Setting out from the site of Canmore he climbed in excess of 3,000 ft. in a northeasterly direction to a summit, noting the top of the mountain had a sharp ridge. The view was like a "magnified geological model", but unfortunately, before he could work out the structure of this portion of the Rocky Mountains, he ran out of time.

Below: the ridge above the helipad. You can spot the trail climbing onto the summit ridge of Lady MacDonald. The summit is out of sight beyond the left-hand top.

16 GROTTO MOUNTAIN — map 4

Long day hike
Unofficial trail & route
Distance 10 km return
Height gain 1365 m
High point 2706 m
Map 82 0/3 Canmore

Access: Bow Valley Trail (Hwy. 1A). Gain Hwy. 1A from the Trans-Canada Highway east exit into Canmore. Turn left (east) on Hwy. 1A, then left (north) onto Indian Flats Road. Keep left (Bow Valley Riding Association stable to right) and drive up the hill to the parking lot of the Alpine Club of Canada clubhouse.

The hole in the ridge that you walk across quite unknowingly. The narrowest part!

The huge mass of Grotto Mountain towering above the Bow Valley has a route up the sloping west flank that is easy *at the moment.* The creeping quarry is coming this way and then you'll need iron ladders bolted to the rock and accessories like belay ropes, slings and karabiners to get you up the first 50 metres. Equally worrying, Ben Gadd seems to think the stripping of limestone from the down-dip edge of the slabs *all along the base* of the mountain could destabilize the slope above and send it crashing down like Turtle Mountain. Best to climb it now, then. The route is a two-piecer: the laborious ascent to the northwest ridge followed by an interesting ridge walk with some mild scrambling. Exposure is nil—the ridge is wider than it looks from down below.

It was named Pic de la Grotto by James Hector and Eugene Bourgeau on August 12th, 1858 while botanizing. Not after the two massive grottos of the west face, but after a cave with a high-arched roof and narrow mouth, the location of which appears to have been lost.

A well-defined trail leaves the upper parking lot, heading up and right on a grassy slope. At the four-way intersection go straight and cross a tributary gully. The trail wends left and continues up the left bank of the main gully (the one issuing from the

northernmost grotto). The ground rises in three grassy steps to the base of the mountain proper. After the first step and on succeeding steps and between benches the trail is augmented by small cairns. At the final bench you should be just to the left of a dry creek, a tributary of the main gully that has turned away to the east.

As of 1995, the laborious pull to treeline no longer involves dragging yourself from tree to tree like a damp washrag. As you climb bow down and give thanks to the Rocky Mountain Section of the ACC, who with pickaxes, hoes and rakes have scratched out one good trail featuring cairns, flagging and switchbacks (now there's a luxury). Start up the grassy rib to the left of the dry gully. In the trees the trail winds about avoiding rock bands and hitting a few grassy openings with views of Canmore. Ultimately you arrive at a belt of slabs where an unavoidable but easy two step scramble gains you a cairn on top. Continue zigging between more slabby outcrops to treeline, a remarkably clean demarcation of trees and talus, and much higher up than is indicated on the topo map.

The talus slope above lies back at a moderate angle. Follow a line of large cairns straight up, then head right on a trail below the ridge line to gain the northwest ridge just before a minor hump.

The northwest ridge is easy, the first bit of scrambling occurring at two protruding rock bands slanting left to right down the west flank. The small one has an easy way through, but the second one requires some inward facing downclimbing on the far side. Alternatively, descend the scree gully on the right a short way, then cut left across easy slabs to the top of the band, which is easily descended in a couple of places. After this comes a longer, steeper pull up rubble on the right flank to gain the upper ridge which is wide and grassy with rocky bits to keep up the interest. Amazingly, this is where you walk over an arch without knowing it, unquestionably the narrowest part of the whole ridge. The final rise to the summit is girdled by innumerable rock bands about four metres high, which are so much fun to scramble up you'd be a moron to stagger up the talus to the right.

The view from the cairn doesn't disappoint. In the words of David Thompson the mountains of the Fairholme Range resemble waves of the ocean in a wintry storm. "Imagination apt to say, these must once have been liquid, and in that state when swelled to its greatest agitation suddenly congealed and made solid by "Power Omnipotent". View all the ridge you've just walked up, plus the cement works, Calgary, and most thrilling, Mt. Assiniboine and the Royal Group.

The summit ridge beyond is broad and easy and you have this terrible urge to run off down the ridge for 3 km to the other end. Unfortunately, descending from the lower summit to Highway 1A is fraught with difficulties, not the least of which is the quarry. By the next revision, though, a well-marked loop will be available. Watch this space!

The upper ridge with the summit in sight.

17 GRASSI LAKES LOOP — map 4

Half-day hike
Official & unofficial trails
Distance 4.2 km loop
Height gain 244 m
High point 1670 m
Map 82 0/3 Canmore

Access: Smith-Dorrien—Spray Trail (Hwy. 742). After passing the Canmore Nordic Centre turn next left towards Spray Residences. Keep left (Grassi Lakes trailhead to right) and drive past the houses to a large parking lot on the left signed 'Public parking for hikers and ice climbers'. This is just before the bridge over Rundle Canal.

One of the rock paintings in the canyon above the lakes.

This little loop makes a nice change from climbing up and down the crowded Grassi Lakes interpretive trail. But even in the midst of a hundred tourists Grassi Lakes is still a worthwhile objective for its varied scenery including waterfalls, two tiny lakes, a canyon, cliffs, rock paintings, pentstock, pipeline and powerlines.

I was hoping to take in Whiteman's Pond, which would have made a much better loop, but TransAlta has surrounded the headgates with impenetrable chainlink fence requiring a Stalag 5 escape routine.

Walk back along the road between the houses and Rundle Canal and get the boring bit over first. After the last building cut through to Grassi Lakes trailhead (picnic tables, biffy).

Follow Grassi Lakes trail which crosses TransAlta's service road, then settles into a gradual climb to a viewpoint looking down onto Spray Power Plant and Rundle Reservoir and up to Chinaman's Peak and the magnificent waterfall below the lakes. The trail twists uphill (congested area), ultimately climbing Rundlestone steps right of the weeping wall to a rustic bench where you can sit and read interpretive signs. Traverse left above cliffs, cross the bridge over Grassi Creek and emerge on TransAlta's service road. Turn right. The gleam of azure you see a minute later is not,

I repeat, *not* Lake Minnewanka as one tourist was overheard to say to another. It is lower Grassi Lake.

Interpretive trails make a figure of eight around both lakes, so it's up to you how you tackle the sightseeing, though most people go around clockwise and make a detour in the crossover to visit Grassi's plaque. I love coming here to drool over the clarity and colour of the water. Overlooking the upper lake are pockmarked cliffs, remnants of a coral reef riddled with small caves and prehistoric rock shelters where you can eat lunch if it's raining. I'd be leery of eating lunch farther out on the west shore in case you get a car on your head. Not only is the highway directly above (honestly, abandoned cars have been fished from the lake and does the sign 'Hikers below' really deter such idiots?), but I've also seen sheep cavorting about on the edge, dislodging rocks.

The lakes used to be called Twin Lakes when Canmore miner Lawrence Grassi, (best known for his meticulous trail building at Lake O'Hara) built his trail 30 years before construction of the Spray Power

Climbing to the canyon from upper Grassi Lake. Farther away is lower Grassi Lake and TransAlta's service road.

Plant. It started from his house on Three Sisters Drive and followed Canmore Creek to the sulphur spring swimming hole before climbing up to the lakes. Nowadays if you followed the same route you'd have to swim the canal.

To the Rock Paintings From the far end of upper Grassi Lake a mess of unofficial trails climb the badly eroded slope into the canyon above. Facing you on the first large boulder you come to are rock paintings of people and caribou believed painted well over a thousand years ago by ancestors of the Kootenay Indians as part of a vision quest. Beyond the boulders the shortest stream in the Rockies springs forth below

the dam and after watering a few arnicas disappears down a hole below the cliff on the right side. Incredible to relate, in the 1800s this canyon, or to be scrupulously correct, Whiteman's Gap, was the major thoroughfare through the Rockies to Oregon. It boggles the mind to think of horses picking their way over the boulders. More likely the trail climbed up the forested south bank.

Descent Return to the service road below lower Grassi Lake and turn right. Let the tourists descend the interpretive trail. Keep right at this junction and climb to the end of the service road at the pipeline. A trail ducks under the pipe and heads off uphill through a rather beautiful pine forest with moss and boulders. Come to a T-junction with another trail. It has an old established feel to it, which makes you suspect it could be the original trail to Oregon. (Up slope, it ultimately disappears under the waters of Whiteman's Pond.)

Turn left down the hill. After the steepness moderates, you cross a talus gully with a neck-breaking view of Chinaman's Peak. The trail continues, twisting down the side of a talus ribbon, then crossing it (historic spade to left) and cutting across another thin strip of talus to flagging where it turns left and makes a beeline for the powerline right-of-way (flagging). Head for the powerline access road (more flagging).

Turn left and walk the access road under the powerlines. Note a service road heading right past Grassi's sulphur spring to Highway 742, then a disused service road climbing up to the pipeline on the left. Wind down to Spray Power Plant and cross a bridge over Rundle Canal where freed water dawdles along, little suspecting it's going to be to be recycled another five times before reaching Calgary. Turn right at the plant access road and arrive back at the parking lot in a couple of minutes.

Right: No. 2 Mine entrance and the Lamp House.

18 CANMORE TO WIND VALLEY — maps 4 & 6

Day hike
Unofficial trails
Distance 13 km
Height gain 80 m
High point 1432 m
Map 82 O/3 Canmore

Access:
1. Canmore. Start at Bow River bridge. On the west bank is a small parking lot on the south side.
2. Wind Valley. Via West Wind Loop #21A at the T-junction west of Wind Creek bridge.

Running from one end of Three Sisters Resorts to the other, the route follows assorted trails, mine roads and railroads. Complicating the already complicated route is construction of the 'Lower Parkway', housing pods and residential roads, golf courses, hotels and the conse-

quent disappearance or appropriation of parts of the route. It's all a trail writer's nightmare! So not only am I pointing out artifacts from Canmore's coal mining era, I'm also anticipating what's going to be happening in the next few years. Know that the Mine Haulage Road is numbered at important junctions.

Excepting for one stretch along the trolley line, this is not necessarily the route the future Trans Canada Trail will take between Quarry Lake parking lot and Dead Man Flat. As if there aren't enough trails, new ones will be built.

Canmore to No. 2 Mine Head southeast on a wide trail to the Lift Station access road. Turn left. Just before the building cross meadow to a new (1996) footbridge spanning Canmore Creek.

On the far bank turn left onto the CPR spur line, sadly bulldozed to dirt road, and follow it between the creek and the rock cut harbouring bunches of rhubarb and Butter & Eggs. Just before Prospect Properties, a trail crosses the road. Turn left and skirt around the back of houses costing in excess of $300,000 to the bank of the Bow River. On coal spoil the trail edges around No. 2 Mine site which is presently being remodelled as a golf course. Looking west, you can spot two mine entrances and the Lamp House. At the chemical creek the trail is forced right past the noxious 'spring' to a junction.

There are two options. Either turn left and walk past the transformer station up a hill to a four-way intersection with the trolley line (coal cars). Or, my recommendation, nip across to the left-hand mine entrance, actually a fan portal opened in 1903. Now walk diagonally right up an old grassy trail to the Lamp House where the miners checked in and out. Just below is No. 2 Mine entrance, recently uncovered, and slated to become a tourist attraction. I'm not sure whether you'll be offered a ride on a coal car, but you can bet there'll be lots of interpretive signs. The Lamp House is the start of the trolley line, an unmistakable rock cut with ties, pins and coal dust, which can be followed to the four-way junction. En route, look for historic trash thrown down the banks.

No. 2 Mine to Three Sisters Creek At a four-way intersection go straight (or left if you took the first option). The lovely stretch through pines is due for a takeover by the 'Lower Parkway' and a Marriott Hotel which means the future trail will be re-routed to the riverbank. But for now you intersect a grassy road, then watch for a road coming in from Riverside Mine on the banks of the Bow. At a power pole, just after an old powerline right-of-way comes down off the hill to the right, the trolley line divides with a spur heading left to No. 4 Mine. You are going to go right but are forced by a willow thicket to go left initially. Where a road forks left off the spur line, head right by the side of a biffy to rejoin the main trolley line. Turn left. Shortly cross waterless Three Sisters Creek. The grassy road on the right and the cutline following are the routes to Three Sisters Creek (#19).

Three Sisters Creek to Stewart Creek The pin-strewn trolley line inclines gently up-hill to 9 where it crosses the Mine Haulage Road at a powerline right-of-way. At the next powerline crossing a road heads right to the future clubhouse for Stewart Creek Golf Course, to be sited on the hill above. You'll see why. After passing Dry Lake you round a bend and overlook a reclaimed strip mine (later Canmore's garbage dump, soon to be golf course), the deep point of the dump semi-circled by a cliff with salt lick. You can imagine golfers sitting by picture windows (you can now see Pigeon Mountain), sipping aperitifs and exclaiming over Bighorns tee-tering about on the edge of the carefully arranged salt lick that was transplanted from Dry Lake after decontamination.

Just before the cliff, the trolley line has a temporary hiatus at a dip, but picks up again around the bend (*not* the road running along the edge of the cliff). In this section the surface looks like a stream went through. It did. The result of a diverted Stewart Creek coursing down the trolley line and over the cliff to put out a fire in the dump. In future this is where you'll don hard hats, because the Trans Canada Trail will head straight through the middle of the golf course. Right now, disregard construction roads to right and left. Back in trees, intersect the dry bed of Stewart Creek and Fall Creek road. Beyond the wide gravel outwash is the four-way intersection with Stewart Creek exploration road. The Mine Haulage Road is a few metres away on the left at 15.

Right: Upper Spray Falls.

Stewart Creek to Wind Valley Road The trolley line continues straight ahead, hugging the foot of Wind Ridge. Cross a road heading to a relay station, then the creek where Henry Smith found coal in 1906. Shortly, a minor road turns off to the right and the trolley line makes a finishing loop. Take the left leg to the Mine Haulage Road at 16. A right turn gains you the environs of No. 3 Mine, a large meadow with a very fine view of Grotto Mountain. Upslope are a couple of grassy roads, the left-hand leading to the entry, the right-hand to a building, as well hidden as a Mayan ruin, which houses a water tank. Preceding No. 3 in 1885 was Marsh Mine in nearby Marsh Creek.

A little further on is a very important road junction at 17. Keep right for West Wind Loop and Wind Ridge. Go left otherwise, plunging down by the side of coal spoil past a gate and across Cairnes Creek to a low point. Start the insufferably long climb back up to West Wind Loop. There's no need to go far. At the road's nearest approach to the powerline (seen through the trees on the left) a flagged trail dekes through to the right-of-way. Cross, angling right, to the start of a grassy old road at a berm. Keep left a little way in and emerge at

three large rocks marking the T-junction with Wind Valley exploration road.

To Dead Man Flat Turn left, then almost immediately right off the dirt road onto a much pleasanter track that lingers below a ridge of Douglas firs, before winding down to the Trans-Canada, almost but not quite rejoining Wind Valley road at the road sign 'Dead Man's Flat'. Lest you think the hamlet is named after some hiker who got run over while sprinting across two lanes of traffic to the Bighorn Food Store, let me assure you it was named after John Marret. Before 1904 this part of the coal company's land was called 'The Frenchmen's Cabin' after John and his brother Francois who was a bit of a weirdo. He had this problem with Chinook winds (something Stephen King has not yet tapped into) and night after night he would lie in bed listening to the 'whirring electric machine' coming to get him. He finally cracked on the night of May 10th, 1904. Convinced John was behind the plot, Francois picked up an axe and killed his sleeping brother.

To West Wind Loop and Pigeon Mountain Trailhead Turn right. Pass a road to Thunderstone Quarry on the left. At junction 23 the route follows the road to the right across the powerline right-of-way. However, you'd have to be on your last legs to turn down a detour to Upper Spray Falls.

Keep left, then, at 23. At an intersecting road turn left into a camping area in a clearing. Turn left and walk through to more camping spots under the trees. From here a good flagged trail runs along the bank top to the three-drop falls, then continues downstream to the fabulous viewpoint used in the Three Sisters Resorts brochure. Return to the intersecting road, but instead of turning right towards 23, cross and join the other road at the powerline right-of-way. Turn left and in less than a kilometre come to the T-junction with West Wind Loop on the west bank of Wind Creek.

For Pigeon Mountain trailhead cross the bridge, then turn left across Pigeon Creek. Follow the old road out to the parking lot.

19 THREE SISTERS CREEK — map 6

Day hike
Unofficial trail, creek crossings
Distance 4.9 km to forks from access 1,
4.4 km from access 2
Height gain 300 m to forks
High point at forks 1615 m
Map 82 O/3 Canmore

Access:

1. From Canmore follow Three Sisters Drive into Three Sisters Resorts. Drive past Homestead Properties to a junction at the information centre and park. The road under construction to the left is the 'Lower Parkway'. The road beyond the gate is the Mine Haulage Road.

2. Trans-Canada Highway (Hwy. 1).
Westbound: Bow River Campground. Drive to the far end of the loop by the river near site #15. A trail heads under the highway bridge to the track accessed by eastbound vehicles.
Eastbound: Just after Bow River bridge (southeast of the Canmore interchange) turn sharp right on a track doubling back to the river.
Also accessible via Canmore to Wind Valley (#18) from the trolley line just east of Three Sisters Creek.

The valley northwest of The Three Sisters has been mucked up by humans ever since the loggers first got in about a century ago. Relics of that era and more recent changes brought about by Canmore Mines can be seen at various locations to well past the forks. I've literally stumbled over a cable near the junction with the tributary at GR153547! Know that a fault prevents all but the most determined hiker from going too far up the valley. Very determined hikers have the dubious pleasure of climbing to Three Sisters Pass and making a point to point with route #63.

Access is through land owned by Three Sisters Resorts who are busily constructing roads, housing pods and golf courses for the next 20 years. In the next few years the most likely scenario is that the Lower Parkway will intersect access 2.

The fault waterfall.

1. Canmore Access 2.2 km. Walk or bike the Mine Haulage Road to Three Sisters logging road, which is positively identified by the number 8.

2. Trans-Canada Highway Access 1.7 km. Brooke will be pleased this doesn't involve climbing fences posted with 'No Trespassing' signs. On the bank of the Bow River west of the highway bridge a good trail starts at a large rock and follows the bank top. Pass a survey marker, intersect a trail, then turn left into a flagged cutline.

Follow the cutline, en route intersecting a minor road and trolley spur line heading to No. 4 Mine. A little further on, cross a grassy road and a few seconds later reach the trolley line (#18). Continue up the cutline to the Mine Haulage Road, turn right and follow it past 8A and Three Sisters Creek to Three Sisters logging road at 8.

3. From Canmore to Wind Valley #18 0.8 km. Shortly after crossing Three Sisters Creek, turn right up a grassy road. At a T-junction with a minor road connecting Riverside Mine to 8A on the Mine Haulage Road (arrow-shaped blaze) turn right. Back at Three Sisters Creek turn left and walk easily up its stony bed to the Mine Haulage Road. Turn right and walk to 8.

Three Sisters Creek to the forks 2.7 km. At 8 the Three Sisters logging road heads south across the powerline right-of-way and climbs steadily up the bank west past branching tracks to where the valley pinches in. At this point Three Sisters Creek has water and scattered old wood flumes. A little further on wade the creek below a dam and reservoir to the southeast bank. Keep left (Bench trail to right) and in a few minutes come to the impasse, a small waterfall marking a major fault where the road has collapsed into the creekbed.

With no ladder available, alternatives are a crumbly ledge on the left or the slab right of the fall which has a reputation for bloodying thighs when people in shorts slide off. Personally, I use the mossy alternative, unattractive though it is: a steep detour up-down above the left-hand cliff.

Regain the road at a cairn. Cross the creek to the northeast bank, then keep left three times. Pass two mossy springs and pieces of metal lying about like buckets and drums. Keep right (road downgrades to trail), then cross the creek and back again. Below a cliff there's a gap in the trail (use dry creekbed), but it soon reappears and takes you to the forks at GR157552. This occurs where a deeply incised tributary comes in from between the Ship's Prow and a similar cliff to its left that is just as dramatic. Amazingly, both are mere buttresses of five-summited Mt. Lawrence Grassi. A few metres upstream on the southeast bank of the main fork you'll find the ruins of two loggers' cabins, and artifacts composed of the usual rusted pails and cans.

GOING FARTHER

Three Sisters Viewpoints A picture postcard view of The Three Sisters demands a strenuous climb in excess of 350 vertical metres up either the right or left bank of the deeply-incised tributary. The left bank has helpful old logging roads that start from a little higher up the main creekbed on the right.

Three Sisters Pass 2262 m 2.4 km to pass from forks, 620 m height gain from forks.

The best way to the pass is from the other side via #63.

One of the cabins at the forks. The Prow pokes up above the trees at upper right.

20 STEWART CREEK & MIDDLE SISTER — map 6

**Day hike to the forks, long day
scramble to Middle Sister
Unofficial trails, creek crossings
Distance 7.5 km to forks from access 1,
3.8 km from access 2
Height gain 335 m
High point at forks 1645 m
Map 82 O/3 Canmore**

Access:
1. Canmore. Follow Three Sisters Drive into Three Sisters Resorts. Drive past Homestead Properties to a junction at the information centre and park. The road under construction to the left is the 'Lower Parkway'. The road beyond the gate is the Mine Haulage Road.
2. Trans-Canada Highway (Hwy. 1). Park at or opposite the sign 'Visit Canmore' northwest of Dead Man Flat.
Also accessible via Canmore to Wind Valley (#18) where it intersects the Stewart Creek exploration road.

Unlike Three Sisters Creek, the going up the valley between The Three Sisters and Wind Ridge to the forks is easy, though five creek crossings might deter golfers. Conversely, Middle Sister is a long strenuous trip on scree requiring prior planning.

Supposedly the creek was named after George Stewart, the Dominion land surveyor who became Superintendent of Rocky Mountain Park in 1887. I remain unconvinced. At the time there were more than enough Stewarts in the Canadian Anthracite Coal Company at Canmore to choose from, including directors McLeod, Archibald and John. I fancy Archibald, the only director to live in Canmore, who got everyone drinking water from Canmore Creek in preference to the Bow River which was contaminated with water pumped out of the mines.

Access is through land owned by Three Sisters Resorts, who are constructing roads, housing pods and golf courses for the next 20 years. At the moment none of the accesses are affected.

1. Canmore Access 5.3 km From the information centre, walk or bike up the Mine Haulage Road to the Stewart Creek exploration road which is positively identified by the number 15.

2. Trans-Canada Access 4.3 km From the eastbound lane cut though to the powerline and turn right. A short distance along turn left on an exploration road. Cross the berm at the forest's edge to a T-junction. Go right. At a Y-junction turn left past the sign and emerge on the Mine Haulage Road at 14. Now in the past I've always cut across to the trolley line, but the road opposite is destined as a golf course, so I'd advise turning left and walking up the haulage road to 15. All this is bikeable.

Stewart Creek to the forks 2.2 km At 15, turn right (south) up the Stewart Creek exploration road. Straight off, cross the trolley line (#18) and halfway up the hill ignore a side road heading left. When the road forks alongside Stewart Creek go right and cross the creek. In May of 1992 the gravel intake was the site of an environmentalists' camp-in protesting the diversion of Stewart Creek, which instead of disappearing into the depths of a mine will soon squirt out of sprinklers onto golfing greens.

Keep left all the way up the hill into the valley confines (all right forks lead to nearby Fall Creek which has wooden flumes and a waterfall worth looking at). During the long straight on the northwest bank look for a concrete dam, water flume and trestle bridge. The road temporarily disintegrates to trail, then crosses the creek where it reverts to road for an equally long stretch on the southeast bank. Ahead is a spiky peak with no name. En route you pass a couple of game trails heading up Wind Ridge, one overgrown road and one rather pretty waterfall. Where the road ends at a prospect, a trail carries on. Either struggle straight ahead through undergrowth or take the right-hand detour which crosses the creek twice before getting back on line. Cross a side creek, then Stewart Creek. A final stint along the northwest bank ends at the forks (cairn). By this point most of the water is travelling via the underground.

Middle Sister 2769 m

15.4 km return from Hwy. 1, total height gain 1458 m. Be up at the crack of dawn for this one, a long but surprisingly easy trudge to the middle summit of The Three Sisters. Neglected no more, thanks to Alan Kane, Middle Sister now sees about a dozen parties on a sunny weekend, so quite a trail is developing, and where there's no trail, there are cairns. Expect plenty of scree-covered slopes as arid as the Sahara Desert, so carry *lots* of water. Biking up Stewart Creek will save you a couple of hours.

At the forks turn right up the stony creekbed. Level with the next side creek a trail starts between two cairns and leads to the avalanche area. Stay on the right side trail. Between here and the upper forks use snippets of trail on one side or the other or just flog up the creekbed from cairn to cairn. You'll be spellbound by the sight of First Sister girdled in cliffs; this is definitely its photogenic side. To its left Middle Sister looks equally impregnable and it's sobering to think that before you can even set foot on the mountain you've got to get that long line of cliffs behind you.

When you turn right at the upper forks the going gets rough. Gouged between scree slopes, the bed's full of boulders rolled into it and small rock steps with bypass trails on the right side—the cruxes! Ultimately the gully bends left and unfolds at a large cairn at the edge of the scree basin.

Middle stretches of Stewart Creek below the forks. Not Middle Sister. Looking towards the spiky peak with no name.

Finally you get to set foot on the mountain. Turn right and head up the large scree fan to the left of the great cliffs, a number of vague trails coalescing into one corkscrewing trail, which above the level of the cliffs turns right onto easy-angled scree slopes stretching almost 2 km to the col between Big and Middle Sisters. As you can see, the cartographers have got the contour lines all a bit wrong at this point; some of the higher ones should be taken out and inserted lower down. Follow bits of trail or cairns, little ups alternating with long traverses, ultimately floundering up the draw in the orange rock zone where the slope takes a steeper turn. Save lots of water for this bit. At the top cairns guide you to the second lowest col between Big Sister and your objective.

Above: A boring but reassuring photo for people unsure about climbing Middle Sister. It shows the rising traverse across easy-angled scree slopes and up the shallow orange-coloured gully. The summit peeks over the top. Easy, eh?

Below: Close to the summit is a fantastic view of Little Sister. Wind Ridge to right.

The final slope is a gigantic helipad slightly tilted to the northwest. A trail hugs the edge of the precipice to the right, where you get your thrills looking across a bizarre array of pinnacles to Little Sister. At the summit cairn a large chunk of the Bow Valley is revealed, including Canmore, and all of Mt. Lawrence Grassi, thus enabling you to sort out the route to Three Sisters Pass from Three Sisters Creek. Unfortunately, I'd have to rate the view a 9 because Big Sister hides the mountain that should be in every view, Mt. Assiniboine. The other thing Big Sister hides is approaching thunderstorms. At such times it helps to have Steve Rothfels up there with you to advise about weather.

The other thing about Middle Sister is that helicopters are continually whirring over West Wind Pass on your left and Three Sisters Pass on your right. The person who had to put up with none of these nuisances, but then he didn't have a trail either, was Mont. B. Morrow, operating officer of the Canmore Mines 1914-1926, who on August 12th, 1921 was the first person on record to climb Middle Sister. That's him in the metal box.

21 WIND VALLEY TRAILS — map 6

I'm not surprised if you can't keep up with developments in Wind Valley because I can hardly keep up myself. Basically, K Country controls the south end of the valley and the Town of Canmore the north end. Three Sisters Resorts, a private landowner within the town, used to hold the surface rights to the north end, but after NRCB recommendations that nothing be built in the valley, did a land swap with the town and will now be building all around Quarry Lake instead. It does, however, still hold the mines and mineral rights. Others with a jurisdictional interest in the valley include the divisions of Alberta Environmental Protection (like Fish & Wildlife), various conservation groups, Parks Canada and the Stoney Indians.

On August 3rd, 1995 it was designated a Natural Area under the Special Places 2000 initiative, which means you're still liable to run into OHVs, hunters and helicopters.

Many people are pushing to upgrade the status to Ecological Reserve which would do away with most of the above. Sounds good. However, hunting and trapping would likely be allowed "for the management and preservation of the animal and plant life" and as "a management tool for decreasing the risk of animals becoming habituated" to new housing development on the fringes.

There's also a danger for people en foot in over regulation with restrictions so complex you'll need to consult a computer. "Let's see, Wind Ridge is closed September to April, the access trail is open July to April. But we can't do a traverse because the valley is closed May to July, which leaves just August". I am not making this up! In the past, hikers have been limited naturally by the state of the trails, lack of signposts, intermittent bridges allowed to wash out and rough terrain. With new development on the fringes, environmentalists have this huge worry about the valley being overrun and to counteract this are proposing to upgrade (gravel) certain trails, erect signposts, blinds, benches and put in an interpretive trail with signs showing you what you might see if you were allowed onto Wind Ridge, thereby attracting the very people who would only hike there in the first place because of upgraded trails, signposts, blinds, benches and interpretive trails with signs. The thought of overzealous stewards giving me a ticking off for setting foot past a blind makes me want to throw up. The solution? Dress like a hunter and carry a bow.

Windtower from Wind Ridge trail.

21A West Wind Loop

Half-day hike
Unofficial exploration roads
Distance 8.6 km round trip
Height gain 335 m
High point 1737 m
Map 82 O/3 Canmore

Access: Trans-Canada Highway (Hwy. 1). At Dead Man Flat interchange, follow signs to Alpine Resort Haven. At the final bend turn right to Pigeon Mountain trailhead and park before the hiking sign. The trail is the continuation of the dirt road.
Also accessible via Canmore to Wind Valley trail (#18) at junction 17.

This quartet of mine roads hardly qualify as an interesting walk by themselves. My advice is to use the loop as access to the other three trails that are much more interesting. Mind you, if you're out just to get fit and don't care a hang about scenery, this loop is just the ticket. I guarantee it'll have you on your knees by the time you get back to the parking lot. Know that the return leg is presently being driven by Three Sisters Resorts employees with keys to the gates.

To Wind Creek The dirt road leads to the powerline right-of-way where Skogan Pass trail turns left. Follow the road across the right-of-way, around a logged meadow, through a gate and down to Pigeon Creek crossing (culvert). At the four-way junction with Mt. Allan trail on the southwest bank turn right and cross Wind Creek on a bridge to gain the main Wind Valley exploration road from Dead Man Flat. Trail #18 turns right, you turn left.

Valley Leg Soon after a gate keep straight (return loop comes in from the right). After this junction the main valley dirt road is obvious. It stays on the northwest bank while grassy side roads peel off to the left across West Wind Creek. The second (first obvious) road to left after a couple of glades leads to the hoodoos. At the sixth (fifth

obvious) junction your road turns right. Almost straightaway Wind Valley trail turns off to the left.

Up Leg The next stretch of road is a grunt: 215 vertical metres gained in a little over a kilometre. One or two Douglas firs signal the final steepening to a flagged four-way intersection at the high point. Just the place where you need a bench for collapse, but you won't find one. After recovery it pays to wander out onto Wind Ridge meadows for a rewarding view of Windtower as shown on the previous page.

Down Leg At the four-way junction turn right. Back in the pines, the way is all downhill. Pass a grassy road to left. When you come to a blazed tree and trail on the right, stop. Officially you're supposed to carry on down the road to a T-junction with the Mine Haulage Road at 18. Why bother when you can take the shortcut trail on the right?

Of course, if you're headed for Canmore then you have to take the road to 18. On reaching the Mine Haulage Road turn left down the hill. Keep left at junction 17 and follow route #18.

Return Leg Should you find yourself at 18 on the Mine Haulage Road, turn right and climb past an intersecting cutline to the top of a hill where the shortcut comes in from the right (having saved you a climb).

All is now downhill. Three roller coaster hills leave you in no doubt as to why this road flunked the test for residential street. Shortly after a grassy road takes off to the right and a road comes in from the left you arrive at the T-junction with Wind Valley exploration road. Turn left through the gate and return the way you came.

Wind Ridge from Wind Valley.

21B Upper Wind Valley

Half-day hike
Unofficial trails
Distance 1.3 km from West Wind Loop
Height gain 35 m
High point 1524 m
Map 82 O/3 Canmore

Access: Via West Wind Loop at the end of the valley leg.

An easy alternative to West Wind Loop. Know that grizzlies are attracted to the fens occupying the other half of the valley, so stick to the trail.

A kilometre-long trail leads into the big meadow with its million dollar view of Windtower and Wind Ridge. Pick up a trail at the far right-hand corner (blaze) and follow it through two smaller glades and a stretch of aspen forest onto open slopes below Wind Ridge where it peters out at a blazed tree. Look across to West Wind Pass which in preliminary plans for K Country was earmarked for a grade 7 bike path.

21C Wind Ridge

Day hike
Unofficial trail & route
Summit 7.7 km from trailhead
Height gain 762 m
High point 2164 m
Map 82 O/3 Canmore

Access: Via West Wind Loop at the high point.

From the Trans-Canada, the dark timbered mass of Wind Ridge doesn't look too interesting. On the other side of the mountain, though, hidden from view, grassy slopes wearing crags like necklaces provide a beautiful route to the summit with one pitch of scrambling.

Turn left onto a nice flat road and with much anticipation traverse out of the trees onto the lush meadows of Wind Ridge's southeast face. Ahead is a breathtaking view of Windtower, best seen in late afternoon light when the sun picks out every rib and gully. Hard to believe this dramatic summit is an easy walk up the backside. The road, deteriorating quickly now, curves

Above: the crux. Gaining the ledge.

uphill and ends at a new vantage point for Wind Ridge, Rimwall, West Wind Pass, and behind Windtower the original Wind Mountain (now peak #1 of Mt. Lougheed), named by James Hector during the Palliser expedition of 1858. Historians would have us believe that while Hector was busy discovering Kicking Horse Pass for the Trans-Canada Highway, Eugene Bourgeau climbed Wind Mountain while botanizing. More likely he was running from one new flower to another on the lower grassy slopes of Wind Ridge, having a marvellous time. In damper facets Blue-eyed grass grows in abundance like a blue haze.

A trail continues up to the saddle on the east ridge. Turn left at the T-junction and peruse the ridge ahead. It marks the demarcation of north side trees and south side meadows where horizontal sandstone bands give the mountain an attractive castellated appearance. One rock band will prove troublesome to non-scramblers. But first it's easy going on grass under occasional Douglas firs leaning into the slope. A steeper winding climb between outcrops leads to

Below: looking towards the summit ridge from above the crux.

the crux which weeds out people with short legs and weak arms. An obvious ledge makes a rising traverse from left to right, but how to get onto it, if, like me, you can't put your left foot where your left ear is? Options farther to the left aren't any better, so get someone to give you a shove. Above, the trail continues in much the same way as before, winding around outcrops with a selection of alpines my friend would like to take home. All climbing at an end, walk the flat summit ridge to the cairn, geodetic survey marker, and if you're unlucky, a helicopter disgorging heli-hikers. A new view has opened up to the north. Here's a chance to examine the route up Stewart Creek to Middle Sister.

Most people descend the same way, a few traversing the ridge to the col under Rimwall from where it's easy enough to drop into Wind Valley and make a loop with #21B, should you be so lucky to find the end of the trail.

21D South Wind Hoodoos

Half-day
Unofficial trails
Distance 3.2 km from trailhead
Height gain 200 m
High point 1600 m
Map 82 O/3 Canmore

Access: Via West Wind Loop, valley leg.

I first saw a photo of these hoodoos in a 1949 geology bulletin, otherwise I'd still be ignorant of their existence. Actually, if you know where to look, you can pick out The Obelisk from Wind Ridge. They make a good half-day objective early or late in the season when the weather is rotten higher up. Expect a moderately strenuous climb on exploration road.

As indicated, turn left off West Wind Loop's valley leg onto a grassy road that crosses West Wind Creek on a bridge. You're going to be following the new road throughout. It's the one with tread. Keep straight and

The Obelisk.

cross a cutline. A little farther on, in a large clearing, be sure to look behind you for a fabulous view of Wind Ridge. Keep right. Proximity to South Wind Creek signals the start of a stiff climb up the left-hand bank. In no time at all, the river is far below in a deep V-shaped valley. Cross another cutline. Just after the following left-hand bend, a cairn indicates a sketchy hunter's trail into South Wind Creek. In case you're wondering, it doesn't provide a good viewpoint for the hoodoos.

Keep straight. When the incline moderates, peer over the bank at lines of capped hoodoos aligned like sentries up and down the slope to the creek. Another steep pull, then the road divides. From the short-lived right-hand road descend the mossy slope to a drop-off and hold onto trees. If you've hit it right, you'll be stunned by the view of The Obelisk. In the running for the world's highest hoodoo, it puts the Monolith in Bremner's Gravel Pit to shame.

22 SKOGAN PASS (Dead Man Flat to Ribbon Creek) — maps 6 & 7

Day hike
Official trail
20 km to Ribbon Creek, 9.5 km to pass
Height gain 670 m
Height loss 625 m
High point 2073 m
Maps 82 O/3 Canmore,
82 J/14 Spray Lakes Reservoir

Access:

1. Trans-Canada Highway (Hwy. 1). At Dead Man Flat interchange follow signs to Alpine Resort Haven. At the final bend turn right to Pigeon Mountain trailhead and park before the hiking sign. The trail is the continuation of the dirt road.
2. Kananaskis Trail (Hwy. 40) at Ribbon Creek. Follow signs to Nakiska ski area and pull into the south parking lot on the left just before the road loops at the entrance.

If the Canmore and Bow Valley Chamber of Commerce had its way, a four-lane highway would sweep across Skogan Pass from the south end of Canmore to Nakiska and Kananaskis Village. It's scary the way development spreads. Just over a hundred years ago Pigeon Pass, as it was called then, was a quiet, undisturbed place crossed by an old Indian trail shown on George Dawson's map of 1886. Likely it was the same trail, by then called the Kananaskis Pack Trail, that was widened in 1936 by the Forest Service to carry the telephone line linking Dead Man Flat ranger cabin to Boundary ranger cabin at the mouth of Ribbon Creek. Henceforth it was known as the Canmore Boundary Telephone Line Trail over Dead Man Pass. Since then, the trail has been obliterated by mine roads, logging roads, Marmot Basin project roads, ski access roads, ski runs, and most of all by the powerline right-of-way and its access road which is currently the new route. Strangely, none of the old pass names stuck and it was left to Don Gardner who was reconnoitring the Ribbon Creek ski trails in 1972, to name it Skogan, a name that has since come into general use. Trans-

lated from the Norwegian, it means a magic forest with elves and trolls.

There is no accounting for people's tastes. I did talk to someone whose idea of a good walk was to follow a powerline right-of-way. I have to admit, though, that it sports one or two great viewpoints.

Pigeon Mountain trailhead to Skogan Pass
Continue along the dirt road. At the powerline turn left up the right-of-way access road, shortly making a lengthy foray into the forest. Ignore two side roads on the right, enter K Country at a gate and regain the right-of-way at a signpost where the trail to Mt. Allan (**A** route) turns off towards Pigeon Creek. Turn left.

Game trails you can rely on to make sensible decisions, but powerline right-of-ways built by man do illogical things, as you'll find out 2.5 sweaty kilometres later when you reach the skyline. On the brink of a great dip, the access road, thankfully, turns off to the left in uphill zigzags. Watch for Pigeon Mountain junction at a cairn.

A sign warning motorists the road ahead is closed to traffic precedes the meadow traverse which should be savoured because never again does the route escape the clutches of industry. Take a break in the long grass and enjoy a panorama incorporating The Three Sisters in profile and Collembola's north ridge in awe-inspiring close-up. Back in the forest, you pass two geologically interesting slumps on the uphill slope, then the trail to McGillivray Creek at a small blaze.

The road wends right into a dip. To the left is Skogan Pass proper. If you want to shortcut, a trail (likely on the line of the original) cuts across to the road on the south side of the pass, thereby avoiding extraneous climbing. If you stay on the road, it climbs to Skogan Pass, a vague spot in the pines determined solely by the downhill inclination of the road in front of you. I recommend a five-minute detour to the summit powerpole, where every great view is ruined by powerlines. Sorry Ruthie.

Skogan Pass to Nakiska parking lot As the road descends it crosses the powerline (a chance to examine the crux pitch on Collembola), then swings right around the head of Lorette Creek, seemingly in no hurry to descend, entering the northern boundary of what was once the Marmot Basin Project at a gate. Climb *uphill* to a junction with the powerline right-of-way and the road to the meteorological station (right), now one leg of a ski trail called Skogan Loop. You can understand why confused people coming in the opposite direction think this is the pass. It's the same height.

Descend the road that twines about the powerline right-of-way. At the bottom of the hill, the road breaks away to the right through spruce avenue, passing the lower

junction of Skogan Loop ski trail. Enter a large cutblock. I say 'cutblock' from habit. After two editions it's become a plantation, but luckily the pines don't yet obstruct your first real look at the mountains about Ribbon Creek—the third great view of the route. You're about 15 years too late to view a string of historic wooden tripods running down the right side of the road, holding up the telephone line between ranger stations. Pass High Level trail on the left and 900 metres lower down, Sunburst trail at the powerline right-of-way. Now if you're headed for Stoney Trail (#35) why not use the powerline access road that spews you out just north of Marmot Creek?

Continue winding down the road to Two Ton bridge over Marmot Creek. Keep left at the junction immediately following and beyond a gate join the wide Marmot Basin road, now in the pay of Nakiska ski resort. Keep left. Forgo Skogan Pass ski trail turning left and continue down the road. Lower down it crosses Powderface ski run, then Chinook ski run under the Bronze Chair. At the left-hand bend following, leave it and make a beeline under

Descending the north side of the pass. The Three Sisters seen from the meadow traverse.

Olympic Chair for Nakiska's day lodge. Likely you'll hit flat ground just to left of the first-aid building. The meadow in front of the lodge is the setting for a wildly popular orchestral concert 'Mozart on the Mountain', and on Labour Day you too can enjoy a few free bars as you walk to the parking lot.

Above: McGillivray Creek chockstone. Note figure.
Below: The south side of the pass. View from the cutblock of The Wedge (left) and Mt. Kidd.

OPTION
McGillivray Creek

I'm not advocating you start up McGillivray from the Trans-Canada Highway. The first third is an obstacle course used by Lac Des Arcs Climbing School with ropes and slings to help you through a narrow canyon. The penalty for failing, or for the rope failing (as is what happened to us) is an impromptu bath. What you have to do is sneak in from the side two thirds of the way up.

A narrow trail turns off Skogan Pass trail at a blazed tree and shortly gains the watershed meadow at unofficial campsites used by horse parties and boy scouts. Water springs out of the ground a little way down the ongoing trail into McGillivray Creek. At the meadow you're in a good position for exploring upper McGillivray Creek and assorted ridges above treeline. There's only one good reason for heading downstream, and that's to stand under a huge diamond-shaped chockstone neatly slotted in a canyon and pointing downwards like the dagger of doom in an Indiana Jones movie.

*The summit as seen from
the lower summit.*

23 PIGEON MOUNTAIN — maps 7 & 6

Day hike
Unofficial trail & route
Distance 7.7 km from trailhead
Height gain 990 m
High point 2394 m
Map 82 O/3 Canmore

Access: Via Skogan Pass trail (#22).

Pic des Pigeon, named for the obvious reason by the Palliser Expedition of 1858, is a very easy ascent to a superb viewpoint. As a diversion from Skogan Pass trail (#22) it is 4.8 km return and 550 m height gain!

Follow the Skogan Pass trail for 5.3 km. At this point it has left the powerline and is zigging uphill. At the cairn, turn left up a narrow, well-trodden trail. It climbs to the top of a triangular-shaped grass spur—a prominent Pigeon Mountain landmark, then settles into a slowly rising traverse through meadows where you might be lucky enough to spot a few sheep. To the west the panorama is superb, taking in Skogan Pass, Mt. Collembola showing its most attractive side (you can pick out the

crux), Mts. Allan and Lougheed, Windtower and The Three Sisters poking up above Wind Ridge. Reach the saddle between the two tops. The lower summit to right requires a scree scrabble that most people forgo, preferring to stroll up easy grass laced with scree to the main summit (once slated for a teahouse). A bird's-eye view of the Bow Valley allows you to check on construction and count golf courses.

It's probably best to return the same way unless you're an old hand at bushwhacking and willing to risk knocking 4.4 km off the route on the strength of a compass bearing. Start from the survey marker further along the ridge and make a beeline for the old Pigeon Mountain ski runs that are being infiltrated by time-share cabins. Walk down to Alpine Resort Haven, turn left and arrive back at Pigeon Mountain trailhead.

24 MOUNT ALLAN FROM THE NORTH — maps 6 & 7

Long day hike
Official trail with red markers on trees,
paint splodges on rocks and cairns
11 km to summit, 19 km to Ribbon Creek
Height gain 1415 m
High point 2819 m
Maps 82 O/3 Canmore,
82 J/14 Spray Lakes Reservoir

Access: Trans-Canada Highway (Hwy. 1). At Dead Man Flat interchange follow signs to Alpine Resort Haven. At the final bend turn right to Pigeon Mountain trailhead and park before the hiking sign. The trail is the continuation of the dirt road.
Also accessible via Skogan Pass trail (#22).

The complete traverse of Mt. Allan from Dead Man Flat to Ribbon Creek (or vice versa) is one of the most wonderful ridge walks in the Canadian Rockies, a very long day indeed, requiring two vehicles but with the bonus of cafes and pubs at both ends. Take plenty of water.

Most people, though, go up one side and return the same way, which is why you'll have to turn to #47 for info on the southern half. The northern half of the 'Centennial Trail', as it is called, calls for an early start if you wish to make the summit and back before dark. Start even earlier if making a loop with Collembola (#25). Expect some easy scrambling and occasional mild exposure at the Black Band traverse which is tricky when snow-covered early or late in the season.

Thanks to Peter Pocklington there are three different starts (labelled A, B and C) to the K Country boundary at GR240520. The trail beyond the junction of A, B and C is closed April 1st - June 21st for lambing. However, if you want to do a training loop with A, B and C or drop into Wind Creek, that's OK.

Know that a less strenuous option is the cirque between Allan and Collembola harbouring Jubilee Tarns.

Start A Built at the time when the traditional start was out of bounds, it remains the official K Country start to Mt. Allan Centennial Trail. It leaves the Skogan Pass trail (#22) at the signpost and briefly heads out to a viewpoint lusted after by Three Sisters Resorts for the Marriott Hotel. The drop into Pigeon Creek is galling, though far worse in the opposite direction when you're knackered. Cross Pigeon Creek and join the Pigeon Creek exploration road (start C) on the southwest bank. Turn left. A little further on, turn right at the arrow and climb steep muddy trail, later moderating, to the signed junction with B's exploration road on the ridge. Turn left.

Start B From the parking lot the dirt road takes you out to the powerline right-of-way. Cross and continue around a logged meadow, through a gate and down to Pigeon Creek crossing (culvert). At the four-way junction on the west bank with another exploration road turn left. As you can see by the red trail markers, you've joined the traditional route from Dead Man Flat.

Going is easy to the junction with Pigeon Creek exploration road (start C), which takes off from the left side at a bend. This signals the start of a 518 vertical-metre climb up the north ridge of Collembola to road's end. It goes on forever, with just Lodgepole pines to look at and the odd cheery Arnica spotlighted by a ray of sunlight. Best to start an intense discussion with your friends to last an hour or two. There's some relief at the K Country boundary where the road into Wind Valley turns right, and A and C come in from the left at a signpost.

Bottom: The final stretch of the north ridge to the summit. Route #25 follows the left-hand skyline.

Top: Approaching the Black Band, which is circumvented by a traverse on the left side.

Start C As indicated in B, leave B's exploration road at a bend and follow the gently-inclined Pigeon Creek exploration road along the southwest bank of Pigeon Creek. In about a kilometre A comes in from the left. Follow as for A, turning right at the arrow, etc. In my book, C is the start of choice, particularly for the descent when your feet are sore from pounding down the road.

K Country boundary to summit Continue labouring up B's exploration road which steepens even more after coal dust corner. Ignore every descending cutline and side road. At a levelling intersected by a cutline, the steep open ridge of Collembola can be seen rising ahead, an exhausting prospect should you be headed that way. A dip, one final uphill, and the road dwindles to a trail. Spirits pick up.

The trail heads right, crossing the lip of the cirque between Mts. Collembola and Allan (cairns and posts) where people bound for Jubilee Tarns should head left.

Bracing yourself for much climbing yet to come, zigzag up a steep grassy slope onto the north ridge of Mt. Allan. Turn left and walk up to the foot of the Black Band. To get around this impasse, traverse slightly exposed grassy ledges on the left (east) side (tricky, even dangerous, after a whiff of snow), then scramble to a large cairn on the ridge top. The easy section following is terminated by a row of red pinnacles straddling the ridgeline and dipping down the western flank. Slip through a gap on the right side and regain the ridge by any of numerous trails climbing the rocky slope where Nodding saxifridges grow in tiny pockets of soil among the boulders. Arriving at a false summit, you discover the real summit is still half a kilometre distant across a slight dip—a final upheaval of orange screes served by a trail that, in the way of all sheep trails, forgoes the slim pickings of the summit and contours around to the southeast ridge beyond. Branch off at the appropriate place and climb to the cairn.

The view from the summit is a little disappointing; the panorama you might expect from a 2800 m peak is severely limited by the great height of Mt. Loughead. Nevertheless, another window has opened up to the south disclosing the lovely country about Ribbon Creek. In the afternoon sun second Memorial Lake 'the emerald' glitters tantalizingly like fizzy Crème de Menthe.

OPTION
Jubilee Tarns

From the lip of the cirque a faint trail follows the right bank of the creek through fields of dwarf willow and Delphiniums (where I found pale blue variants) into the hanging valley between Collembola and Allan. Higher yet, the inner cirque is a labyrinth of small grassy hills and muddy ponds, the farthest one, tucked under Mt. Allan, graced with the name Queen's Tarn. As a destination Jubilee Tarns are not worth the effort of the long walk in, but the valley is lovely, bounded by grassy slopes and seven-star flower gardens on the lower slopes of Collembola.

From Queen's Tarn, you'll notice the north ridge of Mt. Allan is easily accessible via a steep grass slope. Should the need arise, it offers an easy escape route off the ridge in sudden storm. Similarly, a reasonable slope leads to the col between the two summits of Collembola. Besides acting as an escape route, it offers the timorous a way to the highest summit; one that misses out the crux.

Opposite: View from the north summit of Mt. Collembola showing the col between the summits and the south (lower) summit ringed by cliff bands. Using the description you can easily trace the route to the top. Route #25 continues up the facing ridge to the summit of Mt. Allan (centre right). The right-hand ridge is the north ridge ascended by route #24, the left-hand the Centennial Ridge followed by route #47. The high peak directly above Mt. Allan is Mt. Sparrowhawk (see route #67).

25 COLLEMBOLA TRAVERSE — maps 7 & 6

Long day hike
Unofficial scramble
Distance 11.3 km to Mt. Allan
Height gain to Mt. Allan 1646 m
Height loss 253 m
High point 2819 m
Map 82 J/14 Spray Lakes Reservoir

Access: Via Mt. Allan from the north (#24) at the 5.9 km mark.

The traverse of the two summits of Mt. Collembola is a demanding ridge walk, a much more serious undertaking than the traverse of Mt. Allan. Not because the ridge is a knife edge (far from it), but because route finding is tricky in two places and there's one unavoidable step of exposed scrambling. Traversing south to north means downclimbing the crux, not a good idea if you don't know where the route goes. Combined with route #24, it's guaranteed to leave you dead on your feet and ready for a holiday at Club Med. Alternatively, without going to the summit of Allan (or even to the south summit) you can hop off into Jubilee Cirque or, with two cars, head down Marmot Basin to Ribbon Creek via route #46.

The name Collembola is pronounced COLL-<u>EM</u>-BO-LA and derives from 16-eyed snowfleas regularly mown down in their millions by cross-country skiers.

NORTH TO SOUTH

To north summit Follow any option to the end of the coal exploration road. Go a little further up the Mt. Allan trail to where it turns right, then transfer to a short-lived trail on the left that takes you to timberline. Ahead lies the hard work of the day, 600 vertical metres of consistently steep ridge, bounded on the right by grassy slopes rolling tamely down to Jubilee Cirque and on the left by the precipitous east face, furrowed and faulted, ringed with alternating bands of sandstone and shale—all the strata of the Kootenay Formation exposed in one go. High up a couple of small rock bands are easily managed.

Looking up at the crux below the north summit. The route gains the prominent notch (discernable trail), then takes to the steep east face.

East face crux. Note the figure on the ledge. The route up the second tier starts further to the left.

Finally the ridge levels and you look down on Skogan Pass, noticing below you on the east face a tiny pond on a bench, the result of a slump. To your right is Mt. Allan and its north ridge, eclipsed by the four great peaks of Lougheed. A series of gentle rises reveals the north peak of Collembola guarded by a diagonal rock band. The nearer you get the more impossible it appears, but the alternative, dropping into the cirque then plodding all the way up the gully between the two summits, is too shameful to consider. There is nothing for it but to take a peek at the east face.

A trail heads up right, then back left below the band to a notch on the left-hand skyline. Step foot on the east face. Above is the crux: two tiers of cliffs separated by a wide ledge. Scramble up the first step. While climbers seem eager to tackle the chimney to the right, I like to walk left a bit. At the obvious place gain a narrow rock ledge (please replace the handholds for others to use), then traverse left into a recess. At the narrowest point you can wrap your arms comfortably behind a large flake. Scrabble up the back of the recess to a large grassy ledge and walk out right to above the rock band. Finish up grass and scree to Collembola's highest summit. A fresh view is disclosed of Collembola's south summit which is likewise immune to a frontal approach.

Descend yellow shale to the col between the two summits. On your right is the easy escape gully into Jubilee Cirque. Ahead, the lower Collembola resembles a fortress that's been knocked about a bit by rocks hurled from a medieval trebuchet, a bizarre sight caused by massive conglomerates from the Blairmore Group sitting atop the Kootenay. Since a frontal approach is obviously out of the question, it requires careful route finding to gain the summit without going all the way around to the easy southwest ridge. Starting from the col, traverse the east face under the cliffs until you are lower than the col. At a break climb a swath of scree (faint trail, cairns) to a broad sloping ledge. Wend left a bit, then ascend an easy-angled scree gully through the second tier. The gully in question can be distinguished by an odd-shaped pinnacle on its left wall. At the ledge turn right and traverse until you can break through the dwindling third tier without resorting to scrambling. A cairn marks the exit. The summit is just to the right.

All difficulties at an end, stroll down the broad southwest ridge to the Collembola/Allan col where you look down on Queen's Tarn. From here the escape into Marmot Basin is described in route #46.

The 300 vertical metres to Mt. Allan's summit via the northeast ridge is more than one would wish for at this stage, but the going is easy enough up broken rock and shale and you top out right at the cairn for a well-earned collapse.

26 WIND POND — map 6

Day hike
Unofficial trail & route,
creek crossings
Distance 10.2 km from trailhead
Height gain 825 m
High point 2210
Maps 82 O/3 Canmore,
82 J/14 Spray Lakes Reservoir

Access: Via Mt. Allan from the north (#24).

The pond was first noted by M.B.B. Crockford and Gordon Scruggs in 1946/7 while investigating the geology of the Ribbon Creek area. Unmarked on the topo map and hidden by a fold of the hills from the eye of the ridge walker on Mt. Allan, the pond remained undetected by the vast majority of hikers (though not by climbers doing the Lougheed traverse) until 1972 when Harry Connolly's much publicized attempts to reach the lake by snowmobile and on foot were splashed across the pages of the Calgary Herald. Liberal use of the words 'impossible' and 'impenetrable' was alarming and seemed to put it in the same category as Stanley's forays into darkest Africa. There is, in fact, a quite reasonable route.

Follow #24 using route B up the coal exploration road. After route C turns off to the left, you're going to be turning first right. Or in other words, a few metres before routes A and C rejoin the exploration road at a signpost, turn right onto a side road.

Keep right a little way in and walk gently downhill into Wind Creek. The road continues up valley on the east bank, passing a road heading right and intersecting a cutline. Cross the creek on a log and continue to a T-junction with a cutline at about GR242499. Now you can either head into the bush at this point on a game trail or turn right up the road and make two zigs before traversing into the valley on a trail stamped out by the Boy Scouts. (The road, by the way, loops back to the valley road, its high point offering a passable way onto the ridge northeast of the pond.)

Wind Pond and the fourth summit of Mt. Lougheed.

Trails peter out after a while and you're left to make your own way to open ground under the far-flung shadow of Mount Lougheed. Leave the creek at the point where it turns southeast towards its source on the colourful scree slopes of Mt. Allan and head off in the opposite direction towards the col at GR227476, an easy climb once you tear yourself loose from the clutches of head-high willow bushes on the lower slopes.

The pond, actually a composite of several deep springs joined one to another like florets, lies in a hanging valley beyond the col. Take any route down meadows patched with spruce, fir and larch to the lakeshore. The upper layer of water seem quite tepid and teems with tiny red freshwater shrimps.

If you feel up to it, drop off the end of the valley to Wind Creek, a saving of approximately 1 km.

Grotto Canyon near Illusion Rock.

The Bow Valley

27 GROTTO CANYON — map 5

Day hike
Unofficial & official trails, route, creek crossings
Distance 6.3 km to end
Height gain 670 m
High point 1981 m
Map 82 O/3 Canmore

Access: Bow Valley Trail (Hwy. 1A). Although Grotto Pond day-use area is the official start to Grotto Canyon interpretive trail, why walk extra kilometres when you don't have to? At a bend in the highway 1.1 km west of Grotto Pond turn north into a large parking lot. The unofficial trail starts opposite the entrance.

Grotto Canyon is the epitome of imposing rock scenery with the added bonus of Indian rock paintings. Because it's reached with the minimum of effort, it attracts huge numbers of people ranging from first time walkers on the interpretive trail to rock climbers and their entourages. If you're bothered by crowds you'll find peace in the 90% of valley beyond the first canyon. A word on water levels. Normally the creek idles along and is easily crossed on rocks. During flash floods, however, it becomes a raging torrent and has been known to trap people behind the canyon.

The unsigned trail heads across to the powerline left of Baymag Plant 2, thereby cutting out most of the cacophony suffered by walkers walking in the official way. Cross the powerline right-of-way and walk up grass (reservoir below your feet) to where the trail continues, shortly to join the interpretive trail at a T-junction. Turn left.

You reach the creekbed and with mounting excitement follow the trail into the narrowing confines of Grotto Canyon, crossing and recrossing the creek several times. All the way along entertainment is provided by lycra-clad sport climbers clinging to overhanging cliffs with names like Hemingway Wall and The Peanut. Two-thirds the way along on the left the eagle-eyed will discern faint red ochre figures of Indian warriors dancing across a smooth slab about two metres up from the ground. A precursor of sport climbers? Around the next bend the canyon opens out slightly into an amphitheatre at the forks where the official trail ends. A few years ago and at a time of day when most climbers are only thinking of getting out of bed, the cantata 'Stones', the first phase of The Canyon Shadows Project with music by Robert Rosen and words by poet Peter Christensen made its debut at this unlikely spot. It was snowing at the time and all the performers wore ponchos.

You'll notice that most of the water in Grotto Creek comes from a waterfall in the right-hand cleft. A huge chockstone precludes all but the most determined explorer from going any further in that direction, so you turn left, threading a hitherto unseen passage below Illusion Rock where walls on either side reach their greatest height.

After the theatrics of the canyon the valley opens out into Dryas mats and forest. The cliffs are still there, but mostly further away and higher up, part of Grotto Mountain's precipitous east face. A trail carries on, crossing and recrossing the creek right up to GR234617. Points of interest? Straight off on the left is a large buttress of pale orange till eroding into hoodoos, the first of many incipient hoodoos and by far the most bizarre with its prominent cave. A little farther on is Garden Rock and Armadillo Buttress and another 15 minutes walk beyond Armadillo, Grotto Slabs on the right.

The upper half of the valley has the same stony creekbed, the odd incipient hoodoo, one small canyon, plus a rare view of Grotto Mountain embattled with cliffs.

82

28 EXSHAW PASS — map 5

Long day hike
Unofficial trail & route,
creek crossings
Distance 12.5 km to pass
Height gain 900 m
High point 2210 m
Map 82 O/3 Canmore

Access: Bow Valley Trail (Hwy. 1A) at Exshaw. Just east of the bridge over Exshaw Creek turn north onto Windridge Road. Follow the road, turning left at its end onto Mt. Lorette Drive. At the end of the Drive, park on the right side just before a footbridge over Exshaw Creek.

The long walk up Exshaw Creek to Exshaw Pass and back will wear your legs down to stumps. Luckily, the going is generally easy, with one steep uphill on grass at the end. Creek crossings are no big deal. In fact, later in the season you may be pushed to find water. An alternative to the pass is to hike halfway and return along the ridge to the east, a strenuous undertaking especially if you include Exshaw Mountain.

When Lafarge Canada is blasting, there is a faint possibility of rocks showering the first kilometre of trail, so if worried hike the trail on a Sunday.

Cross the footbridge and turn right on a trail running between a chainlink fence and the creek. Where the fence turns away in an open area you have a choice of routes. Alan Kane advocates following the pipeline track along the creek, which entices then leaves you stranded below the dam built in 1906 by Western Canada Cement & Coal Company. Getting out re-

Below: Looking down the full length of Exshaw Creek from Exshaw Pass.

quires a stiff scramble up the right bank. Alternately, and my preference, is to cut left across the open area to a road starting at a pile of boulders. It's here where you might get a rock on your head, but it's worth the slight risk, because, readers, this road takes you to the top of the dam.

From here I usually walk up the shingle in the creekbed, using two snippets of forest trail if the water level's high. At the end of the shingle a trail starts on the left bank. Before an outcrop the trail crosses to the right bank via logs weighed down by rocks. En route to Fable Creek, you cross the creek another five times in the same fashion, though it appears you can omit crossings 3 and 4 by staying on the left bank. After crossing 6 is a rock belonging to someone called Hawthorn, who on July 10th, 1967 carried up a can of white paint. Do not cross the next bridge. A long stretch on the west bank sees you past the wide mouth of Fable Creek (GR264623), the climbers' access to shapely Mt. Fable that has been framed between banks for the last few kilometres. It was named in 1947 by the first ascent party after the would-be first ascent party got lost in the bush and returned to tell a tall tale, "Oh, yeah?". At km 5, this major tributary is an obvious turning back point if you just want a short day.

Under the cliffs of Fable's east buttress, between Fable Creek and the next creek to the west you hop back and forth across the dwindling stream five times, finally ending up for good on the right (east) bank. Beyond here the trail is intermittent. First comes gravel flats offering a first view of the pass and to the left the two Mythic Towers first traversed by Kananaskis guru John Martin, who is as much at home on sport climbs as he is in ticking off every ridge in K Country. Then come meadows with slower going between creekbed willows and grassy sidehill where grizzlies are busy digging for yummy hedysarum roots. Water is plentiful, the grasses luxuriant. Arrive at the foot of the final rise. There are actually two gaps separated by a grassy hill, Exshaw Pass being the right-hand one. Got there? OK,

now drag yourself to the top of the hill in the middle for a stupendous view back down Exshaw Creek.

The V-shaped valley on the north side of the pass is not the best way into the South Ghost. What you do is traverse in a northwesterly direction to a higher pass at GR238698 seen from the top of the hill, then, using sensible sheep trails, descend the east slopes of the new valley direct to the hunter's camp.

OPTIONAL RETURN
Exshaw Ridge 2088 m height gain from the creek 680 m including Exshaw Mountain. An alternative to the pass is to make a loop with the ridge between Exshaw and Jura Creeks. While access is easy, the ridge is without exposure and there's no actual scrambling, this is not an option for walkers who want to keep their pants clean and pressed. The going is rough and time-consuming, with no trail apart from an intermittent sheep track.

After Fable Creek cross the creek either once or three times, then strike up the east slope (easy-angled trees, then grass) for about 500 vertical metres, aiming to top out on the ridge at about GR275632. This is the widest part of the ridge, all grass with spruce creeping up from the Jura Creek side. What a view! All the way up Exshaw Creek to Exshaw Pass which *"looks bloody miles away"*, and across to Mythic Towers and Mt. Fable, a splendid pointy peak available to determined scramblers. On the other side of the ridge lies Jura Creek and an equally fascinating line of peaks: 'Morrowmount' after Pat Morrow who was the second Canadian up Everest and as far as I know the first person (along with Steve Jennings) to do the complete round of peaks surrounding the Archie Simpson Memorial Hut in CMC Valley. That was in 1972. Next along is the crux of the round 'Hassel Castle' (the Hunchback), then Goat Mountain and at the tapering end, mere bumps, Loder Peak and Door Jamb Mountain.

Head almost due south along a lovely grassy ridge, now looking towards a jumble of summits south of the Trans-Canada Highway. The ridge undulates over four tops, its character gradually changing, becoming rockier with trees flooding over from both sides. At a couple of narrow points where slabs sweep down on the right side it's easy enough take to the trees on the left. From the final top drop 400 vertical metres to the col between the ridge and Exshaw Mountain. Emulate the sheep and use the rock rib.

Exshaw Mountain 1783 m Just when you thought you'd finished ascending, there's Exshaw Mountain. Luckily, the 120 vertical metre height gain to its summit is easy. From what historians can deduce, this is the mountain David Thompson of the North West Company climbed with Gabriel Dumond and Duncan McGillivray on Sunday Nov. 30th, 1800. I can just imagine Thompson, his long black hair cut square across his eyebrows blowing in the wind from under his hat pulled down tight, curs-

ing the rock in his Welsh accent, but writing later, "Where the rock was solid, it was extremely rough and full of small sharp points like an enormous Rasp. This enabled us to mount places very steep, as the footing was good and sure, but it cut our shoes, socks etc., all to pieces in a Trice". I'm curious as to what the etc. was, but I can imagine the trio hobbling back to their horses with their behinds shredded to ribbons and some poor Stoney woman faced with a mammoth repair job. As you descend on the village of Exshaw in a southwesterly direction you have to get around some of these slabs. Likely you'll drop onto a gravel lane that runs along the bottom of the hill. Turn right and walk out to Windridge Road, then follow it to the parking area.

Exshaw Ridge. View from the grassy north end of upper Jura Creek, Morrowmount (centre) and Hassel Castle (right).

29 JURA CREEK — map 5

Jura Creek's celebrated false fault.
Exshaw Formation on the left, Palliser
Formation on the right.

Day hike
Unofficial trail & route, creek crossings
Distance 7.5 km to end
Height gain 670 m
High point 1981 m
Map 82 O/3 Canmore

Access: Bow Valley Trail (Hwy. 1A). Park at the entrance to Continental Lime.

A short, rough hike up a geologically interesting valley in the Fairholme Range. Of course, the creek's name should really be Devon or Carbon, or Paleo. When named in 1913 it was thought the prominent black shale outcrop was of Jurassic age in the Mesozoic. It was later proved to be late Devonian and early Carboniferous/Mississippian in the Paleozoic Era. So what if the geologists were out by 200 million years.

Cross the highway and a strip of grass to the powerline right-of-way. Turn left. Very shortly a good trail marked by a stake turns off to the right and heads up valley to the wide, stony creekbed of Jura Creek. On the opposite bank is a 50 year-old wooden hopper used for screening gravel. The trail continues faintly up right bank Dryas flats to the narrows where the valley pinches in between Exshaw Mountain and Door Jamb Mountain, leaving a mere one metre-wide passage. Anyone with a shred of curiosity will take the canyon route. A tree at one point helps you climb to an upper level. With water coursing down, though, your only choice is the laborious bypass trail on the left bank.

Back in the creekbed, follow a trail on one side or the other past a campsite on the left to GR291614. Here, left-hand cliffs and right-hand slabs meet in a V. It certainly fooled me; I thought it was a fault. It's not. On the left the Exshaw formation, comprised of Jura's infamous black shales 'rests discomformably' on smooth pale slabs of Palliser formation on the right. At the contact geologists have found bone fragments of extinct armoured fish that grew as long as 10 metres, called Arthrodirs. Surprising to me, the stream glides from bathtub to bathtub down the Palliser and not down the bottom of the V where you'd expect it to be.

Higher up, bigger deeper potholes force a bypass trail up the left bank.

The trail made by geology students more or less ends at a side creek to right (east) at GR289616. After the dramatics of the canyons, it's back to flat, wide, stony creekbed all the way to the valley head under 'Morrowmount'. On the right slabby summits, including the celebrated 'Hassel Castle', alternate with stony avalanche tongues swallowing up Balsalm poplars. To the left Exshaw Ridge is a six-decker sandwich of cliffs and forest.

OPTION

Loder Peak 2097 m 2.2 km from Jura Creek, height gain 925 m. While gaining the col between Loder Peak and Goat Mountain is a straightforward trudge to a viewpoint, it's worth making the extra effort to win Loder Peak for a far superior view and the satisfaction on getting to the top of a named peak.

Turn up the side valley to the east at GR289616. A trail on the right side takes you into the narrows, leaving you to stumble another kilometre up stony creekbed to a side gully on the right at GR296619. If you inadvertently pass the gully you'll fetch up against a rock step in a small canyon.

Climb the moderately-inclined gully to the col at GR303617. High up where the grass and slabs start, go either left or right at vague forks, or start up the left then cross to the right above its initial rocky step. Your reward is a vertiginous view of the Bow Valley with not a mountain in sight.

From this side Loder Peak (the summit to the south and 70 vertical metres higher than the col) is guarded by a diagonal rock band. As you can see by the trail, climbers tackle the band at the left edge where it's highest. I recommend the security of a rope, particularly for the descent, where a six-metre tumble can kill you just as easily as if you threw yourself down the abyss on the left. If the route doesn't appeal, follow the band downhill and scrabble up where it's lower and easier. The trouble is, the lower you get, the steeper and more rubbishy the slope above the band, and, of course, all the lost height has to be regained. (If you plan on taking a lower route contour across from halfway up the right-hand gully, forget about visiting the col.) The angle eases towards the top and from two summit cairns you look down the connecting ridge to Door Jamb Mountain. This is the scrambler's route from Highway 1A.

Loder Peak from the col.

30 YAMNUSKA RIDGE & CMC VALLEY — map 5

Day hikes
Unofficial trails
Distance 3.5 km to ridge
Height gain 436 m
High point 1798 m
Map 82 O/3 Canmore

Access: Bow Valley Trail (Hwy. 1A). 2.1 km east of 1X Highway turn north onto the quarry road. Almost straightaway keep left. Drive past assorted cutlines and minor roads. Opposite a camping/overflow parking area in a meadow, the lake road turns off to the left. Keep straight and arrive at small parking area with biffy just before the locked gate.

This extremely popular trail takes you to a superlative viewpoint on the open ridge east of Mt. John Laurie, more usually known as Yamnuska, or Yam, a derivation from its Stoney name Iyamnathka, meaning Wall of Stone. It's the ideal early season hike. Although snow still lies deep on the Front Ranges to the west, the blooming of the prairie crocus in the meadows and the drumming of the grouse in the forest tell you that spring has arrived at Yamnuska. Alas, spring also brings that unwanted hitchhiker, the wood tick, which seems particularly voracious in this area.

Continue along the road beyond the gate. Keep straight, climbing up the hill to the quarry operated by Lafarge Canada, who are steadily chipping away at the sandstone escarpment. If the place looks familiar you probably watched the TV movie 'Legend of the Ruby Silver'. Keep left twice as the road sweeps around to the left, then back right to the top of the quarry. Filtering down from the great cliff of Yamnuska above are the calls of climbers shouting things like, "off belay" and "slack". On the left, the old road comes in and the climber's access trail goes out. A little farther on, turn left at some flagging onto a wide horse trail. In a few metres keep right (to the left is another climber's access trail).

The trail up Yamnuska ridge. Yamnuska in the background.

The horse trail heads through aspen forest to a dry gully. Climb the slope to its right, bearing in mind the trail variations nearest the gully are easier. At half height traverse right on a bench above outcrops. Another climb through trees leads into a higher traverse across meadow. Almost at once the trail divides. Either grit your teeth and climb directly to the ridge-top trail, or if you want an easier time of it, follow the bench to the next junction and then turn left. There exists a third alternative for people ready to call it a day. Follow the gently rising bench trail to the corral at the boundary fence with Stoney Indian Reserve—a fabulous viewpoint for the Bow Valley. Who would have thought there were so many ponds sprinkled about the forest? (The horse trail continues, dropping in gobbets of mud down the far side of the ridge, mostly alongside the fence, to a logging road at a gate. Here it turns left, following the flat logging road to the junction with the walker's trail to CMC Valley.)

GOING FARTHER

Walk west along the ridge-top trail towards Yam. A short steep step precedes the junction with CMC Valley trail.

Going left, the trail winds uphill to the base of cliffs at the point where a climber's access trail plummets to the horse trail near the quarry. Return this way if you like! Not far beyond this point the trail downgrades to a scrambler's route up the northeast ridge of Yamnuska. One tricky pitch of downclimbing puts it beyond the scope of this book, so I won't bother you with any further description. Read Alan Kane's 'Scrambles'. However, it's worth walkers coming this far for the view of CMC Valley and the fantastic array of cliffs lining the north side.

CMC (Loggers) Valley

End of valley 7 km return to ridge-top trail, height loss/regain 150 m. The valley at the back of Yam (actually the south fork of Old Fort Creek) can only be approached from the ridge-top trail.

Go right at the aforementioned junction and wander over to viewpoints, then descend through spruce forest to a junction identified by cabin ruins. Keep left and arrive seconds later at the junction with the logging road-horse trail. Drop straight down the hill to valley bottom, the trenched trail bearing more than a passing resemblance to a stream. All the water coursing down the north flank pools on the terrace above the creek and it's here where the trail divides and becomes nebulous. Slosh left, noting a rectangle of grey ash on the right—the residue of Archie Simpson's Memorial Hut, one of the ruins rebuilt by the Calgary Mountain Club when CMC Valley was in vogue as a climbing area. After 25 years of service it was razed to the ground in June of 1995. In a couple of minutes head right to a fire circle on the bank top, then drop left down the bank to the south fork of Old Fort Creek where a tree makes a very convenient bridge to the north bank.

Turn left up a logging road, degenerating in places to trail as it travels upstream. Above the road, bone dry meadow rising to sun-kissed cliffs with names like Bilbo Buttress and The Runes are a startling contrast to the soggy forest of the south slope and the shadowy cliffs of Mt. Doom. As you progress the mountains encircling the valley head come into view: Goat Mountain, Hassel Castle (The Hunchback) and Morrowmount, for which there is an explanation on page 84. The road climbs above a large beaver pond and ends on grassy slopes. You're now in a position to pick out Yamnuska's descent route down the screes of the west ridge to the Yam/Goat col. Should you feel inclined, you can hike up the side valley opposite to the col and return to the quarry via the scree run.

But back to CMC Valley. A faint trail continues where the road leaves off, climbing over a side ridge. I like to leave it here and climb the grassy ridge to a levelling at GR306667, a heavenly spot overlooking the side valley emanating from the great cliff of Ephel Duath—the Mountains of Shadow if I remember my Tolkien correctly.

Top: CMC Valley. The end of the trail at GR306667 under the great cliff of Ephel Duath.

Bottom: upper Heart Creek Valley. A typical scene: open creekbed, forest, unnamed ridges.

31 HEART CREEK — map 7

Day hike
Official trail, then unofficial trails &
creek crossings
Distance to trail end 5 km
Height gain 350 m
High point 1660 m
Map 82 O/3 Canmore

Access: Trans-Canada Highway (Hwy. 1). At the Lac des Arcs interchange drive to Heart Creek parking lot.

The first part is easy, the Heart Creek interpretive trail replete with signposts, bridges and interpretive signs. To go farther up this valley is a culture shock to anyone not used to rough forest trails.

Heart Creek Interpretive Trail
Follow the Heart Creek interpretive trail under the powerline and down the hill to Heart Creek bridge. On the east bank is a four-way trail junction just metres away from the Trans-Canada Highway. Turn first right, heading into the valley. Crossing and recrossing the stream seven times, you wind between high rock gates introducing each new twist of the canyon floor, finally coming to a full stop below a vertical step in the creekbed. End of interpretive trail. Within earshot is a waterfall hidden by a twist in the canyon wall, a grand sight available to the determined hiker equipped with waders and an umbrella.

The Upper Valley
Choose from two unofficial trails to get above the rock step.

Left easier (east side) Hop across the creek to the left of the rock step. Not to be confused with a muddy rake below the ascending cliff line, is the forest trail farther to the left that takes you to the top of a little ridge. Turn left, then at second right drop back to valley bottom, en route passing a wondrous spot where half of Heart Creek wells up in a very large spring, an icy cold nectar devoid of chloride and fluoride. If this wasn't K Country you could set up a stall at the end of the trail and sell genuine Heart Creek spring water to interpretive trail trippers. On reaching Heart Creek, cross to a better trail on the west bank.

Right harder (west side) Just before the end of the interpretive trail turn right up a side valley on a trail. Shortly, it turns left and you grovel up steep hardpacked shale to a high point, then make a gradual descent into Heart Creek above the canyon. Viewing the waterfall is perilous in the extreme since it entails hanging onto trees on the canyon rim. I've warned you so don't sue if you kill yourself. Back at creek level the trail crosses the creek four times on logs; if you find a lens cap it's mine, one of several donated to K Country. I've noticed other people donate lens caps as well, but they never fit my camera.

Both routes join on the west bank opposite the spring. Follow the trail past a tributary to where the valley turns sharp left. At this point it's worth detouring along the shingle bed to a small waterfall emerging from a stunning series of potholes.

Back at the bend, climb into the forest. Go either way at a split, keep straight, intersect a trail on a bit of a ridge and drop back down to the creek above the potholes. Tramped by Boy Scouts, the trail remains clear to a camping spot used during the 15th World Jamboree in 1983. Thereafter, it deteriorates, alternating between banks to the bathtubs, then fades away in dense forest.

32 HEART MOUNTAIN HORSESHOE — map 7

Day scramble
Unofficial trail & route
Circuit 10.5 km from parking lot
Height gain 930 m
High point 2149 m
Map 82 O/3 Canmore

Access: Trans-Canada Highway (Hwy. 1). Via Heart Creek trail (#31) at the four-way junction on the east bank of Heart Creek.

Heart Mountain is good fun, a popular scramble available quite early on in the season. Its rocky northwest ridge is one of those places where experience decides how high you should climb. Some people quit halfway and have a sit-down in view of the cement works, some reach the summit and a few go on to complete the horseshoe. I highly recommend the latter; nowhere are there difficulties comparable to those of the ascent.

You're standing at the four-way junction on the east bank of Heart Creek. The trail, second from right going counter-clockwise is obvious as it starts up the ridge. After a short, moderately steep step the ground levels momentarily, then steepens and narrows, a tenuous trail winding up scree and broken rock above cliffs plummeting into Heart Creek. At one point slightly exposed slabs can be avoided by a detour into the trees to the left.

When the ridge flattens a second time, you must transfer onto the upper ridge above you to your left. In the past so many people have gone wrong at this point the false trail up the bench is quite good. Climb four metres of vertical rock on good hand and footholds to a small cairn.

The upper ridge, easy at first, steepens into slabs that climbers like Pete and Tony greet with enthusiasm while I'm searching desperately for an easy way up. The easiest route is to follow the trail into the security of the yellow scree gully to the left of the slabs,

and when the gully steepens into loose broken rocks escape to a small tree on the gully's right-hand edge and step around onto easier ground above all difficulties. Walk up to the first summit known as Heart Mountain. After the drama of the ascent it seems strange to be greeted by meadows, trees and ground squirrels after your lunch.

The Horseshoe The trail continues over minor humps with views into upper Heart Creek. Suddenly the ridge narrows to a stony ramp with slabs on both sides, a suitably impressive approach to the highest summit of the day at GR318550. This one has a summit register in the cairn and a view of Barrier Lake.

Heading northeast, descend broad grass slopes to a gap, then, regaining all lost altitude, climb to another cairned summit. Traverse to a further top (GR323558) marking the culmination of another northwest ridge—your descent route.

The Descent Contrary to its scary appearance from the Trans-Canada, this ridge is broad, easy and, apart from the initial talus slope, set at a much gentler angle than the ascent route. No scrambling is required as you hotfoot it down a rough mix of rock, scree and grass past the odd dead tree. As you reach treeline the traces of man's passage strengthen into a trail that can be followed all the way down to the powerline right-of-way. Walk left to a side stream and follow it downstream a few metres until you intersect Quaite Creek trail (#33). A left turn will return you to the four-way junction at Heart Creek.

Heart Mountain, the ascent ridge. Inset: the crux at the two-thirds point.

33 QUAITE CREEK TO JEWELL PASS — map 7

Day hike
Official trail
6 km via official start, 4 km via
unofficial start
Height gain 290 m
High point 1630 m
Map 82 O/3 Canmore

Access: Trans-Canada Highway (Hwy. 1).
Official start Via Heart Creek trail (#31).
Unofficial start From the eastbound lane of the highway, opposite the Loder Peak sign, pull off at the Quaite Creek logging road. A gate precludes car travel up the road.
Also accessible from #36 Prairie View and #37 Jewell Pass.

This is a popular trail with mountain bikers and youth groups headed for a backcountry campground not too far from civilization. For walkers Jewell Pass is a rather boring objective best combined with Prairie View trail (#36) to make a point to point.

Official start From the junction on the east bank of Heart Creek the trail heads east, parallelling the Trans-Canada Highway. This is a surprisingly pleasant section through aspen forest. You pass a pond and duck under the powerlines twice. Arriving in Quaite Valley, cross the creek and join the logging road on the east bank. Turn right.

Unofficial start Not far beyond the gate the official trail joins in from the right.

Head up the narrow valley, the logging road squashed between the creek and steep slopes dappled with slabs of white Palliser limestone that for the easily fooled look like snow. After 1.2 km the valley opens into a meadow (cutblock) where Jack Quaite had a sawmill for purposes of experimentation. Incredibly, the Federal Government's Forest Experiment Station reached over Jewell Pass to this valley. The campground is located across the meadow in the trees. Ahead rises the high point of McConnell Ridge crowned by Barrier Lake Lookout.

The road shortly divides, both branches converging on Jewell Pass like pincers. The right-hand branch that crosses Quaite Creek is the official route and the shorter. It climbs moderately steeply, eventually levelling out to a four-way junction with signpost. Go straight and in seconds come to the junction with Prairie View (left) and Jewell Pass (straight). All this occurs in the trees. Bud Jewell, by the way, had a lease to log Douglas firs still standing after a fire.

Jewell Pass at the four-way junction. In the background is the final summit of Heart Mountain Horseshoe.

34 YATES ROUTE TO PRAIRIE VIEW TRAIL — map 7

Day hikes onto McConnell Ridge
Unofficial trails
Distance 1.6 km to Prairie View trail
Height gain 520 m
High Point 1860 m
Map 82 O/3 Canmore

Access: Trans-Canada Highway (Hwy. 1). At the Seebe interchange follow signs to Camp Chief Hector and Yamnuska Centre. For route 1 use the parking lot opposite Bowfort Lodge. The trail starts by the signboard. For route 2 drive further along the road and park near the end in a loop road on the right opposite the access road to Hector Lodge. **Also** accessible from #36 Prairie View.

Short steep trails connecting Yamnuska Centre and Camp Chief Hector to Prairie View trail are undoubtedly the fastest ways onto McConnell Ridge. But apart from their directness, there is little else to recommend them unless you're heavily into botany. As you can see by the map, the two trails can be connected to make a loop.

Route 1 via Yates Route Follow Bowfort trail uphill to the junction with Big Tree trail. Turn left and in a few minutes turn right onto an unsigned trail that is Yates Route to McConnell Ridge. I'm not sure if Emily Yates (a New Yorker) actually used the trail, but she did own the Diamond Cross Ranch that was located on the site of Yamnuska Centre.

Initially, the climb is reasonable, particularly where the trail makes a traverse interspersed with small uphill gains. When there's no view you have to narrow your perspective to the forest floor, which in this case grows Baneberry, Western violets, False Solomon Seals and Blue clematis draped artistically around stumps. Where

the trail turns uphill the angle steepens alarmingly. Take a rest at the junction with route 2 (flagging), then continue slogging it out until the northeast ridge is gained. Here, the trails turns right and reaches Prairie View trail at a cairn and yellow flagging. Turn right.

Route 2 from Camp Chief Hector Continue along the road that shortly splays into three short stubs. Take the centre stub, then at the edge of the big meadow follow the right-hand trail, keeping right past the teepee area and water trough to a signed T-junction with Hector trail. Turn right. (A left turn leads to Barrier Lake.)

Follow Hector trail only a short way before turning left onto a new trail. A dip precedes a very steep climb to a flagged junction. Continue winding uphill, then make a long traverse right (view behind of Whale Lake), and join Yates Route at some flagging. Turn left uphill.

35 STONEY TRAIL — map 7

Day hike
Official trail with signposts &
red markers
Distance 15 km from Barrier Dam to
Nakiska access road
Height gain 80 m
Map 82 O/3 Canmore,
82 J/14 Spray Lakes Reservoir

Main access Kananaskis Trail (Hwy. 40) at Barrier Dam.
Northern accesses
1. Rafter Six Ranch Resort. Trans-Canada Highway (Hwy. 1) at Seebe interchange. Follow Rafter Six signs to a four-way junction and turn left. Drive to the ranch parking lot.
2. Camp Chief Hector. Trans-Canada Highway (Hwy. 1) at Seebe interchange. Follow signs 'Camp Chief Hector, Yamnuska Centre' to a four-way junction and turn right. Drive past Bowfort Lodge (Yamnuska Centre) and park near the end of the road in a loop road on the right opposite the access road to Hector Lodge.
Southern access Kananaskis Trail (Hwy. 40). Turn west onto the access road to Nakiska Ski Area. Keep straight at the junction (left-hand road leads to Kananaskis Village and Ribbon Creek), then just before the intersecting powerline turn right into Stoney Equestrian parking lot.
Also accessible from Jewell Pass trail (#37) and Prairie View trail (#36).

As K Country freely admits, Soapy Smith trailhead in Bow Valley Provincial Park South is nonexistent despite what is shown on some brochures. Bow Valley Park South is in fact closed except for jamborees. It's a huge pity 'cos you miss out on a bit of Marilyn Monroe memorabilia, meaning the very peculiar Whale Lake cabin built 40 years ago for the movie 'The River of No Return'—exterior scenes only.

Most people, then, start (or finish) at Barrier Dam. If you want to use the northern accesses, Rafter Six (rated 1991's 'Super Resort of the World' by Japan Airlines) is the better choice, especially if you can arrange the trip around a scrump-tious meal in the Mad Trapper dining room (open until 9 pm).

What about the trail? Let's just say that dining at Rafter Six might be the highlight of the day. Powerline access roads are boring, though views are good and you travel past a large number of unnamed valleys and ridges up and down the west side of the lower Kananaskis Valley. So use it also as access to better things and don't grumble when overtaken by horses and bikes. Be aware that between Barrier Dam and Ribbon Creek there's no escape to Highway 40 unless you're willing to wade the Kananaskis River.

NORTHERN APPROACHES
1. From Rafter Six via the River Road 8.3 km to Barrier Dam, height gain 152 m.

The route starts to the right of the lodge as you face it (really a continuation of the access road) and, suddenly faint, crosses the campground meadow into trees at the far end where it reasserts itself and climbs over an esker to the boundary fence with Bow Valley Provincial Park South. Don't try getting through the gate. A convenient trail passes through a gap in the barbed-wire fence to the left and rejoins the road on the bank of the Kananaskis River. Keep left. You're on River Road, the very first Highway 40 constructed in 1934 between Seebe and Kananaskis Field Stations, which at that time was a camp for the unemployed.

Shortly after a gate a horse trail takes off to the right, an enticing shortcut to be weighed against detouring to a point of historical interest. This occurs at the end of the second side road to the left—the con-

Stoney Trail. One of the nicer sections where the powerline access road runs below Mt. Lorette.

tinuation of Highway 40—and is, or rather was, the road bridge over the Kananaskis River. The stringers have pretty well gone now, but the abutments, protected by metal gabions, still stand firm.

River Road now swings away from the river, climbing and winding a little. The horse trail comes in from the right and leaves on the left. Keep straight at the white post and after a gap of perhaps one kilometre, keep straight at a powerline access road, then intersect the powerline right-of-way. Strangely, the road makes a loop back north—I hate it when trails do this—and at the apex joins with the route from Camp Chief Hector. Keep left and again head south.

A long stretch sees you past Prairie View trail to right, then left. If heading for Barrier Dam, this is where you'd turn off and not wait until you hit the official Stoney trail that joins the road in about another kilometre. Above you on the right is a long line of cliffs marking the top edge of McConnell Ridge.

2. From Camp Chief Hector 5.5 km to Barrier Dam, height gain 122 m.

Continue along the road that shortly splays into three short stubs (see map on page 95). Take the centre stub, then follow the right-hand trail, keeping right, past the teepee area and water trough to a T-junction with Hector trail. Turn left at the sign reading 'To Barrier Lake' and follow it uphill to a T-junction with an old road from Bow Valley Park South. Turn right. After more climbing, the road levels and runs though a gap between low hills to the T-junction with River Road. Turn right.

Stoney Trail from Barrier Dam

Cross Barrier Lake Dam. Intersect powerline number one, then in a reclaimed meadow keep right and uphill. Just before reaching powerline number two, turn left on the access road that weaves around the second powerline, then the first powerline, both lines converging and running straight to a three-way intersection. Turn right towards the cliffs of McConnell Ridge. At the T-junction join the road from the northern approaches and turn left.

In less than a kilometre you regain the powerline right-of-way and enjoy a tremendous view across Barrier Lake to Mt. Baldy, previously known as Barrier Mountain, Mt. Baldy and Barrier Mountain in that order. I don't much care for the name Baldy which conjures up a smoothly rounded summit rising above a fringe of trees, not this rugged thing mantled by cliffs. So I think I'll go with Sleeping Buffalo Mountain, thanks, as named by the Indians, unquestionably the best descriptive name of the lot. Possibly this was the bald mountain noted by Isaac Kerr, William Cameron and Dan Donnellan on Thursday, August 16, 1883 when the future president of the Eau Claire & Bow River Logging Company was looking over the timber with a view to starting up a sawmill in Calgary.

The road rises past the 'God is Love' boulder (climber's trail heads onto McConnell Ridge), then veers left of the right-of-way. The second road to right with signpost is Jewell Pass trail (#37).

Cross Jewell Creek in a bay and embark on a long straight to the end of the reservoir, boring if it wasn't for continuing good views of Baldy. The road descends to a stony creekbed at GR344524 (tempting side trip), then climbs to a high point overlooking the end of Barrier Lake, a depressing scene when low water, at the push of a computer key, uncovers a vast expanse of mud flats. A picnic shelter roof on an island indicates the line of Highway 40 pre-reservoir days,

Leaving the reservoir behind, the road makes a big detour to the right to avoid boggy valley bottom, then regains the right-of-way for a long stretch below the craggy east slopes of a mountain much admired by Mary Barclay, the co-founder of the Canadian Youth Hostel movement. Look back at its beautiful strata and gaudy colouring as you cross the creekbed dividing the mountain from Mt. Lorette. Across the Kananaskis River is a final view of the twin valleys Porcupine and Wasootch, divided by Wasootch Ridge.

Continue south into a long flat under shapely Mt. Lorette (named after a World War I battle), which throws down two spectacular rock ridges. The left-hand ridge is a popular rock climb, one that beginner climbers get dragged up regularly. The mountain's other claim to fame is that it's on the Golden eagle migratory route from the U.S. to Alaska. Incredibly, it takes birds zooming up the Highwood and Opal Ranges only half an hour to get from Highwood Junction to the unnamed mountain opposite where, this being the narrowest part of the Kananaskis Valley, most birds cross to Lorette before continuing northward. 'Most' means 800 or so out of a thousand plus counted *per day* during the peak times at the end of March and the beginning of October. At such times this is where you'll start running into eagle counters led by the fellow with the aquiline nose.

The next point of interest is Lorette Creek, listed in "The 10 Worst Hikes in K Country". I wouldn't go up there if I was you. The beaver ponds opposite are much more fascinating if you're into birds, which ornithologists tell include such rarities as Cassin's Finch and Black Swifts.

The final stretch starts by climbing under Hummingbird Plume Lookout hill to TransAlta's Mt. Allan Substation. Immediately after the next bend a powerline goes winging up to Skogan Pass followed by its access road, now a horse trail for horses with Porsche horsepower. Cross Marmot Creek and go through a gate. (For the curious, the trail heading right leads to a broken down bridge.) From here the road slopes gradually downhill into meadows used as parking lots during the 15th Olympic Winter Games in 1988. You intersect Hay Meadow trail, make a detour to the right and ignore a number of ski trails heading right and left. A gate precedes Stoney Equestrian parking lot.

36 PRAIRIE VIEW TRAIL — map 7

Day hike
Official trail with signposts
Distance 5 km
Height gain east to west 500 m
High point 1875 m
Map 82 O/3 Canmore

Access: Kananaskis Trail (Hwy. 40) at Barrier Dam day-use area.
Also accessible from Quaite Creek trail (#33), Jewell Pass trail (#37) and Stoney trail (#35).

This is the usual route up McConnell Ridge, formerly called Yates Mountain after the Emily Yates Ranch located on the site of Yamnuska Centre. This is a very useful trail. You can either make a circuit from Barrier Dam incorporating Stoney trail (#35), Jewell Pass (#37) and Prairie View (#36), best hiked in that order if you want to be surprised by the surprise view, or you can do a point to point with Quaite Creek trail (#33). From the high point, a spur trail leads to Barrier Lake Lookout.

Barrier Dam to McConnell Ridge Cross Barrier Lake dam. Intersect a powerline, then in a reclaimed meadow keep right and uphill. Intersect a second powerline and its access road. At the T-junction following, turn right, then straightaway left on what used to be Pigeon Lookout fire road. Closeted in trees, it winds uphill, passing Yates Route at the end of the 11th and final zig. On gaining the northeast ridge, the road follows it to a level clearing above meadows sloping south, a wonderful viewpoint for Barrier Lake and the site of Pigeon Lookout.

Probably many of you remember the white fire tower, even sat on its steps to eat

The last lap to McConnell Ridge from Pigeon Lookout site.

lunch. In 1984, made redundant a year earlier by Barrier Lake Lookout, it was taken down to the Colonel's Cabin, painted grey and housed with artifacts. The lookout that first saw service as guard tower #8 at POW Camp #130 in the early 1940s had returned to its birthplace. Ruthie Oltmann believes the name, which caused an immense amount of confusion with hikers during its 24 years—Pigeon Lookout was *not* on Pigeon Mountain—was named after stool pigeons.

A trail carries on, climbing to a repeater station on the spine of McConnell Ridge—a much superior viewpoint. Finally, the rationale behind the trail's name becomes clear.

Shortcut An alternative to the winding road is a straight trail which leaves the left side of the fire road close to the junction with Stoney trail. It crosses the road twice, following the route of the old telephone line to Pigeon Lookout. Look for remnants of wire and the odd insulator post. Because of its excessive steepness, I suggest you reserve it for the descent. At the top end, it leaves the fire road about 400 m down from the lookout site and is marked by tree blazes.

McConnell Ridge to Jewell Pass Head down the southwest ridge above a line of crags, keeping an eye out as you go for fat marmots sunning themselves. At a col it's hard to tear yourself away from the view and turn into the forest, following the gently descending trail into Lodgepole pines at Jewell Pass. Left is Jewel Pass trail (#37), right is Quaite Creek (#33).

OPTION

Barrier Lake Lookout 1996 m add 2 km return, 125 m height gain.

From Prairie View's high point an unofficial trail climbs to the summit of McConnell Ridge which is much further away than you think and capped by a lookout. Despite lack of a signpost hordes of people make it to the top, which tends to

make lookouts grumpy. To save asking, the fencing above the big cliff is not to stop people falling off, but to protect nesting Prairie falcons from rocks being kicked off by the hordes straining for a bird's-eye view of the Bow Valley. As you might expect from a lookout site, this little summit excels as a viewpoint.

Prayer flags at Barrier Lake Lookout.

Optional Ridge Return to Quaite Creek
6 km to Hwy.1, height loss 914 m, height gain 213 m. From the lookout experienced walkers not requiring trails can follow McConnell Ridge to its northwest outlier at GR321582.

The euphoria at leaving the crowds is eclipsed by the steep shattered slope below the lookout, but after that the going is easy through open forest. Rising above the trees, the outlier's rocky summit is a heavenly viewpoint for Bow Valley industries, and comes equipped with a locked biffy-shaped hut for which I can offer no enlightenment. Getting down to Quaite Creek trail is tricky. Either backtrack and descend on Quaite Creek campground, or weave between slabs to the logging road gate.

37 JEWELL PASS FROM BARRIER DAM — map 7

Day hike
Official trail with signposts
Distance 6.2 km from dam
Height gain 258 m
High point 1630 m
Map 82 O/3 Canmore

Access: Kananaskis Trail (Hwy. 40) at Barrier Dam day-use area.
Also accessible from Quaite Creek trail (#33), Prairie View trail (#36) and Stoney trail (#35).

As a destination, Jewell Pass isn't up to much. Use this trail in conjunction with Prairie View (#36), making sure you hike the loop in a clockwise direction.

Cross Barrier Dam. Intersect powerline number one, then in a reclaimed meadow keep right and uphill. Just before reaching powerline number two, turn left on the powerline access road that weaves around the second powerline, then the first powerline, both lines converging and running straight to a three-way intersection. Turn right towards the cliffs of McConnell Ridge. At the T-junction, turn left on Stoney trail and in less than a kilometre rejoin the powerline. The road rises past the 'God is Love' boulder (a climber's trail heads onto McConnell Ridge), then veers left of the right-of-way. The second road to right with signpost is Jewell Pass trail.

Shoreline start If the water level is sufficiently low in Barrier Lake, you can reach the same point by walking along the sands and shingles of the shoreline from the end of the dam. At a large bay crossed by the powerlines, transfer to a trail that edges around the bay and finish along the powerline right-of-way to the access road.

Jewell Creek to Jewell Pass The trail crosses the powerline right-of-way and follows the top of the right bank (last view) into the confines of Jewell Creek. If you're

there at the right time—June, usually—look for tasty morel mushrooms growing by the trailside. At the forks, detour left to what some optimist has named Jewell Falls. Let's be honest, the falls are a huge disappointment in mid summer when the streams are dwindling, but it's a pleasant enough spot for a break before tackling the final rise to the pass. The trail follows the right-hand fork, bridges it twice, then eases off for the final kilometre to Jewell Pass. This occurs at no obvious point. Perhaps where Prairie View trail comes in from the right, or at the four-way junction with Quaite Creek trail.

Jewell Falls in summer.

101

38 LUSK PASS — map 8

Day hike
Official trail with red markers,
creek crossings
Distance 8.5 km
Height gain 350 m
High point 1740 m
Maps 82 O/3 Canmore,
82 O/2 Jumpingpound Creek,
82 J/15 Bragg Creek

Access:
1. Sibbald Creek Trail (Hwy. 68) at Lusk Creek day-use area.
2. Powderface Trail at Lusk Pass trailhead.

The old road up Lusk Creek.

This undulating forest trail started out as Stoney Cache trail in the 1920s, then for a long period in its history was a navigable road known as the Jumpingpound Trail, still, I might add, marked as a red line on 82 O/2! It's now completely grassed over and not very scenic, merely a useful link between the Kananaskis Valley and the Jumpingpound.

Its most interesting aspect is its name. Tom Lusk, a refugee from the States with a murky past best not inquired into, was a respected packer and guide for all the early explorers of the Canadian Rockies. Dressed like a figure from Buffalo Bill's Wild West Show, his blue eyes alternately steely or glassy, depending on whether or not he was on the whisky bottle, he was noted for a high temper that scared the hell out of his clients. Martin Nordegg recalls that on his trip to Ribbon Creek coalfields, Lusk introduced himself by saying, "Let us be friends and try to understand each other. If you do, it will be best for you". While lacking social graces, he was real soppy over horses.

West to east
From Lusk Creek day-use area access road, a trail cuts across to Highway 68. Turn right, cross Lusk Creek, then follow the trail up the grassy bank to join the end of an old road headed for Kananaskis Field Stations. On your left is a former gravel pit. Either turn left and walk around the top edge of the pit on an unofficial trail, or turn next left off the road at the red marker onto the official trail, both transferring you to the truncated end of the Lusk Creek road.

For the first 2 km, the road rises step-like through three experimental plots. Pass two side roads heading right to the Old Mill Road (Baldy Pass trail #39). After the second junction in a dip, climb over a small rise to a third ill-defined junction in a patch of grass. Turn left here and cross Lusk Creek.

The road now travels along the east bank of Lusk Creek, eventually turning away and climbing much more steeply up a side valley towards the pass which is devoid of scenic interest—dense match-stick forest sees to that. Down on the right a small meadow with picnic tables marks the actual watershed.

The short descent to Powderface Trail follows the drainage out of the meadow, crossing a branch of Jumpingpound Creek shortly before reaching the highway at Lusk Pass trailhead.

39 BALDY PASS FROM THE NORTH — maps 8 & 7

Day hike
Official trail with signposts
Distance 11.4 km to pass
Height gain 623 m
High point 2032 m
Maps 82 O/3 Canmore,
82 J/14 Spray Lakes Reservoir,
83 J/15 Bragg Creek

Access: Sibbald Creek Trail (Hwy. 68) at Lusk Creek day-use area.
Also accessible from Baldy Pass from the south (#40).

The longer and less interesting forest route to the pass. Options up the south fork of Lusk Creek are a lot more exciting and can be done comfortably in one day by biking the Old Mill Road to the sawmill site.

From the day-use area access road, a trail cuts across to Highway 68. Turn right, cross Lusk Creek, then follow the trail up the grassy bank to join the end of an old road headed for Kananaskis Field Stations. On your left is a former gravel pit. Follow the old road uphill to the junction with the Old Mill Road bulldozed in 1951 by the Olorenshaw Logging company lusting after 300 acres of spruce at the head of Lusk Creek's south fork. As you will see by the sign, this road is part of the "Lusk Creek Tour of logging and reforestation areas".

Turn left up the Old Mill Road under the frowning presence of Mt. Baldy. With many windings behind you, reach a junction at the edge of large cutblock 71-4, where the Lusk Creek Tour turns off to the left. Keep right and a few minutes later, stay left of the fire road. Keep right at the next junction and pass the collapsed remains of what was possibly a weather sub station. A little farther on, during the descent to cross the south fork of Lusk Creek, you're motivated by a glimpse of the pass and the peak to the south. Climb a hill, recross the creek in a dip, then abandon the Old Mill Road that turns left into the south fork (see option).

Keep straight on another logging road that gains height quickly through mature spruce forest. From its end a trail traverses right to the high point on the open ridge (cairn), then drops 30 vertical metres to the pass where #40 takes over.

OPTION
The South Fork of Lusk Creek 6.3 km

Turn left and follow the last kilometre of Old Mill Road to the sawmill site, a huge meadow with a confusing number of logging roads radiating out like spokes in a wheel. In our exploratory wanderings we've found several artifacts, the largest a hoist with a donkey engine.

Ongoing options are available, each building on the one before until you reach the top of a mountain....

South fork hoist and donkey engine.

103

The boundary ridge. Looking towards peak GR403471, climbed by the easy left-hand ridge. Peeking above the ridge is Belmore Browne Peak.

GOING FARTHER

The Meadows add on 1.5 km, height gain from sawmill site 322 m, high point 2029 m. The start is obscure. It's the middle of three roads heading up valley from the sawmill site, starting neither uphill nor downhill, but exactly opposite the road you came in on. It crosses the creek at a flume, and narrowed to trail width climbs up the left bank past a boundary cabin used by researchers from the Kananaskis Field Stations since 1983. Look for it in the 1984 CBC made-for-TV movie called 'Ernest Thompson Seton: Keeper of the Wilds'.

The trail continues climbing into gravelly meadows about the watershed with Jumpingpound Creek's west fork. Not exactly Drumheller, one would think. But amazingly enough, these innocent-looking meadows are designated a Protected Research Site by the Tyrell Museum after Laure Maurel unearthed petrified wood and dinosaur bones. As geological maps show, a thin band of Belly River Formation exists all along the eastern slope of the Fisher Range. This is also where the Government's Surveys and Mapping Branch made a major screw up. Try fitting together map sheets J/14 and J/15.

The following are more difficult options on scree with occasional game trails.

The boundary ridge 2180 m add on 1 km, height gain from meadows 152 m. To the west of the meadows rises the spine of the Fisher Range, a long grey wall of broken rock only about 75 metres high at its low point. Walk up to its base and find the game trail that climbs from right to left past the tree island at half height, and on past a solitary tree to gain the ridge at about GR402482 (cairn).

Peak GR403471 2454 m add on 1 km, height gain from ridge 283 m. Don't let the opportunity to bag a peak slip by, especially one that figures prominently in views from Highways 1, 68, 40 and Powderface Trail. Simply walk south along the boundary ridge and up the comfortably broad and moderately-inclined northeast ridge of the mountain to the summit cairn. Easy! You'll be thrilled with the panoramic view, which, to whet your appetite, includes a preview of a ridge walk described in Volume 2.

To Porcupine Creek Incredibly, the boundary ridge is the gateway to Porcupine Creek! This opens up possibilities of a point to point, or a marathon one day or leisurely two-day loop using #40, 39, 41 and 42. Before dropping off the ridge head north a bit to where easier-angled slopes sweep down into the northeast fork of Porcupine Creek's north fork. Now turn to route #41.

#39. Baldy Pass is the partly treed ridge in the middle distance above the right-hand figure. The peak at GR380492 (see #40) can be climbed via the ridge facing or by slopes right of the snow gullies.

40 BALDY PASS FROM THE SOUTH — map 7

Day hike
Official trail, signposts & red markers
Distance 5 km to pass
Height gain 573 m
High point 1990 m
Map 82 J/14 Spray Lakes Reservoir

Access: Kaniskis Trail (Hwy. 40). 10.3 km south of Kananaskis Country boundary, turn right (west) into Baldy Pass parking lot. The trail starts from the opposite side of the highway.
Also accessible from Baldy Pass from the north (#39).

This is the usual hiking route to Baldy Pass, being considerably shorter and more interesting than route #39.

Baldy Pass.

The trail follows the edge of a cutblock past a logging road on the left to a four-way junction in the trees marked with several large red squares. (The logging road straight ahead is route #42 to Wasootch Creek parking lot. Turn left, and on road gradually dwindling to trail, head into the valley confines. At the mouth of a wide side creek spewing stones, cross to the right bank and begin climbing through mossy spruce forest. A steep avalanche slope is crossed five minutes before the pass is reached.

Barely rising above the trees, the pass offers only marginally interesting views; it pays to follow #39 up the open ridge to the south, a 30 vertical-metre climb to a cairn marking the trail's high point where it slips over onto the north slope. This is a far superior viewpoint for Mt. Baldy and the mountains seen through the V to the west.

OPTION FROM PASS
Peak GR380492 2478 m add 1.2 km from pass, height gain 488 m. Scramblers can head either north towards Mt. Baldy which is miles away at the end of a ridge, or south up an unnamed summit. I prefer the latter, because unless you're a complete klutz, success is guaranteed.

From trail #39's high point on the ridge continue up what is the north ridge of your mountain, navigating through trees and glades right of a widespread rocky area. There's no trail, of course, but you can get an idea of the route from the photo on the previous page. At the steepening, climb the rather indeterminate ridge separating the moderately-inclined north face seamed with shallow gullies and the much scarier east face to left. Low down, unstable rocks in the dark grey zone are ankle breakers, but conditions improve once you start encountering broken up rock bands fixed solidly to the ground. Persevere. You'll be delighted with the narrow summit ridge, a pole and cairn marking the high point. Needless to say, the view is incredible.

For a faster descent (or alternative ascent) start out along the northwest ridge. When past a shallow gully head, drop right down one of several ribs (rocks, Dryas mats) converging into the central gully below the waterfall step, at the point where it turns northwest. Follow the gully out to Baldy Pass trail and turn left.

When recrossing the wide side creek look up to the left for a neck-craning view of the mountain you've just climbed.

41 PORCUPINE CREEKS — maps 7 & 8

Long day hikes, backpack
Unofficial trails & route, creek crossings
Distance south fork 8.6 km to end,
north fork 7.4 km to ridge
Maps 82 J/14 Spray Lakes Reservoir,
82 J/15 Bragg Creek

Access: Kanaskis Trail (Hwy. 40). Park at Porcupine Creek bridge.
Also accessible from Wasootch Creek or Baldy Pass parking lots via trail #42. The north fork is accessible from the boundary ridge via #39.

Northeast fork of the North Fork.

Because of easy terrain, *for the most part,* both forks of Porcupine Creek are popular with people wanting to get off the beaten track. As a bonus, several ridges and un-named mountains are available to hikers and scramblers. For mountains far back, take a tent; nothing is as maddening as finding yourself within 150 metres of an attainable summit when time runs out.

Step out along a gravel road on the north-east bank of Porcupine Creek. Intersect the Wasootch Creek to Baldy Pass trail (#42) and continue along the left bank on an interesting scrambly trail that brings you to the forks at a fire circle.

North Fork to the boundary ridge height gain 783 m, high point 2180 m.
From the forks, a trail follows the left bank into the first narrows. Like the south fork the valley floor alternately narrows and widens, necessitating the usual back and forth creek crossings. As you can see from fixed protection, rock jocks are gradually working their way along the valley's crags within six-pack carrying distance from the road. At GR381471 the valley splits. The main fork to the right ends in a box canyon 2.5 km distant. My own preference is the magnificent northeast fork to the left—an improbable through route to the Jumping-pound and Baldy Pass trail north (see #39).
Straight off, perpendicular walls topped by wafer-thin ridges winging upwards to

unseen summits will have your mouth hanging open. There are actually two distinct canyons separated by scree slopes, both quite easy to walk through apart from the usual problem of creek crossings, the water in this case supplemented by springs bubbling out of mossy banks. Higher up, the valley opens out a bit and you'll come to a questionable fork at GR394478. While the left-hand fork leads to the lower gap in the boundary ridge, you can't get down the other side unless you've come equipped with a parachute, so take the right fork, then head up the last forested rib on the left, a very moderate slope despite converging contours indicated on the topo map. On shale near the top traverse right to GR402482 (cairn).

This is where you join the route coming up the other side from Lusk Creek. The big heap to the south at GR403471 is readily accessible and is described and photographed under route #39. Maybe after a rest....

The South Fork height gain 457 m, high point 1859 m.

A trail crosses the north fork and gets you started along the left bank of the south fork. The valley is typical of the eastern slopes: wide flat floors of Dryas mats alternating with woody narrows, running water and long waterless stretches. At about GR382444, the most scenic stretch where 90% of people will end the trip, a grassy slope entices you onto the left-hand ridge for a close-up view of one of the most instantly recognizable mountains in the Fisher Range, the one crowned with a tiara of cliffs at GR407451. More on that later. A little farther on, at side creek GR384442, it's possible to cross over the ridge into Wasootch Creek east of Wasootch Ridge. If you've brought a tent, it's good to know there's always water around this point.

The dry mid section of the South Fork.

SCRAMBLER'S OPTIONS

Continue up the narrowing valley, crossing and recrossing the stream. After passing a stony creekbed on the left at a bend (GR396445), you run into impenetrable canyon. To circumvent, get onto the left-hand bank while it is easy to do so (just after the stony side creek), and climb diagonally right *through trees all the way* to a forested notch about 130 metres higher up at GR400444, where you can pick up ticks in September and change fallen out of Tony's pocket. Don't all rush at once; it was only a dollar's worth. From the notch it's a short, easy descent to the valley beyond the impasse. Around the next bend, at valley's end, the 2500 m summit on the backbone of the range at GR413443 is available to determined scree bashers. But back to the notch. Here, you're in a terrific position to tackle the tiara peak from the back via the red screes of the southwest ridge. While there's no rock band to contend with, just below the summit there's a steepening right across the south face which is a little worrying when seen from down below. Possibly the angle is easier at the edge of the drop-off. As you may have gathered, we didn't get this far, having run out of time, so let me know how you get on. OK?

42 WASOOTCH CREEK TO BALDY PASS TRAIL — map 7

Half-day hike
Official trail
Distance 3 km
Height gain 15 m
High point 1439 m
Map 82 J/14 Spray Lakes Reservoir

Access: Kananaskis Trail (Hwy. 40).
1. Wasootch Creek parking lot (#43).
2. The parking lot for Baldy Pass from the South (#40).
Also accessible from #41 Porcupine Creeks.

This little connector is particularly useful if you're doing a circuit with both Baldy Pass trails and Porcupine Creek over the Fisher Range.

From access 1 After rounding the end of Wasootch Ridge, join a logging road for the climb over a side hill to Porcupine Creek. Cross and keep straight on a new logging road. Stay right at the next three junctions until you reach a four-way junction blazoned with red markers. Turn right for Baldy Pass, keep straight for Baldy Pass parking lot .

43 WASOOTCH CREEK — map 7

Day hike
Unofficial trail & route
Distance 7.5 km to side creek
Height gain 396 m
High point 1829 m
Map 82 J/14 Spray Lakes Reservoir

Access: See #42 above.

While gravel flats makes walking easy, it's debatable whether the upper valley is worth the tedium. My recommendation is to use this valley in combination with Wasootch Ridge. Its most interesting aspect is its name which derives from the Stoney word 'wazi', denoting 'uniqueness and solitariness'. Possibly it's connected with Wasootch Tower, a valley landmark.

A short trail leads to Wasootch Slabs on the left, a popular practice cliff with climbers. The large white letters at the bottom of various slabs were painted by the Canadian army, who used the slabs for training during the 1950s when guidebooks were still 30 years in the future. The spectacular rock outlier on the opposite side of the valley is Wasootch Tower.

For 7.3 kilometres walk flat gravel flats completely rewritten during the 1995 flood that tore up Dryas mats (unfortunately for the walker), but spared the Balsam poplars. Usually, water is intermittent, disappearing underground for long stretches at a time. At the forks overlooked by Mt. McDougall the scenario changes. The main (left-hand) valley narrows and the trees close in. A trail along the left bank leads to a small canyon with waterfall steps. Circumvent by scrabbling up a gully to the left, then head right over a rib back to the creekbed. A little farther on, a stony side creek to the left is the descent route from Wasootch Ridge.

If going to the valley head (a few meadows), stream hopping, awkward side hill traverses around waterfalls and fights with willow bush become the norm.

44 WASOOTCH RIDGE — map 7

Long day scramble
Unofficial trail, route
6.5 km to summit, 16 km round trip
Height gain 890 m
High point 2323 m
Map 82 J/14 Spray Lakes Reservoir

Access: Kanowaskis Trail (Hwy. 40) at Wasootch Creek parking lot.
Also accessible from #43 Wasootch Creek.

The long ridge dividing Wasootch Creek and the south fork of Porcupine Creek is, in terms of difficulty, more difficult than the Centennial Trail, but easier than Northover Ridge; that is, if you follow the ridge in its entirety. Most people don't, being content to make their objective either the big cairn or the first grassy summit before the scrambling begins. If going for the high point at GR376436, check the ridge from the highway and wait until the snow is off the northeast face.

From the picnic area several rough paths climb the steep hillside; all more or less converging on the forested ridge above Wasootch Slabs. Remnants of a trail can be followed for the next kilometre up a longer, less steep step that leads into a long, almost level section ending at the big cairn. After this, the ridge narrows, undulating above and below treeline, finally shaking free of the trees and rising in a graceful curve to a grassy top—the end of the road for most people. The ridge beyond is for scramblers.

Opposite
Top: Wasootch Creek. Wasootch Slabs to left, Wasootch Tower to right.

Bottom: Wasootch Ridge, looking worse than it is. Route drops off the right end of the easy section onto scree slopes, then traverses to a deep notch not visible. From the notch either follow the ridge crest or climb scree to the left of the ridge. Both options join for the slope leading to the summit.

The upcoming fin of rock is best turned on the left side by a few metres of down scrambling to reach the talus slope below. Unless you're a purist, miss out the next top as well by a traverse on the right side. An easy section through trees ends at a viewpoint where the photo was taken. Although the ridge ahead looks terrifying, be assured that the route I am about to describe, albeit a convoluted one, gets you to the summit without turning you into a gibbering jellyfish. Start by working your way along the first easy bit of ridge. Where it zigs left, drop to scree slopes on the Wasootch Creek side and traverse under the rock wall until it's possible to climb an easy scree chute (use the right-hand side) to a deep notch invisible from the viewpoint and the key to the whole ascent. Now some people who don't mind a little exposure scrabble straight up the ridge to the summit. Alternatively, contour below the rock crest on the Porcupine Creek side (scree) and regain the ridge above all difficulties. Finish up easy rubble.

Return via Wasootch Creek Continue along the ridge, an uneventful descent on scree to the col at GR384432. While you can drop into the south fork of Porcupine Creek, most people elect to return via Wasootch Creek. So head right down a rather unpleasant slope, a mix of slaty rocks, bushes and runnable scree ribbons, into a side creek gained about a kilometre away from the main river valley. On reaching Wasootch Creek (water, finally) turn right and pick up a trail taking you out to the Dryas flats. All that remains is a mind-numbing 7.5 km plod back to the parking lot.

Kananaskis Valley*

45 HUMMINGBIRD PLUME LOOKOUT — map 7

Day hike
Official trail with signposts
Distance 10.5 km loop
Height gain 395 m
High point 1865 m
Map 82 J/14 Spray Lakes Reservoir

Access: Kananaskis Trail (Hwy. 40). Follow signs to Ribbon Creek. Drive past the hostel to Ribbon Creek parking lots.

Mostly a forest walk with one interesting viewpoint and a waterfall. The loop follows four metre-wide ski trails throughout, but just because it's technically easy doesn't mean you won't be puffing up a few steep hills.

Start from the picnic shelter located between the two parking lots. For the first hour you're going to be following signs for Skogan Pass ski trail. Straight off, the trail climbs to the Nakiska access road. Cross and resume walking along the trail, keeping left at the junction with Troll Falls trail. In an effort to be interesting for skiers (though vexing for walkers), the trail undulates all around the perimeter of Nakiska ski area, passing side trails to right and left and intersecting Ruthie's. Cross a branch of Marmot Creek, then climb alongside to join the former Marmot Basin Road. Turn right. (For the curious, the next side trail on the right leads to a Research Council of Alberta groundwater site measuring water flow in Marmot Creek. Downstream of the dam is an unsuspected gorge which is worth a closer look.)

The lookout.

112

Shortly, where Marmot Basin Road turns left, keep straight on the gated Marmot Creek Road. At another junction on the bank of Marmot Creek turn right across Two Ton Culvert. After a kilometre of uphill winding, the trail touches a power-line right-of-way. At this point transfer onto Sunburst ski trail which offers nothing but "sweat, toil and tears", as they say, to the junction with High Level ski trail. The sign isn't much help. Turn right and walk to a small meadow atop Humming-bird Plume Hill.

You missed the lookout in the rush to get seats at the picnic table? The 'lookout' is the shack on the right that doesn't appear to be worth a second glance unless there's an imminent thunderstorm, and then it pays to know the shack is grounded. But take a closer look inside. On the walls are inscribed the names and initials of German POWs from Camp 130: Erich Petrinski POW 17.11.1939, JQ 1941, PW July 6/41. At the time the POWs were salvaging burnt timber from the 1936 fire there really *was* a view from the lookout. Now the pines have grown too high, so what you do is follow a two minute trail from the other end of the meadow to the edge of the 130 metre-high craggy east slope with rock gardens to drool over. Before you is the same view of the Kananaskis Valley, the Fisher Range opposite and a profile of Lorette's south ridge.

Return Return to the powerline. This time turn left and follow the powerline access road twining about the right-of-way on its plunge to valley bottom. Nearly 280 vertical metres lost in minutes.

On hitting Stoney trail (#35), turn right and cross Marmot Creek. At intersecting Hay Meadow ski trail (appropriately surfaced with grass), turn right and in a few metres come to a four-way intersection in the trees with Troll Falls trail and Ruthie's. If you haven't been to Troll Falls, you're in for a treat. Follow the narrow right-hand trail into a gloomy recess filled with spray from water crashing into a pool. For a better

Troll Falls from the ledge.

view of the falls, grub up one of the trails on the left to a ledge below an undercut cliff.

Return to the four-way intersection. Continue along Troll Falls trail, the narrow hiking trail converted in 1982 to regulation four metre-wide ski track. Stay left, then right. At the junction with Hay Meadow trail keep right and climb to Skogan Pass trail. Turn left and return the way you came.

113

46 MARMOT BASIN & OTHER TRAILS — map 7

Long day hikes
Official & unofficial trails, creek crossings
Distance 8.5 km from Nakiska
Height gain 762 m from Nakiska
High point 2286 m at spring
Map 82 J/14 Spray Lakes Reservoir

Access: Kananaskis Trail (Hwy. 40). Follow signs to Nakiska Ski Area. Use South parking lot on the left. Via Skogan Pass trail (#22).
Also accessible from #25, Collembola Traverse.

An assortment of old trails and new logging roads through the Marmot Basin Project area give access to the cirque between Mt. Allan and lower Collembola. You can, if you want, climb both these peaks from Marmot Basin, or make a loop with the Centennial Trail or a point to point with the Collembolas. Trails stop at treeline but the terrain is straightforward. Whatever you decide, you know you're in for a strenuous trip with lots of height gain.

Marmot Basin Road section 5 km Follow Skogan Pass trail as described in this book to the junction of Marmot Basin Road and Marmot Creek Road. Turn left up Marmot Basin Road, now a snowmobile access road to Nakiska's Mid Mountain Lodge. Straightaway stay right, then keep left four times as you climb around two bends. The grind is relentless, calling for a collapse next to the fuel tank where a new piece of road turns left towards the lodge. Keep straight. Shortly Marmot Basin Road descends and turns right to cross South Twin Creek, in the process becoming a ski trail called Marmot Basin trail (returning down Marmot Creek to the Marmot Creek Road).

To Marmot Basin Cross bridges over South and North Twin Creeks, then turn left up the original trail which follows the north bank of North Twin Creek. After passing an uphill grassy road to right, the trail itself bends right uphill and intersects a grassy road of a later date which has come up from

the ski trail. Turn left onto the road. In a few metres, turn left on another road that climbs in a semicircle. Again turn left and climb an even steeper semicircular hill. At the apex, marked by a fallen tree, turn left up a road in slightly worse shape. Zig left, right, then left. Just before it peters out above North Twin Creek, regain the original trail in a flurry of flagging.

What joy to follow an easy-angled trail winding through spruce forest and a patchwork of mini cutblocks. Look for the first larch. After the third intersection with the straight-up trail (the last, a worthwhile shortcut to Fisera Ridge), a long traverse right leads into willowy Marmot Creek at the site of instruments measuring stream flow.

Leave the main trail, which zigs back left, and follow a less distinct trail up the left (south) bank to the spring where Marmot Creek emerges in full flight. Ahead are meadows dotted with spruce thickets and snow pockets in July. People with energy to spare can walk up to the Allan-Collembola col.

Even his friends might be surprised to learn the basin and creek were named by Gordon Scruggs who, as a young university student, assisted M.B.B. Crockford during the geological survey of 1947 prior to the opening of the coal mine. According to Gordon, their camp was overrun by marmots looking for easy pickings.

Optional Descent Use the aforementioned straight-up trail intersected three times by the normal ascent route. Below the intersections it becomes rather steep. Keep an eye out for red and white peppermint flagging where you angle right and hit a flagged

Among the larches on Fisera Ridge. In the background is Mt. Allan. To left is the Centennial Ridge #47, to right the final section of Collembola Traverse #25.

logging road. Turn right. Turn right at the following T-junction and climb the hill to its apex at the fallen tree. Keep left and return the way you came up.

OPTIONS

Fisera Ridge 2320 m 1 km from Marmot Creek, height gain 120 m.

At Marmot Creek the main trail swings back left past a metal sign reassuringly stamped 'Fisera Ridge'. Recross the short-cut and climb up the backbone of the ridge through larches (always a thrill), where Zedenek 'Dernny' Fisera tended to metro-logical instruments no longer around. Higher up where the ridge levels you're into meadows with views all around of the Olympic Summit through Mt. Allan to the lower summit of Collembola. Remarkably, the Centennial Ridge is an easy traverse away, useful knowledge if a storm's moving in and you've got to get off the ridge quickly.

South Twin Creek 1.3 km from Marmot Basin Road, height gain 213 m. A fast direct route to open slopes.

Starts between South and North Twin Creeks. Turn left up a grassy logging road that crosses South Twin Creek twice before ending in a tangle of deadfall. A narrow trail continues. After the fourth creek crossing there's a long stretch along the north bank to V-shaped hillsides where the trail is forced into a steeply rising traverse to gain the rib between the creeks. Here the problem is one of excess flagging coloured blue, red, white and dark red. Luckily the trail is obvious (it follows the dark red) and ends at another instrument site about 60 metres below treeline in the larches. This puts you in a good position to join the Centennial Ridge or cut across to Fisera Ridge.

47 MOUNT ALLAN VIA CENTENNIAL RIDGE — maps 7 & 6

Long day hike
Official trail with signposts, cairns &
red paint splodges on rocks
Distance 11 km to summit,
19 km to Trans-Canada Highway
Height gain 1350 m
High point 2819 m
Map 82 J/14 Spray Lakes Reservoir

Access: Kananaskis Trail (Hwy. 40). Follow signs to Ribbon Creek. Drive past the hostel to the upper Ribbon Creek parking lot.
Also accessible from #24 Mount Allan from the north.

It was 1966. The next year was Canada's centennial and to mark this momentous occasion the Rocky Mountain Ramblers decided to build a trail up the long southeast ridge of Mt. Allan to the summit and down the equally long north ridge to Dead Man Flat. It would be the highest trail ever built in the Canadian Rockies, higher even than Jasper's celebrated Skyline Trail. The work took three summer seasons to complete and culminated in a champagne ceremony on the summit during a snow squall. A large wooden sign was erected but didn't stand for long. Within three months the picas had chewed away the supporting poles and in another two years the sign itself was fully digested. In 1983 an inedible bronze plaque was placed halfway along the Centennial Ridge at the Rock Gardens.

The Centennial Ridge is by far the more popular route up Mt. Allan and like the north ridge has a couple of places requiring easy scrambling. Bearing in mind the strenuous nature of the trip, *start early* from the parking lot. Know that upwards of the Mine Scar the trail is closed for lambing between April 1 and June 21.

To Mine Scar Start up Hidden ski trail and in 300 metres turn left onto the Mt. Allan Centennial Trail, which is also Mt. Allan ski trail. Keep straight a little way in. At

the next intersection climb straight up the hill (the ski trail turns right, only delaying the inevitable), and intersect the lowest of five roads leading to Mine Scar (going right returns you to the ski trail at the cabin). Follow the second road to the right a short way, then continue uphill. Intersect the third road (Coal Mine ski trail). At the fourth turn left. Take the second road to the right and arrive at the sign about trail closures. Getting to this point takes about 30 minutes from the parking lot.

Mine Scar viewpoint can be reached by following any of these intersecting roads to the left; they just lead to different levels of what was almost 50 years ago the Ribbon Creek Coal Mine operated by the Kananaskis Exploration & Development Company, a subsidiary of Martin Nordegg's Brazeau Collieries. Appendix 1 of a brief released by the Energy Conservation Board in April 1975 recommended this mine be re-operational by 1982, but thankfully that never happened, although I wouldn't have said no to a parking lot at this level. Now 20 years reclaimed, the strip mine's a lush meadow with grass not quite matching that of the rest of the mountain.

Centennial Ridge Shortly after intersecting a fifth (grassed) road, the Centennial Trail turns uphill and reaches open ground. The sight of the trail crawling upwards, climbing 610 m in less than 2 km, is enough to make you turn tail and spend the day wallowing in the hay of the Mine Scar, but the grassy rib it follows has its compensations in the marvellous views that unfold, and summer's succession of flowers ending in

Bottom: *Mt. Allan's Centennial Ridge from Olympic Summit. In mid ridge is the Mushroom Garden and the pinnacles.*

Top: *Olympic Summit from the first top. The trail negotiates the cliff band to the right.*

late August with a blue colour scheme of asters and harebells. Take a breather on a shoulder, then zig some more up a shaley slope to the apex of three grass ribs—the start of the Centennial Ridge proper.

The upcoming rock step looks alarming (photo previous page), but is easily turned on the right (north) side by a series of broad ledges and a gully that calls for hands in a few places. Under lingering snow, however, this section can be awkward. When we were there one November, someone had rigged up a rope to the left of the gully.

Having expended much energy in reaching a grassy top pretentiously called Olympic Summit, it's discouraging to find the main summit as far away as ever and separated by a dip that doesn't bode well for the return. But the worst of the climbing is behind you and the most scenic part of the whole route is yet to come. This is where the trail winds through the Mushroom Garden, itself only a prelude to the celebrated passage between the rocky ridge crest and a row of 25 metre-high conglomerate pinnacles that is absolutely spectacular. Through the gaps look down on Memorial Lakes and across to Mts. Sparrowhawk, Bogart and Ribbon Peak.

Some interesting down-scrambling follows and brings you to a section of scree ridge where you can either go over the top or keep to the trail on the left slope. Tackle the final rise to the cairn direct; a solid stone staircase is preferable any time to the shifting yellow scree of the south face, which is where some people go. (In case you're wondering, the trail traversing around the summit block to the north ridge is for sheep who don't have the same urge as humans do to reach a summit.)

Opposite: The crux. Don't worry, you can get to Ribbon Falls without resorting to such tactics. The third chain en route to Ribbon Lake.

Below: Three of the conglomerate pinnacles, the Claw at centre.

48 RIBBON FALLS & RIBBON LAKE — maps 7 & 6

Day hike, backpack
Official trail with signposts
Distance 11 km to Ribbon Falls,
13 km to Ribbon Lake
Height gain 311 m Ribbon Falls
Height gain 588 m Ribbon Lake
High point 2076 m at lake
Map 82 J/14 Spray Lakes Reservoir

Access: Kananaskis Trail (Hwy. 40). Follow signs to Ribbon Creek. Drive past the hostel to the upper Ribbon Creek parking lot.
Also accessible from #70 Buller Pass.

This popular trail follows a spectacular valley hemmed in by cliffs. All is easy to the 10 km mark, where cliff bands give rise to two spectacular waterfalls and cause difficulty and danger to the hiker bound for Ribbon Lake. If hauling yourself and a heavy pack up chains doesn't appeal, use alternative trails to get to Ribbon Lake: Guinn's Pass (#53) or Buller Pass (#70).

To the Forks Head into the narrows past a Rundle Rock quarry opened up by Elmer Smith in the 1960s. At the first bend a remnant of logging road comes in from across the river. No bridge of course. This boisterous stream is an expert at deterrence. The next section of trail was wiped out by the spring flood of 1995, and a little farther on, before K Country erected bridges, adventurers were forced into a perilous traverse high above the river on the right bank. It hasn't yet occurred to trail-closing environmentalists that lack of bridges, not to mention lack of good trails, is the natural way to limit numbers in the backcountry without pissing people off.

On bridges, then, cross and recross the creek back to the right bank. At 2.5 km, Link ski trail turns off to the left across the river. The final section to the forks is through spruce forest affectionately called 'Toad Forest' by early hostellers. About 300 metres before the bridge over the north fork the trail to Memorial Lakes leaves the right side of the trail at a cairn.

To Ribbon Falls Across the bridge is a meadow with interpretive plaque and tastefully placed pieces of scrap iron signifying the site of Eau Claire's logging camp that operated in this valley from 1886 to the beginning of World War II. A couple of kilometres further on explore the ruins of two log cabins. In case you haven't noticed, Mt. Bogart is marked incorrectly on the topo map and should be transposed 1.4 km southwest to the higher summit at GR236412. So the steep hillside presently to your right is Ribbon Peak. Shortly after the second cabin, the trail enters Dipper Canyon, a delightful section of river with alternating cataracts and pools. After this it's a gradual climb across large avalanche slopes falling from Mt. Bogart to Ribbon Falls backcountry campground. Climb farther up the trail to a rocky overlook for Ribbon Falls which is worth every metre of the 11 kilometre slog in.

Ribbon Lake

The trail beyond is very much more difficult, even dangerous. There was a serious accident here in the 1970s before the ropes and chains went in. Hikers with heavy packs, particularly women who generally have less arm strength than men, will have difficulty pulling themselves up the chains. Get the men to carry the packs up. In such places I'm not fussy. I recommend a climbing rope for a safeguard, but of course you have to know how to belay.

From the falls, the trail zigs up the north bank and crosses the head of a gully to a large scree slope. Walk across to the bottom of the headwall. With the help of a chain, climb a moderately-angled corner until level with a large ledge on the left, then traverse three metres of slick slab. Walk along the large ledge to a third chain and heave yourself up five metres of difficult rock, bulging in the middle, onto easier ground above (see photo on previous page). Wend right, then left onto a long horizontal ledge protected with a handrail. As you edge above the big drop, it's disquieting to know a fall from here would definitely kill you. Pass a caution sign for people coming the other way. This doesn't mean you can relax your vigilance; the upcoming steps are greasy smooth and a slip could send you perhaps not over the edge but to the very brink, hanging on to a few bushes like the hero of a 1920 Harold Lloyd movie. In the middle of all this trauma, the upper falls are well-worth a detour.

The ground gradually eases to Ribbon Lake, from this angle backdropped by the unnamed peak between Guinn's Pass and Buller Pass. The campground's at the other end. As you wind around the north shore, look for springs bubbling out of circular depressions in the lake bottom.

Opposite: Ribbon Falls.

Below: Ribbon Lake. Looking southwest to unnamed peak GR218373. Buller Pass at far right.

49 MEMORIAL LAKES — maps 7 & 6

Day hike
Unofficial trails, route & creek crossings
Distance 7 km to Second Lake
Height gain 585 m to Second Lake,
690 m to Third Lake
High point 2197 m Third Lake
Map 82 J/14 Spray Lakes Reservoir

Access: Via Ribbon Creek trail (#48) 300 m before the bridge over the north fork.

Waterfalls, tarns, cliffs. The head of Ribbon Creek's north fork is a magical place and quite easy to get to now the trail's in such good shape 11 years after the second edition. Beyond First Memorial Lake, though, the way remains rough and steep in spots, particularly the slope below the third lake which is a scramble.

To the Waterfalls A pile of rocks marks the entrance to the north fork trail on the right. Not far in is a warning sign with drawings of unexploded bombs. I thought at first this was an environmentalist's ploy to keep people like me on the straight and narrow trail, but discovered it's a precautionary measure taken by Nakiska's avalanche control. A sharp uphill precedes two skimpy traverses of shale banks. After a second uphill the trail divides; go either way. Then it's down to the creek. The second time you go down to the creek you're in for a long stint under five metre-high willows. Use the right-hand trail to cross a side creek.

A barely recognizable logging road comes in from across the creek. Follow it up to a small camping area. A few metres on is a junction. Turn right, climb a few metres of steep ground, then detour left to enter the canyon between waterfalls—one of the day's highlights.

To First Lake Retrace your steps to the main trail and continue grovelling up the slope to a junction with a climber's access trail. Turn left here, traversing above the canyon in which the river is behaving with reckless abandon. Note one long ribbon fall

as you continue around the bend and up a small slab to flat ground where the water is calmly gliding along like nothing's going to happen. Past a confluence the trail splits. Cross the creek, keep left and arrive shortly at First Memorial Lake about halfway along its north shore where there's a break in the willows. It's not attractive, though the setting under Bogart Tower is undeniably impressive. To the tower's left, a waterfall tumbles down the headwall from Third Lake (actually, the water drains underground and bursts forth about a third of the way down the headwall). To its right is the shortcut from Third Lake: the top to toe scree gully immediately left of the tower.

To Second Lake—the Emerald The trail continues, crossing the creek above the lake in a tangle of willow bushes to the south bank (Dryas mats and stones). Turn right and follow the trail up a scree step to flat ground. There are several ways on from here, all involving stiff climbing. At the lip, a trail marked by cairns climbs the left-hand scree slope direct to Second Lake, bypassing valley steps two and three. Alternately, follow the flat valley bottom to just before the trees, then clamber straight up the left slope (messy finish) onto flat rocky ground above the second step. Make for a cairn below the third forested step. On intersecting a game trail headed for the creek, turn left, then at a junction a little way up double back right into trees below a low cliff band. The trail climb steeply, meeting the direct route at the top of the step. Turn right and descend slightly to Second Memorial Lake.

If, like me, you've looked down on this lake with great longing from the summits of

Third Memorial Lake, full to the brim. Ribbon Peak above. Photo Alf Skrastins.

Sparrowhawk or Allan, this is a special moment. The unusual clarity of the water and its brilliant emerald colour coupled with its setting are great inducements for idling away an hour or two. Walk anticlockwise (forest trail) to the willowy west shore for a new perspective of the lake backdropped by Bogart Tower.

To Third Lake Out of sight in a cirque behind Bogart Tower, Third Lake is even more difficult to access, despite the deceptively far apart contours shown on the topo map. From where you first saw the emerald lake, continue traversing on sheep trail past the cove and the rotten gully on the left. You're going to be climbing the slope to the right of the gully using one of two starts. The looser one follows the right side of the gully a bit, then cuts right up trash. The firmer trail follows the obvious left to right diagonal grassy ramp between cliff bands. At the end of the top band where the ramp narrows sensationally, a trail zigs back left and meets the first route. Turn right.

A couple of steep zigs, and a long easy traverse above the gully leads to a mini-cirque rimmed by steep slopes. The trail climbs the grassy rib up ahead. At the top

Memorial cairn.

(or before) head left, aiming for the lightly-treed ridge behind Bogart Tower where you look down into another much larger cirque enclosed by the cliffs of Ribbon Peak and Mt. Bogart. On the ridge between the two rises a curious mitten-shaped pinnacle with a hole in it. Thirty vertical metres below you, turquoise waters lap a fringe of meadow at the very edge of the drop-off.

Close under Bogart Tower a trail descends to Third Lake's north shore. Hopefully by the time you get there the afternoon shadow cast by high rock walls will not yet have spread its pall over the scene, and equally hopefully the water will be filled to the brim so you can delight in the spoon-shaped promontory lined with spruce trees.

On a hummock at the edge of the drop-off is a memorial cairn and plaque remembering the 13 people who died during that dreadful week of June 6-14 in 1986 when two search planes crashed during the search for Orval Pall and Ken Wolff. Read the first and last lines of the sonnet 'High Flight' written by 19 year-old fighter pilot John Magee. Strange how something scribbled on the back of a letter sent to his mother two months before he died during the Battle of Britain in 1941 has endured all this time. You perhaps remember President Reagan quoting this very sonnet after the loss of the Challenger astronauts.

Scrambler's shortcut to First Lake
Starting immediately right of Bogart Tower is a scree gully. If uncomfortable at the top, wade through dense spruce thickets on the right side where it's hard to get any downward momentum going at all. When the gully splits, follow the neck between the two, then continue easily down the right side of the left-hand gully, bypassing a small rock band in the gully bed. Level with the bottom of Bogart Tower, cross to the left side to avoid a small cliff. Below the cliff wend back right (waterfall view) and follow a dribble of scree into forest where game trails continue to valley bottom. Likely, you'll have to step left a bit to locate the main valley this side of the creek crossing.

50 KOVACH LOOPS — map 7

Short day hike
Official signposted trails
Distance 7.4 km loops
Height gain 150 m
High point 1675 m
Map 82 J/14 Spray Lakes Reservoir

Access: Kananaskis Trail (Hwy. 40). Follow signs to Kananaskis Village. Drive to the parking lot for Kananaskis Inn (opposite Woody's Pub). **Also** accessible from Terrace trail #51.

Easy but hilly forest circuits following four metre-wide ski trails.

Start from the four-way intersection west of the parking lot. Turn left onto Terrace trail and walk past Rim trail and the road to the reservoir. At the next junction keep right on the four metre-wide ski trail that's named Kovach, and wind uphill to a junction with Aspen in a damp meadow. Anyone resting at the picnic table will need to slather themselves in Muskol.

At this junction and the look-alike junction following stay to the left, always climbing uphill. Look back for a fine view of The Wedge before rounding the bend and disappearing into spruce forest indicating the upper limit of the 1936 fire. This is the loop's high point. On your way down a logging road built to salvage timber after the fire, a fresh landscape appears to the west: Ribbon Peak, Mt. Sparrowhawk and Mt. Allan showing the Centennial Ridge in profile. A picnic table marks the start of two long downhill zigs to the T-junction with Link trail. Should you go left here you'd join up with Ribbon Creek trail. Turn right.

Finish A via Aspen trail In 300 metres turn first right and climb to a junction. Turn left onto the nicest stretch of trail in the area: aspens, of course, flowery meadows and two fine viewpoints, one with a picnic table. On rejoining Kovach, turn left and return the way you came up.

Descending Kovach trail to the junction with Link. Mt. Sparrowhawk in the background, showing route #67 from the col to the summit.

Finish B via Terrace trail Follow Kovach all the way down past Aspen and Terrace Link to Terrace T-junction. Turn right and return via Terrace trail to the four-way intersection at Kananaskis Village. The going is flat, easy and a little boring. Watch for Terrace Link joining in from the right about 500 metres short of the four-way junction near the parking lot.

Finish C via Terrace Link trail In 1.2 km turn second right onto Terrace Link. The trail rolls across strips of damp willowy meadows before joining Terrace 500 metres before the parking lot.

51 TERRACE TRAIL — maps 7 & 11

Day hike
Official trail with signposts
Distance 11.4 km from Ribbon Creek
Height gain north to south 40 m
High point 1590 m
Map 82 J/14 Spray Lakes Reservoir

Access: Kananaskis Trail (Hwy. 40).
1. Follow signs to Ribbon Creek. The trail starts at the picnic shelter between parking lots.
2. Usual start/finish. Follow signs to Kananaskis Village. Use the Kananaskis Inn parking lot.
3. Galatea Creek parking lot.

Terrace trail follows terraces of the Kananaskis River between Ribbon Creek and Galatea Creek. The northern section is a four metre-wide ski trail, not too interesting on foot, but a useful connector to the usual starting point if you haven't got a vehicle.

Mt. Kidd north summit.

North to South From Ribbon Creek picnic shelter the trail crosses Ribbon Creek and winds up the bank to Kovach trail. Stay left and watch for Terrace Link coming in from the right. At 2.4 km you reach the four-way junction next to the parking lot for Kananaskis Inn. Go straight for Woody's Pub.

Seriously, turn right. Pass a baseball diamond, soccer field, horseshoe pitches, picnic tables and biffies. Keep right at Rim trail. Pass the road to the reservoir, then at your second junction with Kovach turn left.

Head downhill on an older narrower track. At the right-angled bend to the left, transfer to an even narrower trail carrying on in the same line as before. Finally free of junctions, though not yet of Japanese tourists, the trail makes for the lowest terrace overlooking a chain of beaver ponds. This is a satisfying viewpoint looking across the golf course up Evan-Thomas Creek to Fisher Peak, the valley bounded on either side by Old Baldy and The Wedge. I've spent an enjoyable 10 minutes at this spot watching golfers putt into the largest pond,

a small, and some might say petty, revenge for being turfed off the golf course for wearing a Mo Zeegers T-shirt.

From here on the twisting trail rises and falls between various levels of river terraces below the east face of Mt. Kidd, which acts like a giant reflector, throwing the sun's heat back down onto dry prickly hillsides of grass, pine, aspen and scrub. During spring melt, waterfalls leaping down gullies in the cliffs fill small streams crossing the trail. Further on you cross assorted alluvial fans and one wide stony creekbed, the scrambler's jumping-off point for Mt. Kidd. Five minutes before a trail junction the trail makes its closest approach yet to the Kananaskis River. A sloping ledge dipping into the water is a fine place for a few quiet minutes before joining the mob on Galatea Creek trail.

Keep left and cross Galatea Creek. Shortly cross the Kananaskis River via suspension bridge and climb the wretched hill to Galatea Creek parking lot.

52 GALATEA CREEK TO LILLIAN LAKE — map 11

Day hike, backpack
Official trail with signposts
Distance 6.5 km
Height gain 492 m
High point 1630 m at lake
Map 82 J/14 Spray Lakes Reservoir

Access: Kananaskis Trail (Hwy. 40) at Galatea Creek parking lot.

Galatea Creek was once a place for adventurers, being fraught with difficulty and uncertainty. In the early morning, low water levels in the Kananaskis River would entice people to wade across to the 'trail'. On returning in the late afternoon, they would sometimes find the river a raging torrent after the opening up of the sluice gates at Canyon Dam, and be forced to spend the night trapped on the west bank within sight of their cars.

Now the trail has been rebuilt with 10 bridges, every man and his dog goes to Lillian Lake, including part-time summer rangers who pick up garbage and tick off anyone with a dog not on a leash. So the clientele has changed. Nevertheless, it's worth dodging the crowds up this moderately strenuous trail to view beautiful Lillian Lake. Lovers of solitude can climb higher to Galatea Lakes. The trail is usually closed until June 30th.

Descend to the suspension bridge over the Kananaskis River and cross. On the west bank the trail crosses Galatea Creek to a junction with Terrace trail and turns left. After an up-down, the next four creek crossings come in quick succession under the precipitous gable end of Fortress Ridge. Between bridges 3 and 4 a chasm opened up during the spring floods of 1995 when the river was making a new bed for itself, forcing K Country to reroute the trail even as I write. The name of this disgracefully behaved piece of water is for once appropriate. It appears

Galatea, meaning 'milk white', was a sea nymph who turned her beloved Acis (killed by Polyphemus with a rock), into a river that forever after bore his name. OK, so it was named after a battleship named after the nymph.

A long stretch on the north bank traverses grassy avalanche slopes above an impassible gorge, taking a line much lower

Lillian Lake.

127

than the original trail but still worthy of the tag 'viewpoint'. En route, a side trail leads to a dangerous viewpoint for a waterfall.

Bridge 6 signals the start of spruce forest. A few minutes later, bridge 7 at the forks ushers you into the northwest fork. I find this final stretch the most draining of the whole route. Coming back down you always meet families, almost on their knees, wanting to know "How much further is it to the lake?" Guinn's Pass trail takes off from the bottom of an avalanche slope 800 metres before your destination.

Circle the north shoreline to the back-country campground at the west end. Every summer weekend, the environs of the lake takes on a festive atmosphere from the mingling of campers and day trippers who are fishing, socializing, even swimming in chartreuse-coloured waters shallow enough to retain a little of the sun's warmth.

GOING FARTHER

Galatea Lakes add 1 km and 183 m height gain. While Lillian Lake is beautiful, the surroundings don't turn me on and I have to climb higher to that fascinating alpine country at Galatea Lakes.

The (unofficial) trail starts behind campsite #11 and climbs a steep scrubby slope to the left of the forest edge. At the top cross the tiny creek and walk up gently-inclined talus to lower Galatea Lake, a beautiful blue tarn ringed by pleated rock ridges. The big mountain at the end is The Tower.

While there is nothing to stop you from wandering along the stony north shore, a trail of sorts continues along the south shore jumble of outcrops, meadows and scrubby subalpine fir to the ridge separating the two lakes. Down below, the upper lake is cradled in a grassy hollow.

Lower Galatea Lake from the ridge between the two lakes.

53 GUINN'S PASS — map 11

Long day, backpack
Official trail with signposts
Distance 3.3 km
Height gain 457 m from Galatea Creek
Height gain 259 m from Ribbon Creek
High point 2423 m
Map 82 J/14 Spray Lakes Reservoir

Access: Via Galatea Creek (#52) at the 5.7 km mark, and via Buller Pass trail (#70) 1 km west of Ribbon Lake.

Alvin Guinn.

Many years ago, Rick's dad, Alvin Guinn, took a string of 20 packhorses over the ridge from Galatea Creek to Ribbon Lake. Well, not by this route exactly. He went up the avalanche gully further to the right. By the time he reached the ridge night was falling and in the need to hurry he led his horses straight down the scree slope to Ribbon Lake! Next morning he looked for a better route back and that's when he discovered Guinn's Pass, spelt with an apostrophe, please.

If you think the pass is a pushover for those of us on foot, you're wrong. From both sides this is a steep, demanding climb exposed to bad weather. Wait until most of the snow has melted. For day trippers the pass is a worthwhile alternative to Lillian Lake, with the added pleasure of climbing a minor summit to look at Guinn's original route.

South to north The trail leaves Galatea Creek trail about 800 metres before Lillian Lake. You cross the creek and start up a flowery avalanche gully that soon becomes a stony gully, a suffocating furnace at midday when the sun bounces off white stones. In theory, backpackers should aim to put the gully behind them early in the day, but are usually found lying about in various states of heat exhaustion, greedily lapping up water from the gully bed. Higher up at treeline you transfer to a bit of scree on the right side, then (gully faded out), zig back and forth on close-cropped

turf pungent with sheep droppings. A tremendous panoramic view opening up behind you is a good excuse to stop often. Ahead, the eye is caught by the peak delineating the west side of the pass, which fully reveals its massive eastern precipice only when you reach the cairn.

No greater contrast between the two sides of Guinn's Pass could be imagined. The north slope is grassless and treeless, just plenty of stones and likely lots of snow early in the season. Under the eye of the precipice make long sweeping zigzags on easy-angled talus into a barren basin, all bumps and hollows, one of which holds a shallow pond. On the bench an unofficial shortcut to Buller Pass heads left. The official trail descends the bench to the signposted junction with Buller Pass trail in upper Ribbon Creek. This occurs where springs gush out of the grassy hillside, a joyful resurgence of melted snow trickling into the pond.

OPTION
Peak at GR237374 2606 m distance 800 m from pass, height gain 180 m.

A simple walk up the stony ridge east of the pass gains you an even better viewpoint. To the south is a welter of peaks, Galatea and The Fortress among them, shadowy shapes among which Lillian Lake and lower Galatea Lake glow like coloured jewels. In the opposite direction you can inspect both Buller Passes, Mt. Bogart showing the scrambler's route, and the long connecting ridge to Mt. Kidd South which makes you yearn to carry on.

Strangely, this insignificant summit, marked by a cairn and pole, is the scene of momentous happenings, from Guinn's adventurous crossing to the tragic loss of Orval Pall and Ken Wolff which started off K Country's largest search. The col to the east is where Guinn first crossed over the ridge with his packhorses. For variety some people descend his ascent route, down the heathery hillside to the south and into the grassy avalanche gully that flows into Galatea Creek not far below Guinn's Pass junction. We once made the mistake of following the forested ridge to the left of the gully. Don't. Not only is it rocky and steep in its lower part, but we suddenly realized we were looking down the cliff where Wolff's Cessna crashed exactly a year ago to the day. Some places are better left alone.

Looking down on Guinn's Pass from the lower slopes of peak GR237374.

54 LOST LAKE — maps 10 & 11

Lost Lake from the bluffs above the south shore. Rummel Pass at top left.

Day hike
Unofficial trail
Distance 7.5 km from trailhead
Height gain 500 m
High point 2018 m
Map 82 J/14 Spray Lakes Reservoir

Access: Kananaskis Trail (Hwy. 40). Via Galatea Creek trail (#52) at the forks.

Want to get away from the hordes trudging to Lillian Lake? This is a quiet forest walk to a lake in Galatea's southwest fork.

Just *before* you cross Galatea Creek for the seventh time at km 4.3, leave the official trail and search for a trapper's trail on the left bank. It's higher than you think and initially hidden by deadfall. Almost straightaway you run into the ruins of a cabin built by Alvin Guinn, who also cut the trail. After this the trail improves and is easily followed as it dodges between trees and deadfall, gradually accumulating height in a forest strangely bereft of shrubs. Shortly keep right and cross a side creek with lots of water. Cross another side creek, then

keep left (logs lain across right-hand trail) into a long uneventful stretch ending at the lake. The colour? Olive green. I recommend you climb grassy bluffs on the south side for the greatest view of the lake backdropped by Rummel Pass and The Tower.

OPTIONS
If you're staying around, the high grassy hill at GR238342 begs to be climbed via its west ridge. Rummel Pass is best incorporated with #81 *in a west to east direction*. The side trail at GR248358 is worth investigating. Quite apart from approaching the high hill from another direction, you can hop over the ridge at GR252342 (criss-crossed by trees felled by the 1936 fire) to Fortress Lake and pick up trail #59.

55 EVAN-THOMAS CREEK — maps 7, 11 & 12

Walking up Evan-Thomas Creek to the pass is the least interesting option, though it provides a route through to the Little Elbow. Use the creek as a jumping off point for more interesting options such as Cloudburst Pass and Camp Creek (#55C), Mackay Hills (#55D), Old Baldy (#56), the lower summit of Fisher Peak (#55B) and for exploratory scrambles in the Fisher Range.

55A Evan-Thomas Creek & Pass
Long day hike, backpack
Unofficial trail, creek crossings
Distance 15 km to pass
Height gain 760 m
High point 2180 m
Map 82 J/14 Spray Lakes Reservoir

Access: Kananaskis Trail (Hwy. 40) at Evan-Thomas Creek parking lot.
Also accessible from North Fork of the Little Elbow (see Volume 2).

I have a confession to make: I don't much like this trail. The route (old road, cutline) is a long boring trudge best done by ski or by horse or by bike to the Camp Creek turn-off. Additionally, it's heavily used by trail riders and hunters on horseback who've made a muddy mess of the cutline section. It's debatable whether the pass is worth the trauma unless you're backpacking into the north fork of the Little Elbow or heading up to the tarn under Mt. Potts, or crossing the delectable Paradise Pass into the west fork of the Little Elbow. So desperate am I to avoid this trail, I'm still piecing together remnants of ancient logging roads, hunter's trails and old Indian trails on the west bank and hope to finish in five years' time.

From the parking lot walk through to Shatto's exploration road, built to George Pocaterra's coal prospects in Camp Creek and turn left. The next 1.5 km of pine forest is slated for golf course "to bolster the three privately operated Kananaskis Village ho-

The side stream at kilometre seven.

tels which have cost the Alberta taxpayers millions of dollars to market and maintain", despite a 1986 K Country Sub-Regional Integrated Resource Plan signed by cabinet reiterating K Country's commitment to maintain fisheries and wildlife in the Evan-Thomas area. Much as I loathe golf courses, I would happily drive up the access road to the clubhouse if it meant omitting the next 1.5 km of exploration road. On the other hand, I'm glad the issue is still tied up in the courts.

What happens at 1.5 km is that the Wedge Connector ski trail takes off to the right and crosses Evan-Thomas Creek on a bridge. Your road bends around to the left. Note two trails leaving the left side just before a side creek crossing. The second is the trail to Old Baldy.

Twice the road climbs high and twice it descends, finally reaching valley bottom above the unseen canyon. At 7 km a large side stream, usually bridged by a log, is the departure point for backpackers bound for upper Canyon Creek. In another kilometre the road crosses to the west bank and passes a camping spot (departure point for Fisher Peak) en route to the Camp Creek/Evan-Thomas Pass junction. Here Shatto's road turns right uphill. Your route is the cutline which dips to Evan-Thomas Creek.

This cutline has all the foibles of its kind. After crossing the creek to the east bank, it climbs high, undulates a while (bypass trails available), then plummets back to creek level. Coming up is the flat wet section, a muddy jaunt through willow brush below the runout zone of large avalanche slopes with seven river crossings, discounting paddling as opposed to fording. This comes to an end on the east bank at the point where the main tributary comes in from the southwest from under Mt. Denny. In the angle is a grassy meadow with a fabulous view of what has to be one of my favourite unnamed mountains, its east ridge built like a ripsaw.

In front are two low gaps in the watershed ridge. The ugly black mess leads towards the left-hand gap. Higher up where the surface reverts to hard pack, watch for a junction offering a choice of routes.

Cutline The cutline straight ahead climbs steeply, passing 50 vertical metres above the gap in open forest, the reward for extra climbing being an unrestricted view of the northern Opals. From the high point, the cutline descends the south slope to another junction with the gap trail, then carries on down the north fork of the Little Elbow.

Gap trail The trail to right dekes neatly through the gap in the forested ridge (the true pass) into the head of Little Elbow's north fork. In the meadow is a junction. Turn right for the tarn, keep straight for the Little Elbow and Paradise Pass.

55B Fisher Peak, lower summit
Long day, backpack
Unofficial scramble, creek crossing
Distance from trailhead 13.5 km
Height gain 1405 m from trailhead
High point 2930 m
Map 82 J/14 Spray Lakes Reservoir

Access: Follow Evan-Thomas Creek trail (#55A). Just before the Camp Creek/Evan-Thomas Pass junction, a camping spot on the left makes a convenient starting point.

I've often been asked if I know anything about Fisher Peak, the enticing peak seen through the gap of Evan-Thomas Creek valley at Highway 40. So I had to go to have a look for myself. I can tell you it's steep in the lower part, unexpectedly pastoral in the middle section and, that after all the effort, hikers can't get to the highest summit.

Walk through the camp site to Evan-Thomas Creek. Ford a bit further to the right where the opposite bank is less high. The 600 vertical metres between the river and the northwest ridge is a strenuous treadmill. You start off in trees, then when the angle steepens link together bits of scree and grass between trees. Don't veer right into a gully or left onto more bouldery slopes. At treeline you should be just left of the gully. A final thrutch up a hodgepodge of grass, scree and rocks gains you the ridge. You'll appreciate its soft grass and sheltering krumholz. Another reward is the view: to the west the Opals, Paradise Pass, Camp Creek and the Mackay Hills (to name only a few recognizable features), and to the east a complexity of cirques and ridges with no names. Now's your chance to check out the route to Canyon Creek.

Unguessed at from down below, this lofty ridge is broad, almost a mini plateau, offering gloriously easy cruising on grass for more than a kilometre. At the end there's a slight descent to a saddle with springs and some patterned ground.

Bottom: Camp Creek from the ridge option near pass GR347296. In the background are the Mackay Hills.

Top: Fisher Peak from the saddle. Route follows curving ridge to the lower summit at right.

After the saddle the rocks begin. Gain the long easy ridge of large scree and boulders (clothed in slimy black lichen) that curves around beautifully to the lower summit. Just below the top, slabs are avoidable, the angle barely steeper than what's gone before despite how it looks from further afield. This lower summit is the end as far as hikers are concerned, the way to the highest point stymied by a rock band. That's the way it is sometimes.

Return the same way. While there are other easy routes off the west side of the broad grassy ridge, it pays to check them out first from down below.

55C Camp Creek

Long day hike, backpack
Unofficial trail, creek crossing
Distance 14 km to Cloudburst Pass,
15.2 km to Camp Creek from trailhead
Height gain 579 m from trailhead
High point 2103 m at creek
Map 82 J/14 Spray Lakes Reservoir

Access: Follow Evan-Thomas Creek trail (#55A) to the Camp Creek/Evan-Thomas Pass junction.

If yearning for meadows and larches, Camp Creek is just the place. What's more, you can take a bike (notice I said 'take') and have a grand run back down. Be aware it's a hunter hot spot, so at such times wear fluorescent pink and swear blind you haven't seen any elk.

To Cloudburst Pass Turn right, continuing up the Shatto coal exploration road. Alvin Guinn remembers as a youth persuading George Pocaterra to build the initial track up the dry north bank of this tributary and not up the muddy south bank where it was likely to be washed out. So thanking Guinn, you climb past an Edwards Coffee can hanging off a branch, note coal spoil down in the forks and game trails heading off to the right, tantalizing for those of us intent on connecting trails up the west bank of Evan-Thomas Creek. You hardly have time to note all these things before you top out in meadows signifying the watershed between Evan-Thomas and Rocky Creeks. I call it Cloudburst Pass after the Cloudburst Coal Company who did some prospecting under contract to Pocaterra in the early 1950s.

Should you leave the road at this point and head west on the longitudinal meadow, you'll reach the summit of the pass at GR343323, which is only marginally higher than the road at 2005 m. But you get to look down Rocky Creek.

To Camp Creek But back to the road. After leaving the meadow it doubles back left, rounding the edge of a ridge and turning south into the main fork of Camp Creek. This is where you run into the first of the hunter's camps and garbage dumps. Wait a hundred years and the dumps will become historic. I can just imagine future hikers sifting excitedly through nose tags, bottles of Palm Breeze light rum and assorted plastic containers. Possibly this was the site of Pocaterra's cabin. A little farther on, the road crosses the creek and splits into two grassy tracks.

GOING FARTHER

So you're standing on the east bank wondering where to go next. You can either head up the valley track into meadows, or turn left and climb to George Pocaterra's coal prospects on a ridge. If you choose the latter, keep left as you climb through the larches and take your imagination with you.

Incredible to relate, Pocaterra spent over 60 years trying to get the coal out. One fact is obvious. Despite the coal testing superior to coal from Drumheller and Crowsnest and interest expressed by the Brits, the Germans and the Japanese, access was a huge problem. That and trying to find backers, the interruption caused by two world wars, and finally the waning market that sounded the death knell.

The prospects mark the start of a longer option taking in both a ridge walk and upper Camp Creek.

Ridge Circuit 5.5 km loop from Camp Creek, height gain 488 m from Camp Creek, high point 2484 m.

Set off towards Pocaterra's coal prospects but at the junction turn right up another track. At track's end a trail heads left, gaining the ridge much higher up. If you haven't been up Fisher Peak, this is a good place to study the various options. The trail continues up the ridge to farther prospects, then fades away near treeline. Climb a steep grass slope interrupted at mid height by a short horizontal ridge of tilted sandstone blocks.

The first top at GR348304 is as broad as a soccer field, not at all the sharp ridge you might imagine from down below, and striped by rock bands you can step over. You can now look right over Evan-Thomas Pass to Mts. Glasgow, Cornwall and Outlaw in the Elbow. To their right is the familiar profile of the ripsaw peak and the connecting saddle with Mt. Evan-Thomas called by the Guinns, Paradise Pass. In the opposite direction the Mackay Hills are naturally of most interest should you be headed that way.

Descend to the pass at GR347296. An elk trail runs across it and down to Camp Creek, then up an equally scrumptious ridge to the west. You can, of course, use this trail as a shortcut.

But why not prolong the enjoyment by carrying on over a higher section of ridge with meadows sweeping down to the left, the most luscious yet. This really is an elk's heaven! Below you rises the true head of Evan-Thomas Creek, crisscrossed by countless game trails some of which emanate from this ridge. (Nevertheless, heading cross-country to Evan-Thomas Pass or to the tarn under Mt. Potts is not as simple as you might think.)

You can get no further than the col tucked under the cliffs of the Opal Range at GR339292, and are forced to drop into the cirque at the head of Camp Creek. A trail runs along the right bank of the stream and takes you out to the flat section of valley below the first col. Walk down meadows and pick up a grassy track on the east bank, which conveniently joins your outgoing track near the creek crossing.

55D Mackay Hills

Long day hike, backpack
Unofficial trails & route
Distance loop 20 km
Height gain 1120 m
High point 2454 m
Map 82 J/14 Spray Lakes Reservoir

Access: Via #55C at Cloudburst Pass.

A beautiful, demanding ridge walk over three grassy summits. According to James Ashworth's 1917 report of the coalfield, the northernmost top is called Mt. Mackay or Mackay's Mountain after claimant Walter Grant Mackay. The penalty for enjoying yourself is an ending so horrible only experienced bushwhackers with a talent for routefinding need think about doing the whole loop. Of course, if camped at Cloudburst Pass you can always climb a couple of tops and return the same way.

Mackay Hills. Centre Peak (left) from the lower slopes of Mt. Mackay. Extreme right: Rocky Creek and Opal Ridge.

The climb up the south ridge to the South Peak starts from behind the little black pond. A game trail zigs left, then right. We went right at a division and followed the trail all the way up steeply-angled forest to open slopes. Sensible sheep. They traverse around to the left to the col between South and Centre peaks. Not so climbers, who must grovel up even steeper grass to gain the summit. Fortunately, there are flowers to identify and views to look at. The lowest of the three summits is a smooth grassy dome where you can spend a happy half hour identifying peaks in all directions.

Walk down to the col. The sheep trail reappears from the left and gets you started up the centre peak before heading off on another traverse. Rather disappointingly, this summit doesn't look up to much. On gaining the top, though, you discover the northwest ridge dropping away to the next col is much more interesting. In fact, it's hard to leave the summit. Detour to the right, then traverse back left below a rock band to gain the ridge. As I've said, it's an interesting descent and I was fascinated by

its fragmented red cliffs and shiny sheets of black coal against which clumps of Alpine cinquefoil dazzled.

From the col regain the 183 vertical metres in the simple climb up Mackay's Mountain which is joined by a saddle to The Wedge. On topping out, you're greeted by a fabulous aerial view of the Kananaskis Valley. Linger a while before starting, most reluctantly, down the grassy north ridge.

Finish 1 North Ridge

When we first did this route we decided to be purists and follow the north ridge all the way down, a grade seven bushwhack that none of us has ever been able to forget. In the steep upper part you squeeze between matchstick lodgepoles with spears for branches, grovel under alders and whiplash willows and climb over trees collapsed in heaps. Low down in willowy clearings you wallow along waterlogged moose trenches. If you're lucky like me you'll stumble over the ancient 7-Up bottle, then hit the end of a logging road square on. Follow this road. At a junction keep left and downhill to Wedge Connector ski trail. Turn right and arrive in due course at the footbridge over Evan-Thomas Creek. Wind uphill to Evan-Thomas Creek trail and turn left for the parking lot. If you're not so lucky, you'll undoubtedly hit the Wedge Connector at some point along its length.

Finish 2 East Slope

All sensible animals leave the ridge before the trees start. I recommend dropping onto the east slope at the demarcation of white and green shading shown on the topo map, and heading down one side or the other of the big, deeply-incised gully to about GR328358, where you'll intersect the old Indian trail travelled by Pocaterra, Amos and Mackay to stake their claims in 1910. Of course, you can intersect the trail anywhere between this gully and the next big gully to the south at GR335350, but be aware that in open forest close to the southernmost gully multiple game trails confuse. Should you

arrive here, look for old and new blazes and bright and faded flagging.

Wherever you hit the trail turn left and follow it out to Wedge Connector ski trail at Evan-Thomas Creek bridge, which makes a good seat for pouring the water out of your boots.

See the accompanying topo (start at the bottom) and don't blame me if you get lost. In fact, I expect you to lose the trail.

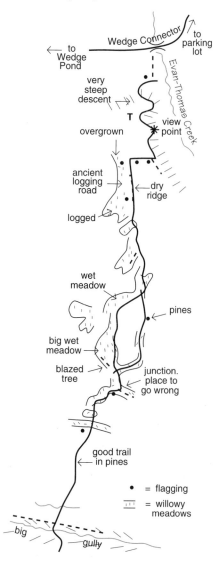

56 OLD BALDY — map 7

Day hike
Unofficial trail & route, creek crossings
Distance 7.8 km to summit
Height gain 860 m
High point 2382 m
Map 82 J/14 Spray Lakes Reservoir

Access: Kananaskis Trail (Hwy. 40) at Evan-Thomas Creek parking lot. Via Evan-Thomas Creek trail (#55A).

This hugely popular trail has a few tricky sections in the valley section, after which it's a straightforward plod up meadows to a grassy summit. Who would think this insignificant summit would be such a fine viewpoint!

Follow Evan-Thomas Creek trail for 1.8 km to the first side creek crossing where a narrow trail turns off to the left at a cairn. Be sure it's not the horse trail passed a few minutes earlier that has no cairn and is going in the wrong direction, anyway. The correct trail follows the left bank of the creek arising from the west slope of Mt. McDougall. Most people seem to call it McDougall Creek.

In the V-shaped section of the valley, the trail established over the last few years is definitely not some boring old logging road. Four times it traverses steep banks that could intimidate anyone who gets wobbly in such places, though I've managed it holding an umbrella with one hand. Easier-angled grass and talus signal your imminent arrival at the forks.

The right-hand branch empties into the confluence in a chain of picturesque waterfalls and pools. The good trail follows the left-hand 'stream', which travels mainly via the underground through a narrow valley. You'll enjoy the next stretch, five trouble-free creek crossings and lots of luxuriant grass and flowers to revel in. After the fifth crossing the trail climbs steeply up the east bank into trees, then levels. At the point where you emerge from the spruce look up to the

right at the optional descent route from peak GR357403. But more of that later. From here it's a flat stroll around the corner to a small seasonal tarn occupying a saucer-shaped depression in the scree. The valley ends not too much farther on, surrounded by a slew of unnamed peaks.

From the near end of the tarn, climb steeply-angled grass, gradually easing, to the col at GR353412 between Old Baldy and one of the unnamed. Turn left. I love the next part, because as you stroll westward along the ridge towards your objective, the mountains rise up one-by-one until finally, from the summit, a breathtaking panorama is revealed extending from Mt. Joffre—the white fang in the south—all the way north to Mt. Aylmer and the mountains of The Ghost. Naturally, the mountains about Ribbon Creek are of most interest.

My best summit day unexpectedly occurred during the horrible summer of 1992. We'd been suffering all the way up. Torrential rain had turned to heavy snow. The temperature had plummeted to -10° C. The umbrellas had seized up. Feeling utterly miserable coming up to the top, we suddenly broke through into sunshine, a sea of clouds lapping all around the bald pate of Old Baldy and mountains poking up everywhere like the islands. It was a wonderful moment.

Optional return via the west flank

Having over the years gone up and down Old Baldy in every conceivable permutation, I offer what I think is the most reasonable return route should you opt for a loop.

From the summit stride down the relatively narrow northwest ridge. Your objective is the top-to-bottom, fan-shaped gully

below you on the west flank. Now you can either drop straight down from the ridge (very steep grass) or come in from the side from lower down the ridge (steep grass). Where the gully narrows and grows shrubs, a trail develops on the right bank and takes you down into forest through the alarming-looking contours shown on the topo map (luckily a fallacy). Always take the down-hill option and with care you'll pass two cairns and emerge in a small clearing with picnic table. A good track leads out to a T-junction with an old dirt road.

You are now in a mess of trails and old logging roads used by Rick Guinn's Bound-ary Ranch. If you're going to get lost any-where, it's here. Turn left on the old road. Keep right twice (road, horse trail) and descend to a T-junction. Turn left. The new road swings around the heads of Flat Creek (hilly), then climbs onto a ridge top. As soon as it flattens cut left a few metres onto another road with blue flagging. Turn left. The rest is downhill. Some way down, turn third left onto a minor road marked at the junction by blue flagging *and* a cairn. This leads to a T-junction. Turn right. Very shortly the road narrows to trail at the point where it turns left. Close to Evan-Thomas Creek parking lot you cross a tiny creek and finish along a few metres of flat-bottomed ditch. Hit the parking lot access road close to the highway.

OPTION

Peak GR357403 2515 m height gain 488 m from the forks. If you've done Old Baldy several times and are looking for some-thing more challenging try this next. It incorporates the two forks and the moun-tain in the middle.

Arriving at the forks, take the right fork. Unless you want to potter about between waterfalls, keep high on the left bank on a bit of a trail. When the terraces peter out transfer to valley bottom. Around the bend barge through willows to the right bank and follow it to the valley head under Mt.

McDougall. There is water and scraps of meadow. Nothing special. But on the west side is this enticing grass slope, not too steep, leading all the way up to a 2515 m summit. Scattered crags high up are easily avoided by heading straight up the draw. From below it appears less tiring to traverse right below the summit crags, then cut left *behind them*, only there is no behind and the jagged right-hand skyline is the northeast ridge. Oops! My excuse to a friend faithfully following along behind was that the resulting scramble made for a more sporting finish. So keep left near the top unless headed for Mt. McDougall.

The summit is mainly turf, a perfect grandstand seat for Old Baldy down below, showing the route from the little tarn (photo above). You'll notice your summit is connected to a ridge circling around to Mt. McDougall. It doesn't look too bad and is on my list to try. If you've already done it, let me know how you got on.

Opposite and above: View from peak at GR357403. It shows the route from the tarn at the head of McDougall Creek to the top of Old Baldy, which is the grassy ridge in the left-hand photo. At lower left is the plateau. In the distance you can identify from left to right: Mts. Bogart, Sparrowhawk, Lougheed, Allan and Collembola. Skogan Pass at extreme right.

Option return to the left-hand fork A more difficult descent route that requires precise routefinding. The grassy west slope lures you down to a squared-off plateau above a drop-off. Now what? Any idea of descending direct to the tarn on the right side is forestalled by cliffs. The left side is similarly cliffy. Ahead, though, at about GR352404, are scree and boulder slopes set at a reasonable angle. Nevertheless, pussyfooting from one tippy rock to another is extremely tedious when you have to concentrate every inch of the way. We ended up in the left fork at last trees mentally knackered, vowing to resist temptation next time. It's your call.

57 OPAL RIDGE — map 11

Day hike
Unofficial trail & route
Distance 3 km to summit
Height gain 1012 m
High point 2597 m
Map 82 J/14 Spray Lakes Reservoir

Access: Kananaskis Trail (Hwy. 40) at Fortress Junction gas station. Park in northernmost parking lot.

Driving up Highway 40, I had often wondered if this route went. Could you get through the cliffs to the ridge top? So one day we climbed it and discovered the 'gates'. We also found out this was no new discovery, but a very well-used route taken by paragliders who jump off the top. As you might expect, it's a demanding trudge to the ridge, but despite its spectacular appearance from the gas station, there's nothing to the ridge itself and no exposure to worry about. Consider an optional return down Grizzly Creek (#58).

From the parking lot hike up a small creek a way, then follow the left bank to the powerline access road. Turn left. Cross a side creek. On your right and facing the highway is a triangular-shaped slope bounded on either side by ridges that meet at the apex. Both ridges go. The northern ridge is narrower and grassier with a belt of trees near the top. But naturally, the nearer ridge is more commonly climbed, so at the flagging turn right onto the paraglider's trail and follow it up the billowy ridge of grass and scree, circumventing slabs when necessary. Meet the other ridge at a levelling and continue up the short scree slope behind to a grassy top with an airy feel of being far above the cares of the world.

From here a rounded ridge connects to the grass slope below huge freestanding cliffs. Can you get through? A trail climbs the slope and in a magical bit of routefinding by sheep wends right and up through 'gates' totally invisible from down below.

You arrive at another meadow, separated from the ridge by a small band of crags. This the trail avoids by traversing way out to the right on orange screes to the low point at GR315281. Another surprise awaits. While the ridge facing Highway 40 is plated in vertical cliffs, the east side rolls in a friendly convex curve down to the meadows of upper Rocky Creek and is mainly grass.

The trail continues up the rounded ridge to the right (south), where I was ecstatic to find clumps of Woolly fleabanes. The two highest tops are rocky and the sheep elect to traverse the east flank. It's much more fun to walk the crest which is easy and has a buffer zone between you and the plunging cliffs so you never have to look down. Ahead is a magnificent view of Kananaskis Lakes and the Opal Range. When we were there it was a day of sun and storm, and across the dark range a constantly moving spotlight was fanning back and forth, illuminating each spectacular peak in turn. Entranced, we sat and watched the theatrics for an hour.

OPTIONAL RETURN
Follow the ridge in its entirety to a much lower top at GR322262, then drop easily into the head of Rocky Creek. Turn right and return via Grizzly Creek (#58). This requires two cars or a 3.3 km walk back to Fortress Junction.

Opposite:
Top: The south end of Opal Ridge, looking down to Rocky/Grizzly watershed and across to the Opal Range. The peak in sunlight is Mt. Packenham.
Bottom: Grizzly Creek from the north bank sheep trail. The trail traverses the treed slope on the right, rising as it crosses the scree slope below the cliff.

58 GRIZZLY CREEK TO ROCKY CREEK MEADOWS — maps 11

Day hike
Unofficial trails & route, creek crossings
Distance 3 km to pass
Height gain 740 m
High point 2380 m
Map 82 J/14 Spray Lakes Reservoir

Access: Kananaskis Trail (Hwy. 40). At Grizzly Creek day-use area.

I knew I'd find a use for this parking lot someday! Grizzly Creek is a demanding hike up a V-shaped valley to meadows. Not the easiest way to reach the glorious head of Rocky Creek, I'll admit, but the fastest. Perhaps it's best used as a descent route from Opal Ridge. This route uses a fairly good grizzly trail up the south bank (one unpleasant section). The obvious sheep trail up the north bank, which entices with flagging lower down, induces vertigo higher up. I've also tried a combination of lower sheep trail then creekbed, but this lands you in an impossible canyon. Another possibility is lower canyon, then the upper half of this trail. Not for novices.

From the parking area you're going to climb straight up the hillside for about 213 vertical metres to a large terrace. The going is easy, aspen benches alternating with grassy risers. At the beginning keep left to avoid small rock bands. On the terrace find two cairns. Go right a little to find the start of the grizzly trail. All the game converge on it from grassy slopes to the right.

The trail descends slightly into aspens at the head of a small tributary, then climbs out of it by a right to left diagonal between rock bands to a shoulder. This is the start of the 'V' section. Traverse the south slope through spruce forest interspersed with narrow avalanche chutes. This easy form of progress ends near the bottom of a high, wide scree slope below a cliff. At this point a game trail joins in from the creekbed, which isn't all that far below. Shortly your trail zigs right, then climbs steeply to the start of another traverse, one that takes you all the way to the meadows of the valley head. But first you must cross the scree slope high up and it's here where you meet my nemesis. You can do something with scree and shifting gravel but till, set hard like cement with a sprinkling of ball bearings on top, is scary. At least grizzlies have built-in crampons. After this the going is very pleasant: trees, bits of talus, the canyon far below and out of sight. The side slope eases as you cross two side creeks. Up on the right is the high col at GR330252 which can obviously be gained by a grassy rib, a useful bit of information to be tucked away in the mind and used another day perhaps. But back to the trail, which finally exits from between two large boulders into flowery creekside meadows overlooked by Mt. Evan-Thomas.

The trail continues along the south bank, then crosses the creek below a small fall and climbs up lush grass slopes, gradually petering out as the angle eases to the watershed between Grizzly and Rocky Creeks. Needless to say, the trail back down to the creek is extraordinarily difficult to pick up in reverse direction.

After the verticalities of the valley, the enormous flat meadow extending north as far as the eye can see down Rocky Creek makes for a nice change. Grizzly diggings are a bit alarming, so keep alert. On the right is Mts. Potts and Denny followed by a string of nameless northern peak Opals. Lining the valley on the left is the much less vertiginous Opal Ridge.

Optional return via Opal Ridge
See #57. From this direction the ridge is an easy ascent up grass.

59 FORTRESS LAKE — map 11

Day hike
Unofficial trails
Distance 5 km via longest route
Height gain 274 m longest route,
369 m shortest route
Height loss 181 m longest route,
256 m shortest route
High point 2331 m
Map 82 J/14 Spray Lakes Reservoir

Access: Kananaskis Trail (Hwy. 40) at Fortress Mountain ski area. Drive to the upper parking lot.

This is a short, strenuous hike through Fortress Mountain ski area to an inky-blue lake tucked under the eastern cliff of The Fortress.

From the top edge of the parking lot walk up the cat track to the right of the T-bar. Turn first left and head through a gap in the ridge. Continue past a road to left, wending left and downhill to a junction. Depending on fitness and inclination, choose from two of the more obvious ways onto Fortress Ridge opposite. Lacking a suspension bridge, both unavoidably dip into Aussie Creek, a dispiriting loss of altitude that must be regained.

Easiest, longest Keep left on cat track, making a very gradual descent (50 vertical metres) across ski runs to the lower terminal of Backside double chair at the head of Aussie Creek. Still on cat track, climb up and right through larch forest to grassy Fortress Ridge. This whole hillside must have been stunningly beautiful once, Glacier lilies crammed into every forest glade. Just before the snow fences begin, cut off left to the low point of the ridge identified by a tarn feeding Devil's Gulch.

Hardest, shortest Turn right and plunge 125 vertical metres into Aussie Creek on cat track. Low down keep right and head to Farside double chair in the valley bottom. Cross the creek. Don't follow the lift up No Mistake Gully, but toil up a horribly steep

Fortress Lake below Fortress Mountain.
Photo Alf Skrastins.

cat track to its right through Sherwood Forest. (In this forest Robin Hood and his merry men would have a hard time hiding from the wicked Sheriff of Nottingham.) From the upper terminal slip through the fence and descend to the tarn at the low point in the ridge.

To Fortress Lake A trail starts from the far end of the tarn, following the right bank of a west-bound creek to a fabulous viewpoint of your objective. Entering trees, it zigs right, then returns to the creek in one steep shale drop. The creek is crossed three times en route to valley bottom meadows where the trail turns left and in less than half a kilometre reaches a junction. Go either way; both trails lead to the lakeshore.

60 FORTRESS RIDGE — map 11

Day scramble
Unofficial trails & route
Distance 5.5 km from ski area
Height gain 550 m
High point 2371 m
Map 82 J/14 Spray Lakes Reservoir

Access: Kananaskis Trail (Hwy. 40) at Fortress Mountain ski area. Drive to the upper parking lot and follow Fortress Lake trail #59 to the upper terminal of Farside double chair.

The ridge extending northeast from The Fortress ends at a superlative viewpoint overlooking the Kananaskis Valley. There is no trail, nor is one needed for the route is obvious and the going easy at first. Later, it becomes more difficult with mild scrambling.

Follow Fortress Lake trail (#59) to the upper terminal of Farside double chair. Walk northeast along the broad grassy ridge to the first summit striped with forget-me-nots and creamy androsace growing in moist runnels. The ski staff call it Baldy, which is very confusing! After the next grassy bump, for convenience called the second summit because it is separated from the first by a definite col, a rocky descent of 120 m brings you to the lowest point of the ridge which is identified by larches spilling over from the east slope. Now climb a long grass slope to the third top. Suddenly, the ridge narrows and the previously friendly slopes on either side steepen into cliff bands. A difficult rock step immediately above the third col is easily avoided by a scramble down a grassy gully on the east side. From the col a steep but straightforward climb gains you the fourth and final summit.

From your island in the sky the Kananaskis Country golf course is spread out below you like a map. Look across to Mt. Kidd and up both forks of Galatea Creek (none of the lakes are visible). Pick out the trail climbing to Guinn's Pass. Of all the mountains in the Kananaskis Range, formerly called the Ship Mountains because a large number of summits were named after ships sunk in the Battle of Jutland, none is more eye-catching than The Fortress, which from this vantage point is seen at its most dramatic.

Looking back at the second summit and The Fortress (right) from the low point.

61 EAST END OF RUNDLE (EEOR) — map 4

Day scramble
Unofficial trail & route
Distance 2.6 km to summit
Height gain 884 m
High point 2590 m
Map 82 O/3 Canmore

Access: Smith-Dorrien—Spray Trail (Hwy. 742) at Whiteman's Gap. Use Goat Creek parking lot.

Here's a chance to impress your non-climbing friends. EEOR at GR107598 is the easternmost peak of Mt. Rundle, the one that looms over Canmore. What your friends don't know is that there's a pretty good trail all the way up the south ridge to the shoulder. After that it's an easy scramble coupled with mild exposure. One or two scree steps above a drop-off could be dangerous if you're not concentrating. Overall, it's a much more serious scramble than Chinaman's Peak across Whiteman's Gap.

Note: the upper section is *not* the Kane route as described in *"Scrambles in the Canadian Rockies"*, and Alan Kane's summit and my summit are different peaks.

The rest spot near treeline. The sharp peak in the background is Chinaman's, climbed by #62 via the right-hand dip slope.

To the shoulder Omit the initial part of the south ridge trail that is for "sheep and goats", according to Brian Carter. Walk back up the highway towards Whiteman's Pond. After the first power-pole and just beyond the sign 'Entering Bow Crow Forest' turn left (arrow) and zig gratefully up a newly built section of trail (yellow discs, arrows, blazes) onto the south ridge. Turn right.

The south ridge trail is fun, flat treed sections alternating with progressively higher slabby risers with route options for all classes of scramblers. Close to treeline is the highest step. You climb a ramp from left to right above a cliff, then head straight for the top, noting a proliferation of small cairns and flagging for the return trip.

On top is an important route feature: two lawn chairs around a fire circle, sheltered from the westerly blast by trees but with a tremendous view of Chinaman's Peak, a neatly folded Sunday newspaper on one seat (when we were there). Leaving is not easy if you've started on the crossword.

Up and off again, enthusiasm returns. For one thing, you're at treeline and after two more risers and a scree plod you reach the shoulder. This is a large meadow with spruce thickets, gently inclined towards the southwest and bounded on the east by a profound precipice of Palliser limestone, which makes you feel sick to look over the edge.

To the summit From the meadow Alan Kane's route climbs straight up the scree, using a ramp through the cliffs. I kind of like the more elegant ridge route myself, and if *I* can do it without whimpering for a rope, anyone can.

Follow the top edge of the meadow graduating to fine shale as it swings round to the left and resumes the form of a ridge. Luckily, by this point the immediate drop-off to the right is not the frightening cliff, but less vertiginous horizontal rock bands partly covered by rubble. Bypass the pinnacle easily on the right side to a notch. The ridge above looks intimidating to nonclimbers like myself, with cliffs starting on the left side. Actually, the stepped rocks are very safe but occasionally awkward for people not six feet high with correspondingly long legs. At the top circle around to the left above the cliffs, and cross a neck (easy). Carefully now, step left across chossy scree, poised above the deep black gash of a gully, to the bottom of a scree slope. Climb the scree to the summit ridge. EEOR is the rocky bump to the right with a cairn, the peak that overlooks Canmore.

From here you're in position to pick off two more tops: GR103598 (Alan Kane's summit) connected by a broad ridge with a pesky rock band across the middle, and GR100602, a much longer jaunt with a 75 m height gain. Although I've never done it, I'm told it's possible to descend the scree gully north of EEOR to junction #73 at the Canmore Nordic Centre.

Looking up the final ridge from the notch to the summit. Figure on skyline is just about to circle left.

62 CHINAMAN'S PEAK — map 4

Day hike
Unofficial trail & route
Distance 1.6 km to summit
Height gain 732 m
High point 2408 m
Map 82 O/3 Canmore

Access: Smith-Dorrien—Spray Trail (Hwy. 742) at Whiteman's Gap. Park in the Goat Creek parking lot.

Looking up the southeast ridge to the summit.

A muscle-aching grind up the back side of a spectacular peak. No scrambling. No exposure. Being unable to locate the trail on the return is a possibility. Incredibly popular. One miserable October Sunday several years *before* Alan Kane's book came out I counted six parties besides ourselves.

Originally it was called 'The Beehive'. Then in 1896, Ha Ling, a Chinese cook working in the Oskaloosa Hotel in Canmore, was bet 50 dollars he couldn't climb up and down within 10 hours. Starting at seven on a Saturday morning with a small flag to place on the summit, he was back in time for lunch. No one believed him. They couldn't spot the flag. So on Sunday Ha Ling led a group of doubters to the top and next to the original flag "proudly flapping in the breeze" set up a 12 foot-high flag pole with a scarlet six-foot square flag that could be seen with the naked eye from Canmore. "As the peak has no name let it hence forth be called Ha Ling Peak in honour of his daring intrepidity". It wasn't, and the name 'Chinaman's' has since come in for a drubbing by a Calgary lawyer of Chinese descent.

We, of course, have the advantage of being able to drive to Whiteman's Gap. Cross the highway, walk up a road to the canal and cross the bridge. The trail starts behind the hut and is quite enjoyable where it meanders through moss forest.

In short time you're climbing straight up the left side of a slabby watercourse. Far too late for aching calf muscles, some token zigs appear, and a proliferation of shortcuts and hideously eroded down routes. Then come the splits on stony ground. I keep right. The last stretch to treeline has several divergent trails all badly defined. If the Alpine Club is looking for another trail to improve, I would like to nominate this mess.

The summit is in view. Some people climb directly up the scree between slabs. Others find it easier to traverse right to a col, then follow the easier-angled southeast ridge to the top. Watch yourself; the cairn is perched right on the edge of the great abyss. For a bird's-eye view of Canmore and the Bow Valley this summit can't be beat. It's also the ideal location to study the entire route up EEOR.

63 THREE SISTERS PASS — map 6

Day hike
Unofficial trail & route, creek crossings
Distance 3 km to viewpoint
Height gain 594 m
High point 2286 m
Map 82 O/3 Canmore

Access: Smith-Dorrien—Spray Trail (Hwy. 742). Just north of your creek at GR128520 is a loop on the west side of the highway where you can park.

When driving along Highway 742 you have to be quick to catch a glimpse of the pass between Big Sister and the fifth peak of Mt. Lawrence Grassi.

Though you can combine this trip with Three Sisters Creek #19, there isn't much point to it unless you're being pursued down Highway 742 by the KGB and just happen to know of this secret pass through to Canmore and the Bow Valley. Anyway, the best part of the traverse is the pass itself (its meadows and viewpoints), most easily reached from this direction in a mere two hours.

The pass Walk south along the highway to the creek. Start up the stony creekbed, shortly transferring to Dryas meadows on the left where good time can be made to the valley entrance.

Continue up Dryas carpet, using a trail on the left bank. On entering the little canyon the trail is forced to the right bank, then back left below the first waterfall step. Scrabble up slabs beside pools and watershoots. I love this part, especially the tub at the left-hand bend. Sculptured out of smooth slab and fed by water coursing down a chute, it's a piece of rockery I'd love to transport to my boring old bathroom at home. Surprisingly, while traditional Japanese inns have hallways like streambeds, the 'pothole bath' hasn't caught on yet.

Beyond the following right-hand bend, all scrambling at an end, use an intermittent trail along the left bank, all

stones and boulders, the whiff of Wormwood mixing with the sulphur smell of rocks. Interestingly, the stream emanates from the hillside to the right, so the final stretch of creekbed is dry, right to the base of the watershed ridge. At the final 'creek' division under Big Sister turn left with the trail into a stand of spruce that reaches almost to the pass, a totally unexpected and easy finish. On the far side of the grassy ridge cliffs plummet into Three Sisters Creek.

The viewpoint So how do you get into Three Sisters Creek without a parachute? Turn left. Even if you aren't going through there's a viewpoint you simply must visit before returning. No need to climb much higher. Traverse a recognizable terrace (grass, stones) below Lawrence Grassi 5 to a notch marking the high point of a grassy basin sloping gently down to timberline in the southwest fork of Three Sisters Creek. The right side of the basin tilts upwards, supported by cliffs, and it's along its undulating edge where you'll find two cairned viewpoints separated by a second (lower) notch. Look across to The Three Sisters and to the four summits of Mt. Lawrence Grassi, those magnificent eastern buttresses put into proper perspective from this vantage point.

GOING FARTHER
To Three Sisters Creek The usual way is to walk down the grassy basin (or its edge) to treeline, then descend avalanche slopes into the southwest fork. A more direct way leaves the lower notch via sheep trail. It deposits you at the head of the main fork below the cliffs before carrying on up Big Sister, leaving the duped hiker kilometres of windfall to struggle through.

Bottom: *Old Goat Glacier from the lateral moraine.*

Top: *Three Sisters Pass. Looking from one of the east side viewpoints towards Little Sister and Middle Sister (right), showing the final easy stretch to the summit.*

64 OLD GOAT GLACIER — map 6

Day hike
Unofficial trail & route, creek crossing
Distance 4 km
Height gain 643 m
High point 2350 m
Map 82 J/14 Spray Lakes Reservoir

Access: Smith-Dorrien—Spray Trail (Hwy. 742). Cross Three Sisters Dam (signed Spray Lakes West campground), turn left and follow West Side road to the creek at GR14949.

Driving along on the other side of the reservoir I was always fascinated by the waterfall splashing down the headwall of this otherwise quite ordinary-looking valley in the Goat Range. The amount of water fluctuated tremendously and seemed greater when the day was stinking hot, which meant…. Grabbing the first coloured air photos of K Country as soon as they were issued, myself and Pat Ronald, the then District Ranger, bubbled over with excitement when we met, because hidden behind high rock walls a glacier was revealed, *almost as long as the Robertson.* The topo map outdoes itself here in not showing even a hint of ice.

Actually, quite a few people knew of this glacier long before myself and Pat cottoned on to it, like Banff Heli Sports, who for a few years used it for heli skiing trips! It was during this time it received its name. Let's just say it's named after a Banff celebrity….

So this not so secretive glacier below the highest peak in the Goat Range is the true north fork of the Spray River? Was. Nowadays it's just another contributor to the hydro scheme, passed by undetected as you drive down the highway.

Getting into the hanging valley is a rough but not difficult walk.

Stand on West Side road and look up the creek. To its right is a small meadow and starting from the end a good trail that joins a cutline a short way in. Alternately, walk up the cutline from further to the right. The cutline ends at a large willowy meadow not too far from the headwall. As you will see, there's only one reasonable way up this impasse: the open slope far to the left between the treed rib and the cliffs.

Continue up valley a bit longer, then cut left across the creek below the falls to gain easy-angled talus. Basically, you follow the edge of the trees around, climbing up the slope behind the rib, using a ribbon of grass when the angle steepens. A final push through trees gains you the hanging valley.

Step onto lateral moraine, first heading left along the ridge as far as you can go for the best view of the glacier down below you, squeezed between steep walls that on the west side rise to the highest summit of the Goat Range, 'Old Goat Mountain' at a massive 3109 m (a ten thousander plus for you people still using imperial). We didn't quite get to the end of the moraine, that spot being occupied by a Bighorn ram posed theatrically against the glacial backdrop. (I believe the view from the col is superb.)

Backtrack past your entry point into lovely country of spruce, larch, meadow—and a green tarn, also not marked on the topo map. Obviously, it was formed by water backed up by terminal moraine after the glacier retreated. But back to our ram. Perhaps it was his first summer on his own and he was lonely for company. Like a pet dog in tow, he followed us all the way to the lake, stopping when we stopped, moving on when we moved. At the tarn lunch stop he nibbled grass and made no attempt to mug us for our sandwiches. He drew the line at our next move, however, which was to descend the right side of the waterfall. I can't really recommend it, though it would be impossible to take a header through such dense scrub.

It's best to return the same way.

65 WEST WIND PASS — map 6

Day hike
Unofficial trail with cairns & flagging
Distance 3 km
Height gain 381 m
High point 2088 m
Map 82 J/14 Spray Lakes Reservoir

Access: Smith-Dorrien—Spray Trail (Hwy. 742). Park 4.8 km south of the Spray District Office at Spurling Creek.

A trail, come into being by the passage of many feet over the years, leads to the grassy pass between two dramatic pieces of rock, Rimwall on the left and Windtower. Careful routefinding is necessary.

Pass implies you can carry on into Wind Valley. Leave it to climbers bound for east-facing precipices. Amazingly, the pass was scheduled for a grade 7 bike trail at one point in K Country's history, and prior to the 15th Olympic Winter Games, for a tunnel conveying the access road to alpine venues, so desperate was the government to avoid reconstruction of the highway between Canmore and Whiteman's Gap.

Two creeks close together cause enormous confusion right at the start. Oddly enough, the right-hand one with copious water is the wrong one. The good trail on its left bank leads only to the spring a little way in. Odder still, this short-lived creek has a name: Spurling Creek, after Calgary Power's J. E. Spurling, survey chief during the initial survey for Spray Lakes Hydro Development in the early 1920s. One can imagine the party filled their canteens at this spot in passing.

So your left-hand creek, which goes all the way to the pass, has no name. Perhaps because it's usually bone dry.

Follow a trail on the left side of the creekbed a short way, then at red flagging take the left-hand trail onto the bank top. The trail, much clearer now, keeps to the edge of grassy banks for the lower quarter of the route, then moves away onto steeper hillsides in the trees. There are many puzzling spots where the trail disappears. Watch for cairns and branches laid either side of the route and across false trails. It's all too easy to climb uphill with the lie of the land and end up on the backside of Rimwall with several layers of rock bands between you and the pass. Of course, the summit of Rimwall may be your intention, but it wasn't mine when I 'guided' some long-suffering friends up to the pass on my third visit! The result of this humiliation was to build a very large cairn at the point where you actually *descend* a little, the trail undulating across rough slabby ground, crossing four fledgling rock bands *in the downhill direction*. Keep alert for more cairns above descents.

Gradually the trail redefines, runs under a rock band, then climbs steeply out of the trees (cairn) and across meadow to West Wind Pass. This is a lovely spot. Limestone slabs make stepping stones across turf starred with tiny Moss gentians. On the Wind Creek side, the ground drops away as if sliced by a knife and growing in a crevice at the very edge of the precipice you'll find a solitary larch, just a young sapling that by some fortuitous quirk of the wind is the first of its kind in this valley.

West Wind Pass. Rimwall in the background.

66 WINDTOWER — map 6

Long day scramble
Unofficial trail & route
Distance 5 km from Hwy. 742
Height gain from Hwy. 1006 m
High point 2697 m
Map 82 J/14 Spray Lakes Reservoir

Access: Smith-Dorrien—Spray Trail (Hwy. 742). Follow route #65 to West Wind Pass.

Windtower. Tower of the Winds. Elegant ridges dividing dark overhanging walls explored by climbers overnighting in hammocks slung from pitons.

From Wind Valley it certainly looks impregnable. The climber's descent route down the back, though, is the hiker's walk-up, barely qualifying as a scramble unless you count the easy rock bands low down. The worst problem is finding the right sheep trail at the start! Exposure is nil, the views terrific. Carry water all the way up from the highway.

Windtower, an awesome sight from Wind Valley.

Start from just below West Wind Pass, about halfway between the trees and the drop-off. Though not presenting its formidable side, Windtower at this point is a jumble of small cliffs. The idea is to traverse right (south) just above treeline to where the west face smooths out into easy-angled scree.

The sheep trail you want is not the lowest, but the next obvious one that can be seen climbing left to right across a scree patch. Into the rising traverse it's soon evident you're cutting across the strata. Step up two rock bands, then avoid the third (steeper, higher with no obvious break) by an uphill detour to a cairn at a junction. Turn right and resume traversing. The fifth band has a few awkward steps. Then comes the easy sixth, a cairn, grass, a few token trees, a seventh band and another cairn indicating the bottom of the ramp leading to the Windtower/Lougheed saddle.

Climb the ramp, a gently inclined slope of grass and scree between the seventh band and a line of low cliffs high up to the right. Stop often and savour increasingly fine views of Spray Lakes Reservoir obscured now and then by travelling clouds of highway dust. At the top of the ramp slip through the left-hand break in the cliffs onto an intersecting sheep trail leading straight to the saddle. Sheep, it seems, take a rather steeper route to this point.

The saddle is broad and flat, overlooked by the first peak of Mt. Lougheed, the original Wind Mountain, or Pic du Vent, as named by Eugene Bourgeau in 1858, but later renamed Lougheed after Peter's grandfather. Recently, the name Wind was transposed to the fifth peak above Ribbon Creek, the rationale behind the name having been completely lost sight of. I wish they wouldn't do that!

From the saddle it's such an easy stroll up the broad south ridge you can carry on a serious conversation with a friend without pausing once to gasp for breath. Tower of the Winds. As you will have gathered by the

155

names hereabouts, the west wind hurls itself over this part of the range into the Bow Valley at Dead Man Flat and is funnelled through the Gap, rocking cars as they round the bends at Lac des Arcs. It's been my experience that no matter how calm it was at West Wind Pass, by the time you near the summit it will be blowing a gale and I'd be cautious when approaching the summit cairn that is perched on the very edge of the 760 vertical-metre drop-off. I stop here, but traversing to the lower summit is an airy option for sure-footed scramblers.

It's satisfying to look down on West Wind Pass and across to Rimwall and The Three Sisters. And surely that's Mt. Assiniboine off to the west!

Left: Spray Lakes Reservoir from near the saddle, showing the easy-angled ascent slopes.

Below: Windtower from the Windtower/Lougheed saddle. Route follows the gentle left-hand ridge to the highest summit.

67 READ'S RIDGE & MOUNT SPARROWHAWK — map 6

Day hike to Read's Ridge & Read's Tower, long day scramble to Mt. Sparrowhawk
Unofficial trails & route
Distance 2 km to Read's Ridge
Height gain 646 m to Read's Ridge
High point Read's Ridge 2353 m
Map 82 J/14 Spray Lakes Reservoir

Access: Smith-Dorrien—Spray Trail (Hwy. 742). Park at Sparrowhawk day-use area.

Read's Ridge is one fantastic viewpoint. And when you tire of lolling around in the meadows there's the option of either continuing to the top of Read's Tower or scrambling up Mt. Sparrowhawk *if you start early enough*. The relentless uphill trudge is eased here and there by trails.

Read's Tower from the notch.

To Read's Ridge Walk out to the highway and turn right (south). In a few metres turn left and climb the grassy bank north of Sparrowhawk Creek to a red survey marker. The Sparrowhawk Creek trail starts here and climbs steadily along the left bank at the edge of pine forest. Where both creek and trail bend to the right, take off into the forest. Head left and up, passing lines of pink flagging indicating a future ski run. Cross a forested draw and climb grassy slopes on its left side to gain Read's Ridge at GR195445. The alternative to all this is to climb straight up the draw from the highway. It's up to you.

So you're standing on a level ridge looking down into Forbes Creek. What's more, you're standing on a pink-flagged trail. Follow it to the right onto steepening ground which to your joy is shaping up into a gorgeous grassy ridge. Who cares if the trail peters out? Long before you reach the culminating cairn at GR201439 you're treated to superb views of Spray Lakes Reservoir and surrounding mountains. Ahead rises Read's Tower and to its left the notch, the gateway to Mt. Sparrowhawk (still looking a hundred miles away). Not so lovely is the view of posts and snow fence strewn down

the south flank, reminding you the west slope of Sparrowhawk was a proposed site for the men's downhill in the Olympic 15th Winter Games. Ken Read, who designed the runs, called it excellent, while the Association of Canadian Mountain Guides took the line that it would "take a nuclear blast to turn it into a recreational slope".

Anyway, after Sparrowhawk was scotched as an Olympic mountain, Kananaskis Pathways Corporation applied to operate a heli-cat skiing operation featuring five warming huts to be scattered around the west face, none of which, I hasten to add, to be available for beer and shelter like the rest houses up Mt. Fuji. The main lodge would be sited near the cairn, but that's a few years down the road, and an environmental impact assessment has yet to be done.

GOING FARTHER

Read's Tower 2627 m 0.8 km and 274 m height gain from Read's Ridge. The tired man's alternative to Mt. Sparrowhawk.

From the cairn traverse right, then plod up straightforward grass and stones to the summit. The tower doesn't connect to the face of the mountain (see photo above...).

Read's Ridge near the cairn, looking up the easy side of Read's Tower. To its left is the notch and a view of Mt. Sparrowhawk.

Mt. Sparrowhawk 3121 m

Distance from highway 4.8 km, height gain from highway 1430 m. You're in for a long day with all those vertical metres to get under your belt before the thunderstorms roll in. Technically, it's an easy ascent until the final scree scrabble up the steeper southeast face which is a mite exposed if you're not used to such places. A consideration: while the west slopes may be free of snow, the southeast face could well be plastered with the stuff, ruining your chances of reaching the summit. If coming from Calgary drive Highway 40 so you can look up Ribbon Creek and assess conditions.

Read's Ridge to the notch From the cairn on Read's Ridge drop into the head of Forbes Creek at treeline, just above the snow gauge. Next, gain the notch between Read's Tower and the main body of the mountain at GR207441. The trail, born again, tackles the scree slope on the right side of the draw, near the top

crossing Last Chance Springs where you can fill up the water bottles.

The notch is another rest stop slated for a warming hut. It's worth coming this far just to look at Read's Tower, which looks absolutely spectacular from this direction. Anyone who's had enough can descend into Sparrowhawk Creek from the notch and return via route #68.

To the col Hiking the slope above the notch takes forever even though the angle is only 18-23 degrees. Make for the col located between Sparrowhawk's head and a formidable line of cliffs circling around to Mt. Bogart. The metal biffy on the col is a RCMP Transmitter Station put up during the Olympic 15th Winter Games. It has a definite design fault in that the doors open outwards. Should snow pile up against it during a blizzard, Harry Connolly worries, anyone inside would be trapped. He fully expects to open the door one summer and have a skeleton fall out.

To the summit Luckily, the cliffs guarding the summit have a weak spot around the back side. Start off up the broad trashy ridge above the col. With four of us we tried different ways and discovered the 'trail' on the far left was better than the 'trail' heading off around to the right. Alan Kane dismisses this last bit as a 'hike'. "Typical climber" you grumble as you throw off a few loose rocks, aware as you gain height of a deepening gulf on the right that climbers never seem to notice. When the ridge abuts against the cliffs, move right onto the steeper ground of the southeast face and stagger at the pace of a tortoise towards the summit cliff band, much reduced this side. The scree is horrible and you suffer. Sharp points of bedrock poking through to the left of the 'trail' help in upward propulsion. Then, unless you want to try the tempting escape gully through the cliffs (one of us, a climber, went this way and was not too enamoured), traverse right under the cliffs to a fan of much easier-angled scree sweeping through a gap onto the summit ridge. Turn right and reach the cairn in less than a minute.

Relief is replaced by wonder at the view, surely one of the best anywhere in the Canadian Rockies. Mt. Assiniboine can be seen, of course, and a huge array of peaks including Mt. Joffre, the Royal Group and the nearby summits of Lougheed, where you can trace the route taken by climbers doing the traverse.

The summit block from the col, showing the trashy ridge. The southeast face is to right.

Looking down the southeast face from close to the summit ridge. Note the figure.

68 SPARROWHAWK TARNS — map 6

Day hike
Unofficial trail & route, creek crossings
Distance 5.1 km
Height gain 671 m
High point 2408 m
Map 82 J/14 Spray Lakes Reservoir

Access: Smith-Dorrien—Spray Trail (Hwy. 742) at Sparrowhawk day-use area.

The cirque west of Bogart and south of Sparrowhawk is a wild rocky place with at least six little tarns to delight in. Just don't go in fall or you'll be disappointed. Initially an easy forest walk on trail, the route later becomes a navigational exercise in rough terrain.

Walk through to the highway and turn right. In a few metres turn left and climb the grassy bank north of Sparrowhawk Creek to a red survey marker. The trail starts here, a really good trail that climbs steadily along the left bank at the edge of pine forest. Shortly after the creek and trail bend to the right is a dip. This precedes the place where everyone goes wrong on the return, blithely following another trail (made by people going wrong) that descends a grassy buttress towards the creek. So lacking a sign 'Keep right you idiots', fix this spot in your mind. A slight descent is followed by a long flat stretch at creek level.

Complications arise when the terrain rises and the trail splits. It seems you can choose any option as they all lead uphill and peter out in a common open area with a view. Conversely, going back down, all trails lead to the main valley trail eventually.

Carry on through willowy meadows below Read's Tower and at red flagging cross a side creek channel choked with willow. Get back to the main creek.

The blue line shown on the topo map is a fallacy. Blocking the way is a massive rockslide. The route with the least amount of rock follows the main creek, then at the point of burial goes up and over a mini-ridge on the right, crosses a draw and ascends the broad curving ridge (Dryas, larches) between the main mass of the rocks on the left and a deep stony draw to the right (alternate route but less attractive). Near the top traverse right on grass. You emerge on a crest between the two forks of upper Sparrowhawk Creek, the rockslide behind you and a view ahead of the cirque backdropped by Mt. Bogart. Down below on the left is a sink lake.

Drop right past outcrops knobbled with Brachiopods to the creek that exits the tarns. A sheep trail follows the left bank meadow under the formidable cliffs of the Red Ridge to a rock step, the first of several to be scrambled up. A higher second step is best handled by making a wide detour to the left to where the crag breaks down. On the terrace above are a couple of reflecting tarns edged with turf and clouds of Red-stemmed saxifridge bobbing over the inlet stream. After sweating your guts out to reach this heavenly spot, it's galling to find it a stop-off for heli-hikers.

Still on sheep trail continue up three more steps, passing to the right of a long, thin tarn enclosed by rock en route to the final two tarns, literally lapping against the face of the mountain. The left one has colour and shelving slabs.

You might think the screes and cliffs a dead end. Not so. See route #69.

Bottom: #69. Red Ridge close to col GR214410 (snow patch). From Mt. GR214405 a fan of scree sweeps down to Sparrowhawk Tarns.

Top: #68. The first view of the cirque backdropped by Mt. Bogart. Sparrowhawk Tarns are out of the picture to the right.

69 RED RIDGE — map 6

Day hike
Unofficial trail & route
Distance 4 km to high point
Height gain 930 m
High point 2636 m
Map 82 J/14 Spray Lakes Reservoir

Access: Smith-Dorrien—Spray Trail (Hwy. 742). Park at Spray Lakes day-use area.

This rocky ridge (highest point GR211417) looks red from the highway. Not a good sign, you think, and sure enough it has a rotten section in the middle. Don't let this deter you. The rest is great walking, rather rough in places with optional scrambling, but neither narrow nor exposed. If combining with Sparrowhawk Tarns (#68), expect steep scree and a smidgen of exposure.

Start from an unnamed creek at GR181427. A few trails on the left (north) bank coalesce into one reasonable trail. Keep left of the old stream channel. At the point where the creek bends right and the ground rises up ahead leave the trail and strike up the hillside. High up, head left up an intersecting game trail that gains the ridge at about GR194429. Too far to the right and you hit a boulder slope.

The ridge climbs in five distinct steps, each section with its own character, separated by dips and flanked on the left side by a long line of cliffs.

Start up easy-angled dinner plates covered in black lichen. I'm not sure what the large cairn signifies, but the view of Mt. Sparrowhawk is fabulous. Next comes the grass 'n' spruce section harbouring a profusion of creamy Bladder Campions (Silene cucubalus), which was astonishing to me since this pale beauty should be growing on waste ground next to parking lots.

A steeper pull up grass and scree with optional scrambling leads into the middle section where the Red Ridge becomes the Rotten Red Ridge. We entered the next dip

off the left side of the ridge. In retrospect you might try the right. The next step looks as if a giant-sized bucket of boulders had been tipped down the slope. Keep well on the right flank which has smaller-sized boulders and strips of terra firma.

It was while I was staggering back up to the crest, hair plastered to my face by sweat, that a 'copter swept by for a few turns of the ridge, heli-sightseers pressed to the windows. For such contingencies (which are becoming increasingly common), I suggest bringing a hairbrush and a sign to hold up like, "drop me a can of Big Rock" if you can't be civil.

The character of the ridge changes once again to turf and gentle slopes rolling down to the valley on the right. One final climb gains you the summit, a small cairn perched on the brink of cliffs. Now you can look down on Sparrowhawk Tarns and across to Mt. Bogart.

Return via Sparrowhawk Tarns (#68), height loss 228 m to tarns.

Walk down grassy ridge to the col at GR214410. At this point the northeast face of the peak at GR214405 is brown shaley scree hanging over a line of cliffs. Fortuitously, a gap in the middle allows a wide fan of scree to sweep down to the foot of the uppermost tarns. To reach the fan follow sheep trails on a downward traverse some distance above the drop-off (you don't actually have to look down it). You'll notice another sheep trail traversing the other half of the face en route to upper Ribbon Creek. You're more on the brink there; I'd definitely need blinkers.

70 BULLER PASS — maps 10 & 6

Backpack, long day hike
Official trail with signposts
6.5 km to pass, 10 km to Ribbon Lake
Height gain 671 m
High point 2484 m
Map 82 J/14 Spray Lakes Reservoir

Access: Smith-Dorrien—Spray Trail (Hwy. 742) at Buller Mountain day-use area. The trail starts from the east side of the highway opposite the access road.
Also accessible from #48 Ribbon Falls and Ribbon Lake, and from #53 Guinn's Pass.

Although the moderately strenuous Buller Pass trail is perceived as being a backpacker's trail to Ribbon Lake, there's no reason why fit hikers can't make the pass and back in a day. The original north pass route was superseded by the south pass trail in 1981, but is still available as an alternative or for making a high-level loop. Snow (cornice on north pass) persists on the east side of the passes well into July.

To the forks Straightaway the trail makes a beeline for Buller Creek. Cross to the north bank and climb steadily up-valley to Engelmann spruce flat. Here the trail crosses to the south bank and zigs up a step in the valley floor. At the top a riverside meadow encourages a collapse, or wait until you reach the waterfall and bowl equipped with automatic blue foaming toilet bowl cleanser. The colour is lovely, and if you can forgive the analogy, this is where you should top-up the water bottles. Beyond this point, water is not guaranteed until you reach Ribbon Creek springs. Soon after, the trail crosses the south fork to a junction with the north pass trail.
Buller Pass Turn right up the south fork. In an amazingly short time the scene changes to flat valley floor (grass and a sprinkling of larches), where quick time can be made to the foot of the headwall. Climb 168 vertical metres of scree up the left side, then make a long traverse right above an area of slabs to the

pass. You emerge over the crest to the million dollar view of Ribbon Lake backdropped by the two peaks of Mt. Kidd (see photo).

Weave down the east side boulder slope, traversing left to gain a grassy rib taking you all the way down to the draw. Here keep right and continue to the brink of a drop-off where you'll spot an unofficial trail shortcutting along the bench to Guinn's Pass trail. Part way down the slope, just after Ribbon Creek bursts out of the hillside in great spouts, you meet Guinn's Pass trail proper at the trail sign.

Waterfall and bowl in Buller Creek.

Turn left, descending all the way to the bottom of the hill. Cross Ribbon Creek and wander through alternating spruce forest and smelly flower meadows (it's the valerian) to Ribbon Lake backcountry campground. En route it's tempting to explore the side valley to the northwest which offers meadows, a tarn, a col overlooking Sparrowhawk Tarns and a 2780-metre summit at GR222406. Save it for a half day option.

OPTION

North Buller Pass 2484 m 6 km from trailhead, height gain 685 m. The original, unofficial route, marked with faded blue paint splodges on rocks, is without the benefit of a good trail.

Left: View from Buller Pass of Ribbon Lake. In the background rise the north and south summits of Mt. Kidd. At extreme right is the first Guinn's Pass, showing the scree slope navigated by Alvin and his packhorses.

Looking down on North Buller Pass. The route traverses snow slopes early in the season to the saddle at bottom left. Guinn's Pass can be seen above the saddle and the lower slopes of peak GR237374.

Across the mouth of the south fork the trail picks up in the trees and can be followed for another kilometre before crossing to the north bank below a box canyon with waterfall. Continue up stones and meadow to the base of the headwall, which is easier than it appears. The reappearing trail climbs a steep ribbon of grass to the left, then cuts right across scree to the pass. The view just misses seven star status: the high peak far to the west being not Assiniboine (which is hidden behind Mt. Buller), but the infamous Mt. Eon. In the other direction you're looking across to Guinn's Pass, peak GR237374 and Mt. Kidd's two summits.

Traverse down right (grass, talus and likely snow), aiming for the saddle at GR217388 between a knoll on the left and the peak on the right that separates the two passes. If you can hack another 100 vertical metres, I recommend taking in the knoll for a superb view of Ribbon Lake. Continue down the draw and join the official trail low down near the drop-off. If making for Buller Pass, traverse right before losing too much height.

71 WATRIDGE LAKE, KARST SPRING — map 10

Short day hike
Official trail with signposts
Distance 3.8 km to lake, 4.4 km to spring, 5.5 km to Spray River
Map 82 J/14 Spray Lakes Reservoir

Access: Smith-Dorrien—Spray Trail (Hwy. 742). Turn west onto Watridge logging road signed Mt. Engadine Lodge, Mt. Shark trailhead. Keep right at all intersections until you come to the end of the road at Mt. Shark parking lot in 5.3 km.

This is an easy walk through cutblocks and climax forest to one of the largest springs in North America. Watridge Lake, en route, has been called "the finest Cutthroat lake in Alberta", and with such an easy (bikeable) trail, portage of canoes and collapsible rubber dinghies is possible.

Watridge Lake and Cone Mountain.

To Watridge Lake Straight off you can see the tip of Mt. Assiniboine from the parking lot which bodes well. Start from the signboard where Watridge Lake trail cuts through to the closed portion of the Watridge logging road beyond the gate. Turn left. The old road is obvious as it cuts through the convolutions of the Mt. Shark racing trails. In brief, keep straight at junctions 2 and 24. Cross Marushka Creek. Keep left at the top of the hill at 23. Intersect junctions 21 and 20 (fine views of Tent Ridge, Mt. Shark, Mt. Turner, Cone Mountain and Mt. Nestor all along this stretch). Just past 14 keep right and descend past 13 to Watridge Creek bridge. Note that the creek is wide and rushing. Turn left at 12 up the hill. Just before you leave the cutblocks for good, transferred onto four person-wide ski trails built in 1988/9, the old trail to the lake takes off from the left side and offers an alternate route if you don't mind stepping over deadfall.

At the junction with Bryant Creek trail (not yet marked as such on the signpost), turn left and drop to the old trail. Turn right. Just after the trail to Karst Spring turns left you reach the pale green waters of Watridge Lake. Take it from me, you'll have mud up to the knees if you try a circuit of the lake, but the bog flowers are beautiful, particularly the white Bog orchids.

Karst Spring If you stand on the north shore, the mountain silence is broken by a continual roar from somewhere in the forest. You'd have to be a pretty dull person not to wonder what the hell is going on up there. Nowadays there's an official trail to Karst Spring, but 20 years ago when Harry Connolly led us to that place the thrill of discovery was still burning bright.

Karst Spring. Photo taken over 20 years ago when Harry Connolly (second left) led us to what he called Grotto Spring.

The first person to set eyes on the spring was Dean Marshall, then foreman of Spray Lakes Sawmills. While making a preliminary study west of Marushka Lake prior to logging in 1967, he stumbled across a creek "so unique" he returned the following day, approaching on a higher line to the source of the noise.

Today's trail crosses the outlet to Watridge Lake on boardwalk. The trickle gives you a clue that this Watridge Creek as marked on the topo map cannot be the same as the one crossed earlier. The mystery is resolved as you plod up the steepening trail to its end. The real Watridge Creek glides out of a gloomy recess on Mt. Shark and thunders down the mountainside in great waves. It's at its most spectacular during early summer; in fall and winter the rate of flow slackens somewhat and reveals boulders carpeted in bright green moss.

Without experimenting with pyranine concentrate or rhodamine WT, one can only speculate where the water comes from. From the valley between Mt. Shark and Tent Ridge? Unlikely. The snow-fed rivulets that vanish into the ground most likely reappear lower down as Marushka Creek. Or could it be this is the resurgence from two deep lakes sited in the basin west of Smuts Pass, erroneously shown on maps as being inside Banff National Park? A lake's water supply could well explain the spring's almost constant rate of flow throughout the year. Nevertheless, it boggles the mind to think of the subterranean stream coursing through stony labyrinths, maybe idling around in an underground reservoir for a while, changing valley and slope, and passing under Mt. Shark *for a distance of six kilometres* before rising again at Karst Spring.

To Spray River Valley, Bryant Creek & Assiniboine via Bryant Creek trail

Back to Bryant Creek trail. At the signed junction continue along the ski trail and in one kilometre reach the height of land at Banff National Park boundary. Wind down to the Spray River, losing 76 vertical metres.

Cross the footbridge to a junction. Turn left for Spray River Valley, White Man Pass, Spray Pass, Leman Lake and Palliser Pass. Turn right for Bryant Creek and Mt. Assiniboine Provincial Park.

72 MARUSHKA (SHARK) LAKE — map 10

Day hike
Unofficial trail
Distance 4.5 km to lake
Height gain 36 m
Height loss 68 m
High point 1920 m
Map 82 J/14 Spray Lakes Reservoir

Access: Smith-Dorrien—Spray Trail (Hwy. 742). Turn west onto the Watridge logging road signed Mt. Engadine Lodge, Mt. Shark trailhead. In 1.8 km park in a small parking area on the right side of the road.

This silky sheet of green water, which I persist in calling Marushka, lies in the valley between Tent Ridge and Mt. Shark. The large cutblock and its access road, which comes uncomfortably close to ruining the setting, provides easy access.

About 100 m farther along the road beyond 'Monica Brook', turn first left onto the grassy Marushka Lake logging road that we used to drive by car. In one kilometre keep straight (route #73 to Tent Ridge turns left), then keep left at the bend unless you wish to descend to Mt. Shark parking lot or visit the helipad. The road reaches a high point, then makes a prolonged descent past skid trails into a large cutblock.

When the road runs out, pick your way across the cutblock towards the sound of water. Drop to Marushka Creek and follow a trail along the left bank to the lakeshore. Now when the guru of the Spray, Harry Connolly, came here donkey years ago with Terry Beck, his cousin from England, Myra Willey and Czech engineer Jozef Turcan, the lake was unnamed. "Is Myra the same as Mary?" Jozef asked, then suggested they use the lovely Czech name Marushka.

Harry, of course, has spent 30 years promoting an alpine ski area at Tent Ridge, his company's proposal used in Calgary's successful bid for the 1988 Winter Olympics. During early days when Bob Niven was president of CODA and Frank King was Chairman, Niven's daughter sadly succumbed to leukaemia at age 12. Frank took Harry aside. "Haven't you got something in your area you can name after her?"

He had. Walk into the upper valley under Mt. Smuts. Heaps of recessional moraines make progress frustrating. But here and there the water surfaces in lovely blue pools at the bottom of sinks called collectively Kirsten Tarns.

The lake, backdropped by Mt. Smuts.

Tent Ridge. View looking south towards the hub of Tent Ridge Horseshoe (shadowy peak at centre right). In the background from left to right: Mts. French, Commonwealth, Robertson, The Fist, Sir Douglas, Birdwood.

73 TENT RIDGE — map 10

Day hike
Unofficial trails & route
Distance 3.5 km
Height gain 625 m
High point 2515 m
Map 82 J/14 Spray Lakes Reservoir

Access: Smith-Dorrien—Spray Trail (Hwy. 742). Turn west onto the Watridge logging road signed Mt. Engadine Lodge, Mt. Shark trailhead. In 1.8 km park in a small parking area on the right side of the road.

If yearning for a great view that includes Mt. Assiniboine, take the normal route up Tent Ridge. It's a relentless uphill trudge with one tricky bit of routefinding.

About 100 m farther along the road beyond 'Monica Brook' (unofficially named after Monica Prociuk by Harry Connolly and Terry Beck), turn first left onto the grassy Marushka Lake logging road. In a kilometre, fork left up a secondary logging road that levels out below a large cutblock reaching far up the slope. At the far end of the cutblock turn right onto a rougher road and climb past umpteen skid trails to the cutblock's top left-hand corner. Look for a wooden signpost and a tree wrapped with green and white candy-stick flagging. At this spot two trails take off into the trees at 12 and 9 o'clock.

The one at 12 appears the major trail and must have cost someone a pretty penny in peppermint flagging. It winds about a good deal (keep right after the first hill), eventually turning left and descending into flat meadow above Gawby Gulch. I much prefer the left-hand trail at 9 whose start is concealed by a fallen tree. It leads in a few minutes to Gawby Gulch and follows it up to the meadow. Easy!

In the meadow trails peter out. (Should you head southeast you'd stumble on the trail that dips into Monica Brook and joins route #74.)

Although you can't see it yet, ahead and in direct line with Gawby Gulch is a gully, one of several parallel gullies scoring the steep larch-covered slope. A good trail starts left of some deadfall and climbs straight up the left side of the gully to a prominent white boulder at the three-quarter mark, a useful marker during the descent when you want to be sure you're on the right route. Continue uphill on Dryas, intersecting three game trails en route to a bench below open slopes.

While you can stagger up the bowl almost anywhere to the summit, reserve this slope for the descent and don't forget to look for my polarizing filter as you go, please. For the ascent I advocate the northeast ridge on the right, which calls for nothing more than strenuous effort up moderately inclined grass and stones. On topping out at a cairn, you'll be thrilled by the magnificent view of Spray Lakes Reservoir. To its left you can trace the route from Mt. Shark trailhead up Bryant Creek to Assiniboine, the great peak itself peeping over the top of Mt. Turner.

Harry Connolly named Tent Ridge aptly I think. Continue along the ridgepole on grass to the highest point, marked by a cairn and white pole, where you can study the ridge walk described in #74 and identify the welter of peaks to the south suddenly disclosed.

Opposite: Tent Ridge Horseshoe. Halfway up the north ridge of peak GR154311. Mt. Smuts to right.

74 TENT RIDGE HORSESHOE — map 10

Day scramble
Unofficial trails & route
Distance for circuit 9 km
Height gain 823 m
High point 2554 m
Map 82 J/14 Spray Lakes Reservoir

Access: Smith-Dorrien—Spray Trail (Hwy. 742). Turn west onto the Watridge logging road signed Mt. Engadine Lodge, Mt. Shark trailhead. In 1.8 km park in a small parking area on the right side of the road.

This is one of the most enjoyable ridge walks you'll ever do. It takes in three summits and one section of easy scrambling coupled with mild exposure. Access is easy (though not straightforward); it pays to be familiar with the normal route to Tent Ridge.

Clockwise (for the best views) From the parking area walk back along the road a short distance, then turn right (west) up a grassy logging road. Round a bend into a logged area with innumerable skid trails branching right like the veins of a leaf. Head right up the first reasonable trail (a few trails in). At the top edge of the cutblock the *correct* skid trail enters a draw from which a regular trail climbs out into the bush. I really must flag this junction. Third time along and to my embarrassment I still turned up a skid trail too soon, and likely you will too, but just head left along the forest edge until you come to the draw.

The narrow forest trail leads to a T-junction with flagging. Turn left. (The trail to right crosses deeply-incised 'Monica Brook', then heads across meadow to intersect the normal route up Tent Ridge. An optional return route.)

The ridge between the hub of the horseshoe and Tent Ridge. Looking down on Watridge Lake and along the length of Bryant Creek. Cone Mountain at centre right.

The left-hand trail cuts across to 'Monica Brook' higher up at the start of the meadows. Follow them up to seasonal ponds in the valley head. Next, gain the ridge to the left (east) by a diagonal climb from right to left at treeline.

Get set for an enjoyable scramble up the north ridge of peak GR154311. Beyond the first rocky knob, identified by a red pinnacle poking up above ridge level on the west side, the ridge pinches in. Above is the first step. The steepest. Tackle it on the right side via slabs or broken rock even further to the right. After this, the route unravels beautifully, long grassy promontories alternating with scrambly rock steps. Rather disappointingly, this exciting form of progress stops short of the summit, which is a boring mound the size of a tennis court with a Surveyor's bench mark and three cairns. But it is a fabulous viewpoint, especially looking south: Tryst Lake (far below) and all of K Country's shapeliest peaks grouped together in one photo frame: Robertson, French, Sir Douglas, Commonwealth, Birdwood, Smuts and The Fist.

Stroll down the broad west ridge to a col touched by fingers of spruce thickets reaching up from the Tryst Lake side (escape route). The upcoming climb to the hub of the horseshoe at GR146308 is not as steep as it looks, the ascent helped by a winding trail in the scree. At the summit a fresh view opens up to the northwest; Marushka and Watridge Lakes set like opals in a dark forest and a view up Bryant Creek to Allenby Pass.

From the hub the connecting ridge to Tent Ridge appears level. It's not. Unseen is one big drop requiring a detour onto the west flank. In fact, vertigo sufferers may wish to follow a trail below the ridgeline on the west side all the way down *300 vertical metres* to the hub/Tent col.

The final pull up colourful Tent Ridge is easy and from the top you're rewarded by a superlative view of Spray Lakes Reservoir. But far more satisfying, in my opinion, is the view of the whole ridge walk you've just completed.

Return to your vehicle via the normal route for Tent Ridge (#73).

75 TRYST LAKE — map 10

Short day hike
Unofficial trail, creek crossing
Distance 3 km
Height gain 260 m
High point 2150 m
Map 82 J/14 Spray Lakes Reservoir

Access: Smith-Dorrien—Spray Trail (Hwy. 742). Turn west onto Watridge logging road signed Mt. Engadine Lodge and Mt. Shark trailhead. In 900 m, turn up the (second) side road to the left and park.

A short steep climb to a typical cirque lake. This is another of those lakes formerly called 'Lost' until Harry Connolly arranged a lover's meeting.

Walk south along the flat grassy logging road for 1.6 km, en route passing a road with orange markers turning right up a hill (Tent Ridge ski trail). About 50 metres before the small stream issuing from Tryst Lake, watch for a cairn indicating the start of the Tryst Lake trail.

Head off through the trees to the creek, gained at the bottom of an avalanche slope. Wallow up the right bank a way, then cross to the left. The trail improves as you climb the steep draw to meadows about the lake. Tryst is wonderfully situated below a peak shaped like a clenched fist, the whole scene becoming magical in fall when the larches turn colour.

Twenty years ago in June, though, the lake was frozen and snow lay on the ground when Harry guided Elizabeth Willey (Marushka Mary's sister) and her fiancee, Jim Springer, to the lake. Enamoured by the wonderful scene, they embraced and Harry took a photo for posterity.

GOING FARTHER

For those of you who don't need trails, it's possible to latch onto Tent Ridge Horseshoe (#74) from the lake. Follow the north shoreline to the upper valley, and at the demarcation of forest and scree climb 244 vertical metres to the col at GR150309. Though steep, the going is straightforward through larches with a permanent lean from the weight of winter snowpack. At the col you're in position to pick off a couple of summits or make a loop with peak GR154311 via its north ridge (a scramble). Better still, do the loop in reverse. What satisfaction to drop in on a lake for a paddle before the long walk back.

Tryst Lake and The Fist.

76 SMUTS PASS — map 10

Day, long day hike
Unofficial trails & route
Distance 5 km via short approach
Height gain 408 m to pass
High point Smuts Pass 2332 m,
High Col 2393 m
Map 82 J/14 Spray Lakes Reservoir

Access: Smith-Dorrien—Spray Trail (Hwy. 742).
1. Long approach Turn west onto Watridge logging road signed Mt. Engadine Lodge, Mt. Shark trailhead. In 900 metres turn up the (second) side road to the left and park.
2. Short, wet approach Park on the shoulder of the highway about 4 km north of Chester Lake parking lot and about 2 km south of Watridge logging road. In other words, opposite Commonwealth Creek.

Commonwealth Creek is the gateway to some superb alpine country that makes you yearn to carry on. With two vehicles you can do just that: continue over Birdwood Pass to Burstall Pass in one day. Whatever you decide, allow plenty of time for looking around. If using approach 1, biking to the end of logging roads is easy and saves time. Otherwise, I'd use the short approach.

---

1. Long approach Add 1.2 km. Walk or bike south along the grassy logging road past Tent Ridge ski trail and Tryst Lake trail to a junction at km 2.2. Turn right.

2. Short, wet approach Cross the soggy flats of Smuts Creek and the creek itself into trees on the other side. Follow orange ski markers (Princess Anne ski trail) up a bank into a large cutblock. Cut left uphill to intersect a major logging road, likely emerging opposite the trail to Commonwealth Lake. You, however, turn right on the logging road that dips to Commonwealth Creek (a four-log crossing), then climbs to a junction with approach 1. Turn left.

Up Commonwealth Creek As you follow the new logging road into Commonwealth Creek valley, keep left, and walk through a sawmill site to a cutblock. At the far forest edge where the road goes winging up a hill to the right, transfer to a forest trail.

The trail descends to Commonwealth Creek at a small waterfall, then seesaws between boisterous creek and rocky outcrops through the narrows. This section ends in a bog. Continue at the demarcation of forest and flat wet meadows where the stream flows majestically over gravel beds in great meanders. To your left is peak GR163287 (see #77), while ahead rises Mt. Birdwood revealing its diminutive north glacier. Farther on you cross the runouts of horrendous avalanche slopes falling from below The Fist and Pig's Tail, and wade through fields of ragworts and cow parsley. Just ahead is another narrows, but you're not going through. Instead, the trail climbs slightly to a stony side creek with cairn at GR150289.

To Smuts Pass Cross the side creek and climb up the left bank on stones to another cairn and white flagging where the trail resumes. Continue climbing fairly steeply, then traverse left into the forest for a flat stretch where aspiring botanists can search for delicate Foam flowers among the rhododendrons. At a junction keep to the right; only guidebook writers would cross a pile of branches laid across the false trail to see where it goes. Two short steps bring you to treeline below the headwall.

Smuts Pass (left), lower lake and Mt. Birdwood from the terrace east of Ice Lake.

Coming up is the steep climb of the day. Make for the scree gully on the right side of the headwall and scrabble up a trail on its right side. Shortly it crosses the gully to the wide, grassy slope and climbs the larch-scattered rib just left of the gully. Near the top where the headwall starts to rear up and become ugly, head off right across easier-angled ground to gain a large, flat terrace above the gully's left fork. High to the left, Mt. Birdwood rises like the thin blade of a knife. On the right the south ridge of Mt. Smuts looks equally terrifying and I can't believe it's a scrambling route, but this is where hard-core scramblers would set off up the first gully. I'll watch from the bottom, thanks! For us walkers there's one last step to go. Short and easy, the trail traverses from right to left to Smuts Pass.

The ground ahead slopes gently down to a sunken valley occupied by a lake. On the terrace above is another lake, frozen for most of the year. In fact, I've never seen it completely free of ice even in late August when enough of the ice had melted to disclose inky blue water. From it, a cord of white water pours into the lower lake, whose waters sink into the ground at the same phenomenal rate to join some vast underground drainage system. This giant sinkhole is bounded on the west by a high ridge that is the true K Country/Banff Park boundary, no matter what the topo map shows. Now if the water could be shown to emerge at Karst Spring….

To High Col The trail continues, climbing beside the stream to Ice Lake, as I call it, and from there to High Col at GR135279, a fine vantage point for the west face of Mt. Birdwood, becoming spectacular if you wander up the west ridge a bit. My favourite viewpoint has to be the terrace east of Ice Lake where an unsuspected tarn mirrors the mountain to perfection. From higher up the terrace, a view above bluffs includes both passes and the lower lake (see photo). Late afternoon light is best for photos, which isn't much help, I know, to those of you continuing on over Birdwood Pass.

GOING FARTHER

Birdwood Pass 2463 m add 2.5 km to pass, complete loop 12 km, height gain from High Col 167 m, height loss 76 m. Making a loop with Burstall Pass trail using Birdwood Pass as the link makes for a very long day. Trails are intermittent, the terrain occasionally steep and rocky with a bit of bushwhacking thrown in. In a whiteout, navigation could be a nightmare unless you're lucky enough to own a GPS receiver.

To Birdwood Pass Start from High Col. Without losing height, head southeast across meadow to the skyline at treeline. Find the game trail that drops steeply through the trees for 10 vertical metres, then cuts left through a diagonal rock band into a long, slightly descending traverse. Between forested ribs you cross steep avalanche chutes crammed with flowers, the whole gorgeous scene looking remarkably like a neo-impressionistic painting by Georges Seurat.

At black shale the trail drops sharply to a flat meadow nowhere near Birdwood Creek (which is farther down the slope in a mini canyon). From this low point restart the climb to Birdwood Pass. Farther right the terrain is extremely complex. Use the draw under the west face of Birdwood, a simple walk up grass, scree and often snow leading directly to the pass at GR146264.

This is a bleak spot, wide open to bad weather. Somehow I can't seem to get here without a thunderstorm gathering. Judging by his photographs, Alf Skrastins has the same problem. But the view is stupendous, not only of where you've come from but looking ahead to the fabulous karst country of Burstall Pass, the smooth slabs of Whistling Ridge leading the eye towards the great peak of Mt. Sir Douglas.

To Burstall Pass trail The far side is a two step scree or scree 'n' snow slope dropping to a grassy bench. Gain the lower, narrower bench sited above the high cliff defending the pass from the Burstall Creek side. It was here, just as the storm was imminent, we came upon a couple of climbing acquaintances with a tent. Unfortunately, we couldn't cram another six peo-

Into the storm. Birdwood Pass, looking towards South Burstall Pass (top, far right). Whistling Rock Ridge rises from left to right towards Mt. Sir Douglas (hidden in the murk).

ple into a tent made for two and had to leave. This means walking to the far left end of the bench (as you look out), where a 'trail' in scree leads down to a four metre-high rock step that can be managed holding an umbrella in one hand. After this you descend under the cliff, heading a long way right to grass where the trail, its duty done, vanishes. Descend where you fancy. The end result is always the same: some tree bashing to gain the Burstall Pass trail in the big meadow. Turn left and follow it out to Burstall Pass parking lot (#79).

OPTION

Birdwood Pass to Burstall Pass 1.7 km, 90 m height gain, 46 m height loss. The traverse has one stretch of easy but potentially dangerous scrambling. I recommend waiting until most of the snow has gone.

Head south along the lower bench and at the obvious place transfer to the upper bench which is of varying width and slant.

Halfway along is a small plot of Indian Paintbrushes, featuring showy bicoloured species.

Unfortunately, the bench peters out and you must climb steep broken ground to gain the south ridge of Snow Peak above. Climb diagonally left uphill, passing below then up the left side of what is almost a permanent snow patch. The scrambling couldn't be easier. The danger comes early in the season when a more extensive snowfield forces you farther left onto ledges above the drop-off. Needless to say, finding the going down place from the uphill direction can be a bit tricky.

Once you've reached the ridge, it's an easy walk down to Burstall Pass. You'll be ecstatic with the panoramic view as shown on pages 182 and 183.

77 COMMONWEALTH LAKE — map 10

Day hike
Unofficial trails
Distance 1.9 km via short route
Height gain 183 m to lake
High point 2042 m
Map 82 J/14 Spray Lakes Reservoir

Access: Smith-Dorrien—Spray Trail (Hwy. 742).
1. Long approach Turn west onto the Watridge
logging road signed Mt. Shark Racing Trails, Mt.
Engadine Lodge. In 900 metres turn left onto a
side road and park a little way in.
2. Short, wet approach Park on the shoulder of
the highway about 4 km north of Chester Lake
parking lot and about 2 km south of Watridge
logging road. In other words, opposite Commonwealth Creek.

A moderately steep forest trail, cleared by
Rudi Kranabitter, takes you to a body of
water formerly called Jeanette, then Lost
and now Commonwealth, a pretentious
name for a small green gem.

*Commonwealth Peak is the
backdrop for Commonwealth Lake.*

1. Long approach Add 1.2 km. Walk or
bike along the grassy logging road heading
south. Ahead, Commonwealth Peak comes
into view and to its right the peak at
GR163287 which is climbed from the optional loop. Keep left twice at logging road
junctions and cross Commonwealth Creek
on a four-log bridge. At the top of the hill
turn right onto a trail.

2. Short, wet approach Cross the soggy
flats of Smuts Creek and the creek itself into
trees on the other side. Follow orange ski
markers (Princess Anne ski trail) up a bank
into a large cutblock. Cut left uphill to
intersect the logging road used by approach
number one, likely emerging opposite the
trail to Commonwealth Lake.

Head up the left (southeast) bank of Commonwealth Creek. Entering forest, the trail
reverts to logging road, crosses the sawmill
site and continues uphill into a jumble of
intersecting and branching skid trails.

Your road is distinguished by tread. Remember that as it levels, bending right,
then back left up a hill. Before it starts to
curve even farther to the left around the
top of a shallow gully, abandon it for a
narrow trail leaving the right side.

Climb steeply through fir and menziesia
to a flat area where the trail winds about a bit
before arriving at the lakeshore (blazed T-
junction). The lake is beautifully situated
below Commonwealth Peak, and as I've
mentioned, it's green, the colour of Granny
Smith apples.

GOING FARTHER
The Loop add on 5.8 km, 290 m height gain.
The fit walker can extend the trip by making a loop with Commonwealth Creek incorporating the col at GR163281 and possibly the unnamed peak at GR163287.
Should you take in the peak add 90 m to the
height gain. This is rough terrain, occasionally steep, with scree, snow early in the
season and only the occasional game trail.

To the col 2362 m It's an easy walk up the valley beyond the lake through forest and flower glades to the larch zone. At the obvious place take to the right-hand hillside and climb steep grass, threading between slabs to gain easy-angled talus leading to the col. One by one Mts. Birdwood, Smuts and The Fist come into view. When we arrived at the col a fierce rainstorm had just passed, the clouds parting theatrically to reveal the steaming rocks of Commonwealth Peak glittering in the sun like Anthracite. Andrew Lloyd Weber couldn't have stage-managed it better.

Up peak GR163287, 2454 m Anyone arriving at the col and not heeding the siren call of the little pointy summit to the north is missing out on a fabulous viewpoint. Start out on grass, promising not to turn around until I say. After scree begins, the ridge steepens and narrows dramatically, with cliffs on the left side and on the right a convenient sheep trail running below the crest to the 'summit', which turns out to be false. Ahead stretches a wide, flat promontory clothed in high altitude grass. Walk to its end—the true high point and

look back. What a place to view the north faces of Commonwealth Peak and Mt. Birdwood! We were here in early July and while winter's snow still lay heavy on the peaks, here all was green grass and flowers and picas running about between our feet.

Completing the Loop Return to the col. Slither down scree and possibly snow into the barren valley on the west side. Follow the drainage down to the first drop-off. Use a game trail on the left side of the creek. Where a side creek comes in from the left, cross to the right bank. Above the second steeper drop-off the trail traverses right across scree into forest, then plummets to valley bottom.

At this spot Commonwealth Creek is meandering across a flat valley floor. To reach the trail on the northwest bank requires a push through willows and a paddle. Turn right and follow trail #76 down Commonwealth Creek to the main logging road you started out on.

Peak GR163287. Looking back along the promontory to Commonwealth Peak.

78 HOGARTH LAKES — map 10

Half-day hike
Unofficial trail, creek crossing
Distance main loop 7 km
Map 82 J/14 Spray Lakes Reservoir

Access: Smith-Dorrien—Spray Trail (Hwy. 742) at Mud Lake parking lot.

This is a very pleasant forest walk around a string of fishing lakes named after Scottish forest ranger James Hogarth. While logging roads make access easy, you may be thwarted by Burstall Creek if the logs aren't in place.

Start out on Burstall Pass trail. Cross Mud Lake dam, then at the bottom of the uphill where the trail turns left, turn right onto the unsigned Hogarth Lakes logging road. In one kilometre cross Burstall Creek via logs slightly downstream.

Now refer to the sketchmap. By following the black line (major road) clockwise under the cliffs of a knoll you come to first and second lakes. Unlike muddy Mud Lake,

Hogarth Lakes are remarkable for their translucent green colour shading to cream in the shallows. Tom Thomson trees around the rims make wonderful foregrounds for the mountains of the Kananaskis Range.

As you can see, the main trail circles around third lake on avalanche slope and returns through forest. This is where you might want to explore the dashed lines indicating a complexity of old roads in varying states of revegetation. Some allow you to reach the west shore of Mud Lake. My favourite runs along the east shore of all three lakes, giving new background views of Mts. Burstall, Murray and Cegnfs. The latter name is not an editorial error, but supposedly the initials of the first ascent party: Findlay, Findlay, Gould, Noakes, Poole and Schiesser. You figure it out!

First Hogarth Lake.

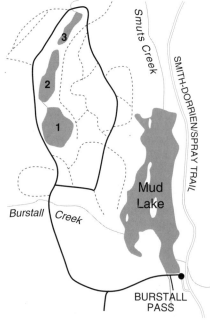

79 BURSTALL PASS — map 10

Day hike
Official trail with signposts
Distance 8 km
Height gain 472 m
High point 2380 m
Maps 82 J/14 Spray Lakes Reservoir,
82 J/11 Kananaskis Lakes

Burstall Pass summit near the signpost. In the background are the lower slopes of Snow Peak, Birdwood Pass, Mt. Birdwood, Pig's Tail and Commonwealth Peak.

Access: Smith-Dorrien—Spray Trail (Hwy. 742) at Mud Lake parking lot.

The Burstall Pass trail takes you effortlessly into that cheerful green and white karst country above treeline. As Joe Kovach and Bill Balmer noted on October 6, 1948, the pass can be easily crossed to the Spray River. Anyone off to Leman Lake, Spray Pass or Palliser Pass could come this way in preference to slogging all the way up the Spray River trail from Bryant Creek. If you don't need trails, use South Burstall Pass for Palliser Pass. For those of you staying around, my recommendation for maximum viewing is Burstall Pass, ridge GR147230 to South Burstall Pass, and a return to Burstall Pass via the benches, a round-trip from the trailhead of about 16 km.

Cross Mud Lake dam and wend left at the unsigned junction with Hogarth Lakes logging road. At the top of the hill is a T-junction with the French Creek logging road. Turn sharp right onto the Burstall Creek logging road which climbs past numerous skid trails, the result of Balmer's visit to look over the timber. When the road levels off, keep left.

The remainder of the road is tedious walking, especially if you used to do your walking by car to the sawmill site. For variety, I like to nip down to First Burstall Lake which is largely ignored by people on a fixed march. Near the sawmill site a trail takes over, heading downhill to a large alluvial flat extending from Robertson Glacier to third Burstall Lake. Cross kitty-corner to where the trail re-enters trees left of the avalanche slope.

A word about the flats. As you will gather from bridges made redundant, the braided streams move around a lot. Right now a deep channel near the forest edge overflows regularly, leaving a large area awash in water and not a bridge in sight. After rain be prepared for a paddle.

Before turning into the trees look back to the Robertson Glacier, suddenly revealed to the south. Unless you're a skier there's little point in stumbling up the stony south fork to the toe. I refer summer skiers to the book *"Kananaskis Country Ski Trails"*.

Climb the timbered headwall, which is a bit of a grunt with overnight gear and a six-pack. 120 vertical metres later you reach the flat meadow below Birdwood Pass and Mt. Birdwood's Lizzie Ridge. Cross the meadow to the mouth of the draw. While winter's route goes into the draw, the summer trail climbs steadily up the right bank into alpine meadows with scattered clumps of spruce and larch. On a flat stretch the main trail turns right (ahead is South Burstall Pass), zigging right, then left, ultimately approaching the pass from the south. A signpost marks the spot.

When the cloud's down this is a hugely complicated terrain of barren ridges, confounded by a deep sinkhole on the west side. In fine weather it's a marvellous place to be. Mountains encircle you, including Snow Peak above the pass, Mt. Birdwood to the northeast and The Fortress seen through the gap made by Burstall Creek. Sir Douglas is preeminent to the south, while to the west, Assiniboine lords it over a welter of lesser peaks.

To Leman Lake viewpoint The trail continues into Banff Park, traversing the left side of the sink to a grassy shoulder. Keep walking until the peacock colours of historic Leman Lake come into view.

OFF-TRAIL OPTIONS
South Burstall Pass 2484 m add 2.5 km.

The slightly higher pass at GR155226 is gained from Burstall Creek trail as mentioned. After the valley trail peters out choose your own route, more or less following the rocky draw (nowhere near as simple as the winter version) to a wide flat area of fissured pavement where a tall cairn marks the pass. Look back. The four dogtooth

mountains: Smuts, Birdwood, Pig's Tail, and Commonwealth Peak have lined up four abreast. What you've really come for, though, is the close-up of Sir Douglas, its north face mantled with glaciers.

Ridge GR147230, 2615 m add 215 m height gain. If motivated by fabulous views, traversing the ridge between the two passes is something you can't pass up.

Getting onto the ridge from the north end is not as easy as you might expect. From Leman Lake viewpoint you must first climb over a big grassy hill, the one at GR145239. From the signpost at the pass head southwest onto the same hill through a break in the rock band. Next, gain a smaller rise by the left edge. Ahead rises the main body of the ridge. Sneak through the obvious draw on its left side, cut back right on steep grass, and finish with a simple scree plod on sheep trail.

Burstall Pass (centre) from the south ridge of Snow Peak. Below Mt. Sir Douglas (left) is South Burstall Pass. At centre is ridge GR147230, to far right Leman Lake viewpoint above the sinkhole.

Except for one short rise before the second cairn, the summit ridge is broad and flat, the right side falling away in cliffs to the Spray River valley. You'll revel in the view that takes in the whole of the Spray Valley from Bryant Creek to Palliser Pass, plus Mt. Assiniboine and all the peaks you could see from Burstall Pass. Look *down* on blue-tinted Belgium Lake, and across the pass to Mt. King Albert, named after the King of the Belgians who died in a climbing accident and not, I hasten to add, a member of the Royal Group. Carry on to the end, dropping slightly to a spectacular grassy promontory that gives you the best view of the day—the classic shot of Sir Douglas shown on page 15.

Return to Burstall Pass From the end you can safely drop off the left (east) side. Three scree steps alternate with two terraces. At the lower terrace head left. Where the terrace slips a notch at mid point, most people descend to the flat meadow and pick up the Burstall Pass trail just below the pass.

80 FRENCH CREEK — map 10

Day hike
Unofficial trail & route
Distance 7.2 km to glacier
Height gain 853 m to glacier
High point 2758 m
Maps 82 J/14 Spray Lakes Reservoir, 82 J/11 Kananaskis Lakes

Access: Via Burstall Pass trail #79.

After years of trampling by provincial team skiers en route to the Haig Icefield (they now have to walk round the long way), the trail is a lot clearer and takes you to the base of the French Glacier. In summer, going further requires all the paraphernalia of glacier travel. Those innocent looking snowfields have snared quite a few people, including a ranger fortuitously accompanied by two search and rescue experts. Rather than freeze to death down a crevasse, I suggest spending more time enjoying the waterfalls.

Follow Burstall Pass trail to the signpost at the top of the first hill. Go straight on the French Creek logging road. Keep straight and climb to the top of a hill. As you descend into French Creek valley, keep left at a questionable junction. Down below are glimpses of French Creek being diverted from its natural course by means of canals and culverts to poor old Mud Lake, a receptacle for all the muck carried down from the Robertson and French glaciers. On the flat, the road runs alongside a French Creek *au natural* to a T-junction just before the creek crossing.

First waterfall up French Creek.

DETOUR to First Waterfall
Turn right at the T-junction and head along the right bank to road's end in about a kilometre. Just ahead is a cliff bisected by the two-tier waterfall.

Back to the T-junction. Cross French Creek via a collapsed bridge and follow the main logging road as it gains height up the left (east) bank to another river crossing above First Waterfall. Do not cross. Transfer to a trail edging along the left bank to Second Waterfall, which occurs at a junction with a tributary to the east. Climb steeply up mud to the left of the fall, then make a gradual return to the creek. Another flat riverside section gains you the base of Third Waterfall, a rare sight at runoff. This time the trail makes a lengthy detour to the left.

Continue along the riverbank. Opposite avalanche slopes falling from 'Piggy Plus' the trail turns away from the river, cutting off the corner as it climbs into scanty patches of meadow and larches below a lateral moraine, one time site of ski camps.

Walk up the trough of the lateral moraine to the top. What a place to view the French Glacier, a little bit of the Haig Icefield spilling through the gap between Mts. French and Robertson, which have to be two of the most spectacular mountains in K Country. As skiers will testify, the gap is a lot farther away than you think!

Rummel Lake.

81 RUMMEL LAKE — map 10

Day hike
Unofficial trail & route, creek crossings
Distance 5 km
Height gain 350 m
High point at lake 2217 m
Map 82 J/14 Spray Lakes Reservoir

Access: Smith-Dorrien—Spray Trail (Hwy. 742). Park on the shoulder opposite the Watridge logging road turn-off.
Also accessible from route #83.

Some people think this little lake, named after Baroness Elizabeth 'Lizzie' Rummel, surpasses Chester in both colour, setting and number of larches. In getting to this delectable spot you'll undoubtedly encounter a few routefinding problems.

For some people, lakes near timberline are only a stepping stone to the alpine above, in this case Rummel Pass. Game trails are intermittent but the terrain is easy enough. If you've got two vehicles, and a willing party who can hack steep slopes and a little bushwhacking, I recommend carrying through to Lost Lake (#54) and out via Galatea Creek (#52) to Highway 40. Total kilometrage 17.3 km.

Starting from the east side of Highway 742, a logging road heads south, parallelling the highway, to a large cutblock. At Peter Lougheed Provincial Park boundary, it turns left, climbing past the odd clump of White rhododendron and Labrador tea to the top left-hand corner. A gangway leads into the upper cutblock, where a trail continues climbing to the top edge. Slip into forest, following the gently-inclined ridge high above Rummel Creek through a wonderfully open forest with soft grouseberry and red heather underfoot. After the third dip, the trail divides and you go left at a junction possibly marked by flagging or by branches lain across the 'wrong' route, which is right route if you're taking the grizzly trail to Chester Lake (#83).

The trail climbs a bit, then drops to Rummel Creek. Round a couple of bends is a rocky bank above a cascade. The traverse is tricky if you happen to be hefting backpacking gear with projecting Therm-a-rest and tent poles, and are being pulled along by your dog. Alternatively, traverse at creek level or go over the top.

After the talus slope is behind you, a minor routefinding problem occurs in willow brush on either side of a tributary issuing from the cirque to the right. From a cairn, some people head left, while others, like me, walk up the creek a way and then cross. Either way, both routes meet in a small meadow distinguished by the 'flag tree' that, sadly, keeled over in the winter of 1990. It must have been a quite magnificent tree in its time, but is now a recumbent trunk of incredible girth, festooned with fluorescent wolf lichen and sheltering all kinds of creepy crawlies within its rotting heartwood.

Climb back into the trees. A short way on cross Rummel Creek below small waterfall steps (log), then climb up the left bank to the lakeshore. However, before you can say "Who's got the lunch?", it's mandatory to read fish catch instructions and a sign about spawning beds, then ponder a line of red flagging that apparently denotes the provincial park boundary for the benefit of hunters. But it would be hard to ruin the scene completely. Rummel Lake is lovely, translucent turquoise waters overlooked by Mt. Galatea and further away by The Tower, a name transposed from The Fortress.

Opposite: En route to Rummel Pass. The second tarn.

GOING FARTHER

Rummel Pass 2390 m height gain 183 m from lake, distance 3 km from lake.

Long before you reach the inlet stream on the northwest shore, climb a draw to a bench (last trees). On a northeast heading, slip between Mt. Galatea and the Tower into the upper valley, a simple walk on grass to the first tarn. From this direction The Tower is considered a 'walk-up', if 777 vertical metres of steep scree appeals. Personally, I would rather loll by the tarn and through binoculars watch someone else's struggle while slurping nectarines.

Another tarn lies above and beyond the boulder field, one that in mid summer is still rimmed by snowbanks and has icebergs wafting about. A trail develops in the scree of the left shore and takes you around a corner to the pass at the edge of a drop-off. There is something in the configuration of the mountains at this spot that squeezes the air and sends it battering like a wild thing on the walls of The Tower. (Heaven knows what this place is like in a full-fledged gale.) So you tucker down over the edge and look ahead to a new dark landscape holding Alvin Guinn's lost lake.

To Lost Lake height loss 372 from pass, distance 2 km from pass.

Find the sheep trail that circles down left over ledges and crosses the big scree slope. Before reaching a ridge, head down a ribbon of grass into the bowl. Exit via sheep trail on the left side of a cement-like slope with ball bearings. Boulders, dribbled down the slope, have fanned out across the flat at the bottom into the trees, which is a trifle disconcerting. Make for the grassy draw. A trail develops on the right side of the fledgling stream that, without warning, plunges over a cliff. Now what? The trail crosses a side creek, descends to the lip, climbs to an overlook on the right, then drops over the edge. While there's no cliff at this point, it's a branch-clinging slither for some 35 vertical metres.

In forest just west of the lake the trail disperses with the animals. Possibly there's a trail around the willowy left shore. We chose to traverse the more interesting right (southeasterly) shore, until dense thickets and cliffs drove us up onto grassy bluffs (fine viewpoint). At lake's end drop to the outlet and pick up the valley trail at the forest edge. See #54 for the route to Highway 40.

Bottom: Tarn two, Three Lakes Valley. The highest peak in the background is Sir Douglas.

Top: Chester Lake.

82 CHESTER LAKE — map 11

Day hike
Official trail with signposts, unofficial
trails & routes beyond lake
Distance 4.8 km
Height gain 310 m to lake
High point 2220 m at lake
Map 82 J/14 Spray Lakes Reservoir

Access: Smith-Dorrien—Spray Trail (Hwy. 742) at Chester Lake parking lot.
Also accessible from route #81 via #83.

Despite a less than aesthetic start up steeply-inclined logging roads, this jade-coloured lake in the larch belt is a popular destination; there's sure to be someone fishing from a rubber raft.

Note: after decades of traditional camping by the lake, backcountry camping is no longer allowed in this area.

The logging road leaves the top end of the parking lot near the biffy. After the gate keep straight, then veer left at the junction with Blue upper leg ski trail and cross Chester Creek. At the next junction turn right. Between here and the next signpost at a five-way junction the route is obvious, taking every uphill option—you aren't likely to stray onto an overgrown skid trail. At the five-way junction, you depart from the ski route and turn right. Keep left up a hill and wend right at the bend into a long straight. Bike locks indicate the end of the logging road section.

Head left up a narrow, twisty trail into the forest. Cross two hummocky meadows. Preceding the lake is a third meadow, much larger, extending right across the creek with a clear view of Mt. Chester, Gusty Peak and The Fortress—all easy scrambles per Kane. This is the place of departure for Mt. Chester and route #83 to Rummel Lake.

At the outlet, the trail splits; one trail bridging the creek into a larch clump and pica rockpile, the other following the west shoreline.

GOING FARTHER

Accessed by game trails, the two options are very much rougher

Three Lakes Valley add 2.2 km to third tarn, 240 m height gain.

From the lakeshore trail, turn left onto a well-used trail that climbs over the intervening ridge of larches and jumbo-sized boulders (Elephant Rocks) to the valley north of Chester Creek. The trail continues upstream to a tarn with damp shores beautified by clouds of silky white cotton grass. Climb the grassy headwall above, noting tufts of goat hair snagged on knobbly boulders. The finger valley between Mt. Galatea and Gusty Peak is a goat hot spot and if you're lucky you can spot them feeding on delicacies in damp slanting gullies high up to the right. Tarn three is a sink lake, often disappointing. Tarn two, though, sited picturesquely on the headwall's brink, is a place to linger by.

Upper Chester Creek add 1 km to lip, 190 m height gain.

Follow the lakeshore trail past the turn-off to Three Lakes Valley. The trail climbs into a grassy draw below Gusty Peak, following the edge of the left-hand scree slope to the lip of a hanging valley. This upper extension to Chester Creek is filled with rocks of all sizes and shapes, piled up in great heaps like unwashed dishes, and going further is unpleasant, not worth the effort if you're only aiming for the pond. Nearer at hand, meadows as immaculate as city lawns border the infant creek which sees daylight for perhaps 50 metres before sinking into the ground below a permanent snowbank.

83 CHESTER LAKE TO RUMMEL LAKE — map 10

Day hike
Unofficial trail & route, creek crossing
Distance 4.2 km
Height gain south to north 60 m
Height loss south to north 60 m
High point 2270 m
Map 82 J/14 Spray Lakes Reservoir

Access: Smith-Dorrien—Spray Trail (Hwy. 742).
1. Via Chester Lake trail #82.
2. Via Rummel Lake trail #81.

Every time I've been to Rummel Lake the normal way I've always met a hiker who's come in from the Chester Lake trail. They are usually found recuperating at the junction and talking in a quivering yet wondering voice about 'the grizzlies'. Don't let this deter you from following this route; there's never been a close encounter and the trail between the two lakes, or to be scrupulously correct, between the two access trails, is surprisingly scenic. But with all those grizzlies around, it's best to be a group.

Chester to Rummel Leave Chester Lake trail at the last meadow before the lake. Strike up meadow to the left and through a few token trees on the watershed to a brown-coloured pond marking the southeast edge of a large, flat meadow which is the mid portion of Three Lakes Valley. The whole hillside between this meadow and Elephant Rocks has been torn apart by grizzlies digging up yummy hedysarum roots. Yet for decades happy campers at Chester Lake seemed blissfully unaware of what was going on less than half a kilometre away in Three Lakes Valley.

Pass left of the pond, following the left (south) edge of the meadow to Three Lakes Valley Creek. Cross. Indistinct at first, a good trail materializes in the grass of the far bank and climbs diagonally from right to left across steep flowery slopes. As it turns northwest into the trees the gradient eases and red flagging appears, indicating keep right at questionable junctions. Cross over the watershed and emerge (red flagging marking the spot) in a draw filled by an extremely long longitudinal meadow between larches. Through the V are blue mountain shapes. To your right rise steep grassy slopes that I like to check for big brown shapes.

The trail continues down the centre of the draw which seems endless. But there comes a point when the meadow fills up with bushes and it's here (flagging) where the trail climbs the bank on the right past a large dead tree into spruce forest. The final stretch is slightly downhill and, except for one short stretch of deadfall, is straightforward to the junction with Rummel Lake trail. For Rummel Lake turn right.

Looking down the draw. Easy meadow walking.

84 HEADWALL LAKES — map 11

Lower Headwall Lake. The mountains through the V from left to right: Mt. Smith-Dorrien, Mt. French, Mt. Murray, Mt. Robertson, Cegnfs, Mt. Sir Douglas.

Day hike
Official & unofficial trails, route
Distance 5.2 km from access 2
Height gain 451 m to upper lake
High point 2341 m
Map 82 J/14 Spray Lakes Reservoir

Access: Smith-Dorrien—Spray Trail (Hwy. 742).
1. Chester Lake parking lot.
2. The logging road on the east side of the highway, 1 km south of Chester Lake parking lot.

This has to be the most delectable valley on the east side of the highway, containing within its boundaries all the finest components of mountain scenery: blue lakes, waterfalls, meadows, a karst pavement. The prerequisite to heaven is a jaunt through Smith-Dorrien's network of skiing and mountain biking trails. Colour-coded logging roads (discs on trees or posts) make access to the valley easy.

From access 1 If you want to be officially correct and add 2 km to the trip it's up to you. Your best bet is Blue upper leg, which turns right off Chester Lake trail just before the bridge over Chester Creek. Climb past Orange and join Yellow above the Blue/Yellow section. Keep left.

From access 2 The old road leads to Blue lower leg in a couple of minutes. Keep right and minutes later reach the junction with Yellow. Keep straight on Blue/Yellow, climbing past a spate of skid trails to the junction with Blue upper leg. Keep right.

191

To the lakes Yellow climbs to a logged area on a ridge, then continues past Orange upper junction to Headwall Creek upper crossing. At the right-hand bend following, continue up the logging road to a cutblock on the left side. Leave the road and walk along the edge, looking for flagging signalling the start of a good trail into the valley.

A stint through forest brings you back to valley bottom. The trail continues below a talus slope, then in a series of alternating steps and traverses, the last on scree, gains the top of the first headwall. Underfoot is a fascinating karst pavement scraped by a passing glacier. Below lies lower Headwall Lake cradled in a rock-girt bowl.

Follow the trail around the east shoreline, then climb a grassy headwall to the right of the tumbling stream that spouts out of the hillside at three-quarter height. The beautiful blue upper lake is the usual place to end the walk, its austere setting under The Fortress a deterrent to further exploration.

Headwall/Chester col looking along the east ridge of Mt. Chester.

OPTION

Chester Lake via Headwall/Chester col 2707 m (GR235314) About 4 km between lakes, 365 m height gain. Round trip 15 km, total height gain 823 m. The col between Mt. Chester and The Fortress enables experienced hikers not adverse to scree to make a round trip with Chester Lake trail #82. Because of steeper slopes on the west side I recommend an east to west crossing.

Traverse the right bank of upper Headwall Lake on talus to the upper valley where you're back to grass. At a pool start up low-angle scree, aiming for the low point on the ridge at GR235314. The slope steepens below the col which, you discover, is not one, but *two* cols separated by splinters of rock with a cairn. What a situation! Apart from being able to look into two valleys at once, Mt. Chester, which normally resembles a pudding, has an east ridge built like a ripsaw.

From the left-hand col drop down the west slope, a much steeper incline with black shale you can dig your heels into. On arriving in upper Chester Creek, boulder-hop to the sink and pick up the trail taking you down to Chester Lake.

85 THE FORTRESS — map 11

*A very foreshortened view of the summit
block from the upper part of the ridge.
The route traverses left below the crags
then climbs up the left edge.*

Long day scramble
Unofficial trail & route
Distance 8.2 km from highway
Height gain 295 m from Headwall/
Chester col, 1113 m from highway
High point 3002 m
Map 82 J/14 Spray Lakes Reservoir

Access: Spray-Smith—Dorrien Trail (Hwy.
742). Via Headwall Lakes trail (#84) at Headwall/Chester col gained more easily from upper
Headwall Lake.

Incredibly, The Fortress, which appears
impregnable from Highway 40, is a walk-up from the back, accessible to hikers who
can handle scree and easy scrambling.
There's even an intermittent trail. For vertigo sufferers there's certainly not much to
be scared of. However, don't think of it as
just a detour from the col; plan an early start
from the parking lot.

The first rise above the col is the crux:
scree on top of slab. That done with, the
ridge broadens and the angle eases
slightly. The scree is still a trial though,
and you may find it easier to stick to the
rocky crest and leave those gaudy orange
slopes on the right for a fast descent.
Higher up, after passing a couple of cairns,
the angle eases even more and you become
conscious of the drop on the right and
then on the left as the ridge tapers.

Approaching the summit rocks, the
trail cunningly turns left, traversing below the cliffs on broken ground. As
you're about to drop off the edge of the
world, scramble diagonally right up big
blocks to a sloping platform of scree and
walk to the summit. The view is superb,
taking in Mt. Assiniboine, of course, and
the white fang of Joffre further south, the
whole of the Opal Range, Guinn's Pass
and Fortress Mountain ski area, to name
just some of the features. With care, Fortress Lake can be spotted 823 vertical
metres below the eastern abyss.

86 JAMES WALKER CREEK — map 11

The lake backdropped by Mt. Smith-Dorrien (left), Mt. Murray (centre) and Cegnfs (right).

Day hike
Official & unofficial trails, route,
creek crossings
Distance 4.3 km to lake
Height gain 259 m to lake
High point 2118 m at lake
Map 82 J/14 Spray Lakes Reservoir,
82 J/11 Kananaskis Lakes

Access: Smith-Dorrien—Spray Trail (Hwy. 742) at Sawmill day-use area.

Like Headwall Lakes, this valley is accessed via the colour-coded Smith-Dorrien skiing and mountain biking network. So it's an easy walk to the lake. Once there, you're within reach of twin upper valleys divided by Mt. James Walker, a much more strenuous option.

Start up the logging road to the left of the biffy. Straightaway peel left onto Red/Yellow/Green. At the boulder go either way—right is more usual—and climb past skid trails to upper Red junction. Keep left on Yellow/Green. Turn right up the next good road, located exactly halfway between upper Red and James Walker Creek.

Follow James Walker Creek logging road through a mishmash of overgrown skid trails to road's end at an avalanche slope. A game trail covers the 1.5 km to the lake, rather vague where it crosses the avalanche slope, but becoming clear once it enters forest (flagging). In the meadow following, keep to the forest edge (larches) and climb over a rock pile to the lake which is obviously the creek pooled behind the rock dam. Nevertheless, it's quite attractive with a touch of colour and a surround of grass.

GOING FARTHER

Upper Valleys 2.2 km, height gain 174 m to tarn. Be prepared for a bushwhack.

Walk round to the inlet stream. A game trail follows the right (east) bank of the creek to an avalanche slope where the trail vanishes under willow brush. Pick your own line up the forested headwall; I recommend a route to the *left* of the major stream, which has the bonus of waterfalls where the two creeks merge.

The left-hand finger valley is the longest, a stony wasteland pitted with sinks storing stagnant water. Conversely, the right-hand branch holds a particularly beautiful tarn in a green and white setting of grass and limestone pavement.

87 BLACK PRINCE LAKES — maps 11 & 15

Day hike
Official & unofficial trails, route
Distance 4.5 km to lakes
Height gain 591 m
High point 2322 m
Map 82 J/11 Kananaskis Lakes

Access: Smith-Dorrien—Spray Trail (Hwy. 742) at Black Prince day-use area.

An easy interpretive trail leads to Warspite Lake where you leave the tourists behind, happily reading interpretive signs and checking for birds while you carry on into the cirque. This involves a steep grind and a bit of a bushwhack should you lose the game trail in the willows.

To Warspite Lake The interpretive trail starts behind the garbage disposal unit. It crosses a logging road en route to a bridge over Smith-Dorrien Creek, then doubles back to the logging road on the southwest bank. Climb the hill to the cutblock. Where the road starts to bend left, a trail turns right to a bench (view of Kent Ridge), then descends to Warspite Creek. Near the bottom of the hill is a junction. Turn left. After Warspite Creek crossing, the trail winds across a boulder field harbouring a good selection of berry bushes. Warspite Lake is contained within the jumble of boulders, its astonishing emerald green colour caused by algae activated by strong sunlight. The outlet takes the underground route. The water can be heard gurgling deep down beneath the trail.

To Black Prince Lakes At interpretive signs #9 or #10 step off the interpretive trail and circle anticlockwise around the north shoreline. Before reaching the inlet, you'll hit a good trail taking you through a belt of spruce into willowy flats south of the lake. Head south to grassy slopes where animals have foraged, aiming for a prominent black slit at the bottom of a cliff. Starting to its left, an elk trail climbs diagonally left towards the creek, then, deeply entrenched, climbs up the right side of Warspite Cascades to the top of the headwall. It's a climb to make you gasp.

At the lip a grassy cirque is revealed with Mt. Warspite at centre stage. When we were there an elk herd was just moving over the ridge to the left. You, however, turn right, climbing another 150 vertical metres up a grass and boulder slope to the top of a terminal moraine where you look down on three appropriately inky black tarns under Mt. Black Prince.

Warspite Cascades.

88 GYPSUM QUARRY — map 16

Day hike to quarry
Unofficial trail, creek crossing
Distance 5.2 km to quarry
Height gain 454 m
High point 2130 m
Map 82 J/11 Kananaskis Lakes

Below: the gypsum quarry.
The prominent peak at top right is
Indefatigable Outlier. To its right
is Indefatigable Col.

Access: Smith-Dorrien—Spray Trail (Hwy. 742) at Peninsula day-use area, far parking lot. **Also** accessible from #104 at the col between Indefatigable Outlier and the north summit of Mt. Indefatigable.

This is a delightfully easy walk up an exploration road to a gypsum quarry. Too bad the bridge is out over Smith-Dorrien Creek. On the other hand, this means less encounters between people and (judging by the scat) large numbers of game using the road.

From the loop at the far end of the access road transfer to the old road. Keep left and descend to Smith-Dorrien Creek, where you find out if the walk's a go. In mid July the water is thigh-deep and this is downstream of the bridge abutments where the river is wider and calmer!

On the south bank the 'road' (long grass, encroaching alder) continues to a junction. The overgrown trail to the left up

Gypsum Creek was the first attempt at getting a road to the gypsum deposit, but came a cropper when it hit a series of rocky gullies. So you turn right.

The road traverses avalanche paths to a junction. Keep left. While a shortcut is available using overgrown roads and game trails, why wallow through bushes when there is a nice grassy road offering views all around? The major road is obvious as it winds up the lightly-treed north ridge of Mt. Invincible. Everywhere between trees grows the White rhododendron, a beautiful sight during blossoming.

Below a steeper step the road levels and runs in a straight line along the right side of the ridge towards the face of the mountain, at the last minute deking left through a gap to the quarry. From a bench scattered with snowy white gypsum you're treated to a

great view: an Opal panorama, and farther to the right Mt. Rae, the Elk Range and a glimpse of Lower Kananaskis Lake below Gypsum Creek.

Versatile stuff, gypsum, which is used in the manufacture of all kinds of things from cement to glass to drugs. This particular outcrop was reported by the Geological Survey in 1964 (Report 65-1), and resulted in a 21-year lease being issued to CP Oil & Gas, who transferred it several times over to the Alberta Gypsum Company. After all the trouble in getting a road to the area, they operated for just a few years until August 1970 when the lease was cancelled, the company having failed to make a cash deposit to cover land restoration costs.

GOING FARTHER
Indefatigable Col GR297329 1.8 km from quarry, height loss 149 m, height gain 354 m. The cross country jaunt to #104 won't suit everyone; connecting game trails have rough, steep sections. Your best bet is to walk right through to North Interlakes parking lot, which, of course, requires two vehicles.

To Gypsum Creek road Cross the bench to the far end of the quarry, then follow hoof prints uphill and left across a gravel slope into some trees. Look for the trail establishing itself in the shallow scree gully beyond. Rising and falling, but mostly falling, the trail crosses treed ribs alternating with gullies. There are a few tricky metres where the trail disappears on steep ground, then reappearing, circles around a large gully manufactured from cement shale. Count three more rocky gullies to Gypsum Creek road which starts (or ends) on the far bank of the third.

The road crosses one humongous avalanche slope divided by a stream leaping down the headwall. Cross the stream (not marked on the topo map despite supplying 90% of the water to Gypsum Creek), then in trees cross the very much smaller creek from Gypsum Tarns.

To Gypsum Tarns Just after the creek crossing turn right off the road, using a trail near the forest edge to gain the bottom of a boulder slope. Intercept an excellent elk trail

The largest Gypsum Tarn under Mt. Invincible.

and follow it to the right (back into trees) towards the creek, at a division climbing either way to the lip of the cirque—a not too onerous task in larch and Glacier lily country. Cupped in grass at the bottom of scree slopes are three small tarns of varying beauty.

To the col A very convenient elk trail heads east up the left bank of the drainage to treeline. While it's possible at this point to climb direct to Indefatigable Outlier via its stony west ridge, the more attractive elk route tackles the grassy slope below the col. Cross the creek and gain height up the right slope, then swing back left (multiple trails) to a grey shale finish right of the orange rib.

Return via Gypsum Creek road? I knew you would ask this question. The dreadful thing is from this direction the first couple of kilometres lures with a clear path through trees. Then, at the point where the road turns away from the valley, instant infiltration: mini spruce, gooseberry bushes, six metre-high alders, deadfall. You'll emerge looking like an escapee from the polar bear complex at the Calgary Zoo. Don't go.

Lower Kananaskis Lake, looking south to Mts. Fox, Foch and Sarrail.

89 LOWER LAKE — map 16

Half-day hike
Official trail
Distance 3.5 km one way
Height gain 33 m
Map 82 J/11 Kananaskis Lakes

Access: Kananaskis Lakes Trail (Hwy.).
1. Canyon day-use area. The trail starts by the boat ramp.
2. William Watson Lodge.
3. Elkwood parking lot.

A pleasant stroll along the east shore of Lower Kananaskis Lake Reservoir. Just don't come in early summer when low water reveals the original lake surrounded by unattractive mud flats. Interestingly, the lake's first name was Thorpe, after a director of Wisconsin's Eau Claire Logging Company who were sizing up the timber berths back in 1883.

From Canyon Dam area the trail passes through a walk-in picnic area to the promontory marking the boundary of this sheltered backwater. Turn the corner and travel south along the lakeshore in the pines, making forays now and then to the waterline (however far that is) for rather splendid views of Mts. Fox, Foch, Sarrail and Indefatigable.

In an area of unnatural meadow growing Foxtail barley, the trail turns inland and follows a stream up a cool damp valley harbouring mature spruce to the paved trails of William Watson Lodge.

Turn left at 5 onto the interpretive trail for the disabled. A short way along at 3, it's worth detouring left to a pond (4), birthplace of the small stream and foreground to a rather nice view of the Opal Range if it wasn't for the powerlines. Return to 3 and turn left.

To William Watson Lodge At 2 turn right. Keep straight (fire circle to right), then straight at 1. Cross the RV campground access road to another trail. Turn left, keep right (cottages to left) and arrive at William Watson Lodge and parking lot at the end of its access road.

To Elkwood parking lot Keep left at 2 and follow the paved trail under the powerline to a junction with Lodgepole ski/bike trail. Turn right and cross Kananaskis Lakes Trail. At the signboard, if not before, nip into the parking lot on the left.

90 KANANASKIS LOOKOUT — map 16

Day hike
Official trails with signposts
Distance 6.4 km from Boulton Bridge,
4 km from Hwy. 40
Height gain 432 m from Boulton
Bridge, 296 m from Hwy. 40
High point 2125 m
Map 82 J/11 Kananaskis Lakes

Access:
1. Kananaskis Lakes Trail (Hwy.) at Boulton. In terms of altitude:
    a. Boulton Bridge parking lot.
    b. Boulton Trading Post parking lots. At the upper parking lot a ski trail runs along the top edge. Follow it to the right and join the trail from Boulton Bridge at a T-junction. Turn left.
    c. Boulton campground. The access road to A loop crosses the trail as does the access road between loops B and D.
2. Kananaskis Trail (Hwy. 40). Park at the entrance to the fire road at GR370118.

There are two reasonable routes to Kananaskis Lookout. Both are wide forest trails that amalgamate for the final steep pull to a fabulous viewpoint. If I'm on a bike I much prefer to zip along the fire road from Highway 40. But as this is a hiking guide I'd have to recommend starting from Kananaskis Lakes Trail at the Boulton area which has campsites, an eating place and lots of people looking for a walk.

Boulton Bridge access For a more interesting start follow Boulton Creek interpretive trail across Boulton Creek and up the bank to the old Fish and Wildlife cabin relocated from Lower Kananaskis Lake. At the T-junction turn left past the garage. At the following junction turn right onto Whiskey Jack trail (the trading post can be seen through the trees). Next, the trail from the trading post parking lots joins in from the left (access b). Climb a hill. Cross campground access road to A loop (access c). Climb alongside the campground road, then cross the road between B and D loops (access c).

All campground clatter left behind, continue on Whiskey Jack trail, which is uphill though undulating because you keep crossing Spotted Wolf Creek and all its tributaries. The most interesting part of all this is the name of the creek which commemorates George Pocaterra's blood brother Paul Amos.

At 4.3 km you arrive at the T-junction with the fire road that has come in from Highway 40. Under its various guises you're going to be following the fire road all the way to the lookout. Turn right on Pocaterra ski trail. In half a kilometre turn right at the junction with Tyrwhitt onto Lookout ski trail. Coming up is the worst climb of the day, a steep grind up the north ridge of lookout hill where total humiliation is to be passed by a mountain biker. The incline eases into a long straight, at the end of which, and with a delicious feeling of anticipation, you climb out of the trees to picnic tables. The hill top is shaved, a green meadow allowing a 360 degree view if you stand by the lookout, 1974 version. Look south to the mountains about Elk Lakes (that's Mts. Cadorna and Swiderski through the gap), west to Mts. Fox, Foch and Sarrail and Kananaskis Lakes, and north down the Kananaskis Valley to Mt. Kidd.

Highway 40 access Follow the fire road in its entirety. Cross Pocaterra Creek by bridge (Lionel ski trail) to a junction with Pocaterra ski trail. Keep left (on Pocaterra) and following in the footsteps of Joe Kovach, who blazed a trail to the lookout site in July 1949, make a gradual climb to Whiskey Jack junction. Keep left.

Top: Kananaskis Lookout. Looking west across
Upper Kananaskis Lake to Mt. Putnik (centre) and
Upper Kananaskis Viewpoint (below Mt. Putnik).

Bottom: The signboard at West Elk Pass.

91 WEST ELK PASS & FROZEN LAKE – map 16

Day hike
Official & unofficial trails
Distance 6.1 km to pass
Height gain 213 m to pass
High point 1905 m at pass
Map 82 J/11 Kananaskis Lakes

Access: Kananaskis Lakes Trail (Hwy.) at Elk Pass parking lot.
Also accessible from Elk Lakes Provincial Park entrance via #92 and from #93 West Elk Pass to Upper Elk Lake.

80 year-old monument at West Elk Pass.

I can't imagine why all those early explorers and travellers insisted on going over North Kananaskis Pass when Elk Pass was so glaringly obvious. Although the editor of 'Survival on a Western Trek' surmised the John Jones Overlanders crossed North Kananaskis Pass en route to the gold fields of British Columbia in 1858, most people believe they went over the Elk. Myself, I'm convinced they crossed Highwood Pass. The mistake is understandable. In the days before photogrammetry, the fact that the Elk Valley and the Highwood Valley ran parallel but on either side of the Divide caused a lot of confusion even to veteran mountain travellers like George Dawson and Walter Wilcox, and has resulted in mountains being misplaced. For instance, is Mt. Fox really Mt. Tyrwhitt?

But back to Elk Pass which surveyor Arthur O. Wheeler named in 1915 after being astonished to find it was nameless. Elk Pass is actually three: East Elk, Elk and West Elk. The secret trail through East Elk to Tobermory Creek was used by George Pocaterra to escape game wardens. I've never bothered to look for it. Too many grizzlies around, thanks! Elk Pass (the highest) is now followed by the powerline right-of-way. West Elk Pass (the lowest) was the usual route and was crossed by an ancient Indian trail headed to hunting grounds in Nyahe-ya-Nibi. Deadfall was always a torment. In 1901 it took Walter Wilcox's party six hours to travel between the pass and

Kananaskis Lakes. And this was in the downward direction! Even 20 years later, in the days of early tourism, forest rangers were always hacking out the trail.

Today we don't have this problem, not since Calgary Power put in the powerline access road and a road built for a tramline that never came about. So 95% of the route to West Elk follows the road (officially Elk Pass ski trail) and 5% the old trail.

Set off along the powerline access road, ignoring Boulton Creek ski trail on the left near the start. The road climbs over a ridge at the powerlines, which sing in the wind, then descends into Fox Creek. Keep right

(Fox Creek ski trail to left). After crossing Fox Creek, again keep right (powerline access road—Hydroline ski trail—to left) and follow a new stretch of road built for skiers. Cross the creek twice more, then settle into a long stretch tucked under the east bank alongside Fox Creek. It's interesting to note the main volume of water enters the valley at the halfway point. Thereafter you're actually following the southeast fork, a slow-moving stream overhung by willows. At a stretch of corduroy keep right (powerline access road—Patterson ski trail to left) and turn a corner. Notice the forest is opening up, allowing views of Mt. Fox and The Turret, both climbed by the Boundary Survey in 1916. Surprising to skiers are the chain of beaver ponds along the valley bottom. Level with a beaver house is the junction with Blueberry Hill ski trail marked by a signpost, picnic tables and resident Whiskey Jacks.

About 100 metres after this junction, just before the road starts its final climb to Elk Pass, is a small sign on the right side reading 'Lower Elk Lake'. So you turn off here, following a trail up the open draw. Higher up, switch to the west side of the meadow and arrive shortly afterwards at West Elk Pass on the Great Divide. This important place is marked by an information board and a boundary cutline crossing the pass at right-angles. On your left is the start of a very long longitudinal meadow from where, with boots slowly sinking in the ooze, you get a tantalizing glimpse of the mountains of the Elk River rising up above the horizon.

Frozen Lake

2 km from pass, height gain 280 m, high point 2185 m at lake. If you're just hiking to West Elk Pass, which isn't too exciting, or even going through to Elk Lakes, why not visit Frozen Lake, a truly worthy objective after the ice melts? True to its name, this gorgeous lake remains frozen for about nine months of the year, so plan on visiting from late July on. The trail is unofficial, quite distinct and steep.

From the information board head west up the boundary cutline. Where #93 turns off to the left just after '1M' monument stay on the cutline. Cross a wet meadow (flagging both ends) and continue up the cutline that climbs very steeply to '2M' monument. Another longer climb brings you to the end of the cutline in the vicinity of '4M'. (Just before '2M' a trail starting between two blazed trees on the left side descends to Fox Lake. Use it as a shortcut to trail #93, should you be headed that way, on returning from Frozen Lake.)

What are these monuments, anyway? Designed by Arthur O. Wheeler, they were constructed during the boundary survey to delineate the Alberta/British Columbia boundary at important passes. Elk Pass was assigned the letter 'M', so with the pass being so wide there's a whole slate of monuments and cairns extending from Mt. Fox to Mt. Tyrwhitt, all with different numbers up to 23. The monument at the lowest point of a pass was always numbered '1'. The Elk Pass bunch were constructed on the spot in 1916 using cement and gravel gouged from a nearby creekbed to make concrete. Unless a flat rock was handy, the concrete base generally extended one metre underground. The heavy zinc cover was painted bright red and filled with concrete, the whole weighing an incredible 2700 lbs!

But back to the trail. From the end of the cutline it turns right, then left into another steep climb. The gradient eases at a new-fangled metal boundary post, also marking the start of meadow and larch country. Traverse a grassy shelf between outcrops (view of Elk Pass and Fox Lake), then climb one final hill into the cirque.

Cradled in the precipitous arms of Mt. Fox, Frozen Lake is an awesome sight, extremely difficult to photograph unless you have a wide angle lens in excess of 28 mm. When we were there last, a good hour's entertainment was provided by another party having an epic circumventing the lake and climbing up the glacier below Mt. Fox (not marked on any map).

Frozen Lake from Taiga Viewpoint. Upper Kananaskis Lake and Mt. Indefatigable (right) can be seen above the north arm of Mt. Fox.

GOING FARTHER

Taiga Viewpoint 2360 m height gain from lake 215 m. This one's for scrabblers. 'Trails' and I use this word advisedly, lead to the col on the south arm of Mt. Fox, and up the outlier Taiga Viewpoint at GR348035.

Starting from the lakeshore head diagonally uphill, traversing two shale gullies into some trees. Climb the tree ribbon to below a rock band, then make an ascending traverse twixt rock and scree to the col.

From the col or before transfer to other game trails that ascend Taiga Viewpoint, the heap of rubble on your left. The summit ridge is beautiful, though, being narrow, long and grassy, and capped by a cairn built by the Boundary Survey who used the outlier as a camera station in 1916.

You'll be thrilled by Frozen Lake which from this vantage point looks more like a caldera lake than a lake in the cirque. Peeking over the top of the north arm are the Kananaskis Lakes. No less exciting is the forested expanse of all three Elk Passes, their complexities made clear. To the south lies Lower Elk Lake backdropped by Mt. Aosta, and the sweep of the Elk Valley enclosed by the wall of the Elk Range. For a view of the latter turn to page 127 in the Report of the Boundary Commission Part 1.

Shortcut to route #93, height loss 487 m. Before you start, know this is a grizzly hot spot. Still want to go?

From the col, head southeast down the avalanche chute. This grassy, flowery gully is not as enjoyable to descend as you might think. Hidden by vegetation are ankle breaking rocks that roll. I hate that. At a steepening a trail appears and takes you into the stony creekbed. Lower down where the incline eases, use meadow on the left side. Intersect #93 about 1.2 km from Upper Elk Lake.

92 WEST ELK PASS TO ELK LAKES PROVINCIAL PARK ENTRANCE — map 16

Day hike, backpack
Official trail
Distance 4 km from pass
Height loss 177 m
High point 1905 m
Map 82 J/11 Kananaskis Lakes

Access: Via West Elk Pass trail #91. Elk Lakes Provincial Park entrance is accessible by road if you have a couple of days to spare. Start from Highway 3 on the B.C. side of Crowsnest Pass. At Sparwood turn north on Highway 43 and drive 35 km to Elkford. Continue up the unpaved Elk River Road, a further 72 km of very rough driving. At the end, keep left into the parking lot.

Boardwalk meadow near Elkan Creek.

The quickest way to Elk Lakes Provincial Park is from Peter Lougheed Provincial Park via West Elk Pass—a mere half-day walk. This, the southern half of the route, is an upgraded Indian trail travelled by such notables as Arthur O. Wheeler, Walter Wilcox and George Pocaterra. Of course, if Highway 43 Association had their way the pass would be crossed by a paved highway, thus doing away with routes #91, 92 and 93, not to mention a half dozen ski trails. One can imagine the park filled to bursting point by tourists catered to by one of those fast turnover eateries with attached gift shop selling scenic place mats.

From the information board, the trail keeps to the west edge of the longitudinal meadow. You cross the infant Elkan Creek trickling out of Fox Lake and about a kilometre farther on draw close to the bank of that creek, which by now has plunged into a deep valley labelled 'Canon' on the old boundary survey maps of 1917. Wind steeply down the hill and at the bottom recross Elkan Creek on a log. In case you haven't twigged, the word 'Elkan' is an acronym of Elk and Kananaskis.

Come to the big meadow (swamp) where I remember lurching from one tussock to another. Now there's this tremendously long boardwalk, so rather than have your eyes glued to the ground, you're free to admire many-buttressed Mt. Aosta, seen in all its gothic splendour across the Elk Valley—the best view of the day. The final stretch of trail heads down a ribbon of firm ground to join the main park trail at a signpost. Turn right for Lower Elk Lake. Turn left for the park entrance and park headquarters half a kilometre away at the end of the Elk River Road.

Elk Lakes Provincial Park was established May 18, 1973 and in 1995 was extended to include all of the former Elk Lakes Recreation Area (meaning Cadorna Creek).

Some regulations to know about: bikes, horses and OHVs are prohibited, hunting is allowed. Leave the fossils where you find them. Trails are regularly patrolled by rangers in residence between June 1st and mid October. Camping is at the three designated campgrounds except in the headwaters of Pétain and Nivelle Creeks where it's called bivouacking.

93 WEST ELK PASS TO UPPER ELK LAKE — map 16

Long day hike, backpack
Official trail
Distance 3.5 km
Height gain 55 m, height loss 152 m
High point 1980 m
Map 82 J/11 Kananaskis Lakes

Access: Via #91 at West Elk Pass.
Also accessible from #92.

This pleasant forest trail is the quick way in and out of Upper Elk Lake and the Pétain Creek area.

The trail near Upper Elk Lake. In the background is Elkan Peak. The splash of white is Castelnau Glacier.

From West Elk Pass head west up the boundary cutline towards Mt. Fox. A few metres beyond '1M' monument, turn left at a signpost. The trail crosses bog on boardwalk and makes a gradual climb to the east shore of Fox Lake. While chiefly of interest as a watering hole, it does have a rather fine backdrop in Mt. Fox. You can distinguish the cirque holding Frozen Lake and to its left the large, grassy hill known as Taiga Viewpoint.

Continue up the trail to its high point at the 1.5 km mark, then start the descent to Upper Elk Lake. Glades allow fine views looking down the Elk Valley. Cross a creek with deliciously icy water, and lower down a wide, grassy avalanche gully where grizzlies are often spotted. OK, don't panic. I just thought I'd warn you this is probably not a good place for a picnic. The trail at this point has been rebuilt following a thorough mashing by trees toppled in the 1991 avalanche.

Nearing trail's end, you cross a talus slope and are treated to a view of Upper Elk Lake backdropped by Elkan Peak and the Castelnau Glacier to the right of Mt. McCuaig. Cross the bridge over the Elk River at the outlet and join route #94.

Turn left for Lower Elk Lake and the park entrance, right for Pétain backcountry campground, Pétain Falls and Pétain Basin.

Pétain Falls.

94 ELK LAKES TO PÉTAIN FALLS — map 16

Day hike from park entrance, backpack
Official trails
**Distance 1.6 km to Lower Lake, 3.2 km
to Upper Elk Lake, 5 km to Pétain
Creek backcountry campground, 7 km
to Pétain Falls**
Height gain to falls 244 m
High point at falls 1981 m
Map 82 J/11 Kananaskis Lakes

*Below: Lower Elk Lake
backdropped by the triad of Mts.
McCuaig, Nivelle and Castelnau.
Below Elkan Peak (centre right) is
The Viewpoint with facing cliff.*

Access:
Via road: Elk Lakes Provincial Park entrance at the end of Elk Valley road. Start from Highway 3 on the B.C. side of Crowsnest Pass. At Sparwood turn north on Highway 43 and drive 35 km to Elkford. Continue up the unpaved Elk River Road, a further 72 km of very rough driving. At the end keep left into the parking lot.
On foot: from Kananaskis Country. See #91, #92 and #93.

This is the easy main valley trail. Make of it what you will; a stroll to Lower Elk Lake with a side trip to the viewpoint, a full day hike to Pétain Falls (the most spectacular waterfall in this book), or as access to tougher trails climbing into the cirques.

To Lower Elk Lake The trail leaves the parking lot opposite the Park Entrance camping area, an entirely unofficial site with no biffy. (Sadly, the habitable cabin built by 'Old Man' Phillips was razed by three drunken snowmobilers in 1989. Too drafty to contemplate is the remaining Baher cabin built in 1943 by hunting guide Mike Baher, who built a string of cabins up and down the Elk River and into Cadorna Creek.)

Walk past the bulletin board, turn right—park headquarters ahead—and descend to meadows. Cross a small creek to the junction with route #92 to West Elk Pass. Keep straight. The main trail crosses Elkan Creek and its meadows, then runs

alongside the Elk River (a rushing glacier-fed stream emanating updrafts of icy cold air) to Lower Elk Lake. This tranquil body of water is sheltered from westerly blasts by a high wall of forest, the highest bump with cliff being The Viewpoint. To the south is fabulous Mt. Aosta, built on Gothic architectural lines.

A boardwalk takes you along the north shore past Lower Elk Lake backcountry campground to the inlet, crossed on newly built bridges. On the west bank of the Elk turn right for Upper Elk Lake, stay left for The Viewpoint.

To Upper Elk Lake The trail more or less follows the southwest bank of the Elk River to the junction with route #93 near the outlet. Keep left and arrive at Upper Elk Lake. Your attention is riveted on Mt. Fox across the water, from this direction an awesome precipice cleft by gullies and knife-edge ridges. See photo above.

The trail **to Pétain Creek backcountry campground** follows the east shoreline. The lake is two kilometres long and fjord-like, squeezed between the forest wall on the left and precipitous slabby slopes on the right, which rise over a thousand metres to the ridge between Elkan Peak and Mt. Foch. It's one of those places improved by a rain. Layers of clouds trailing across the flanks hide starting points of dozens of rills that burst into life and pour in parallel lines down the sodden slabs. At such times the trail tends to be inundated by rising water levels.

Once past the lake crunch along gravel outwash plain to Pétain Creek backcountry campground on the left, the starting place for Coral Pass (#96).

For Pétain Falls cross the bridge over the Elk and continue in much the same way as before along the west bank. Round the bend in a belt of spruce. You break out of the trees and stand spellbound by the scene of not one but many falls plummeting down the cliffs from Pétain Basin. For clarity I call this Pétain Falls viewpoint. For a closer look of the lowest, highest falls, stay left and tramp through meadows, in season a golden carpet of glacier lilies. Crossing Pétain Creek isn't too healthy. Poised above your head like the sword of Damocles is the snout of Castelnau Glacier. Pieces break off regularly with loud bangs that scare the hell out of you and can be heard from as far away as the park entrance!

OPTION
The Viewpoint 1865 m GR348012, 3 km return to junction, 134 m height gain. A worthwhile short day alternative.

From the junction on the west bank of the Elk River, the trail follows the west shore of Lower Elk Lake. At a bay the official trail turns right and, climbing steadily, approaches the summit of the knoll from the back side. On your right is a drop-off and another at the summit facing east, so keep an eye on the kids and the dog. The best view is of Lower Elk Lake and the Elk Valley fading away to the south.

95 PÉTAIN BASIN — map 16

Day scramble from Pétain Creek
campground
Unofficial trail & route, creek crossing
Distance 2 km from Pétain Falls
Height gain 366 m
High point 2347 m
Map 82 J/11 Kananaskis Lakes

Pétain Basin, looking across to Pétain Glacier and Castelnau Glacier (far left). Mts. Castelnau and Nivelle at centre. Photo Clive Cordery.

Access: Via #94 at Pétain Falls viewpoint.

This is one tough climb, a relentlessly steep climber's access trail to the south side of Mt. Joffre. Expect some easy scrambling with no exposure, and snow in the upper basin.

Follow the right-hand trail into some trees. Cross a gully and start up the headwall, a tortuous crawl up vertical bush on the left edge of the gully. In your desperation you'll be glad to haul yourself up with anything at hand; branches, roots, even gooseberry bushes. The terrain eases fractionally at some fallen trees (rest), then continues in much the same sort of way as before. Three quarters of the height gain behind you, scramble up a grassy rib (left of the avalanche gully) that leads into a narrow stony channel between bushes. Ascend the channel for only a few metres before branching left towards a small cairn marking the beginning of the traverse.

Traverse left across grass below talus slopes, then rock bands. The trail descends slightly to the base of a two-tiered buttress that you climb to a cairn. Possibly easier routes can be found to the right; certainly harder variations exist to the left. Topping out into the basin, head left to where Pétain Creek shoots out into space. Pétain Basin backcountry campground is located across the creek *on the edge* and is more safely reached by a lengthy upstream detour below another waterfall.

Now for the secrets of the basin. The lake below the glacier is reached by a circuitous scree scrabble between cliff bands. Similarly, skirt cliffs to gain the basin proper, a heady mix of flowery meadows and outcrops scored by rillenkarren. Low down you'll run into a couple of tarns and the artesian spring dubbed 'Fountain of Youth'. From a high vantage point only 380 vertical metres below the summit of Mt. Foch the view of Pétain Glacier is spectacular.

96 CORAL PASS — map 16

**Day scramble from Pétain Creek campground
Unofficial trail, route, creek crossings
Distance 5.5 km to pass
Height gain 780 m
High point 2515 m
Maps 82 J/11 Kananaskis Lakes,
82 J/6 Mt. Abruzzi**

Above: nearing Coral Pass. View back to the Elk Glacier and Mt. Nivelle.

Right: the headwall from Nivelle Creek. The route climbs the forested slope to the left of Nivelle Canyon, winding between rock bands. Start to the left of the lowest band.

Inset: the crux.

Access: Via #94 at Pétain Creek backcountry campground.

Of all the hikes I've had to do for this book, this was one of the most horrible because we didn't start from the campground at Pétain Creek and it was pelting with rain both going up and going down the headwall. At the time it seemed far worse than the grunt up to Pétain Basin. This is definitely one for the experienced. Route-finding is tricky, particularly on the descent. Expect creek crossings, steep B.C.

bush, snow and a few metres of scrambling. Warning! When we were there, the route was marked by flagging, but don't depend on it being there. The reward for all this trauma is wild untrammelled uplands and the most spectacular fossil beds you have ever seen (hence the name Coral).

Slightly upstream of the bridge over Pétain Creek, at some yellow flagging, a trail heads south into the forest and is good until you cross a small creek. After this follow what is probably an old river channel leading straight to Nivelle Creek. Blocking the way ahead is a headwall with no easy way up. Don't even think of following the canyon choked by snow. We chose the forested slope just left of the canyon, which appears quite innocuous. It certainly fooled us. First, gain the bottom of the headwall at GR329982 (small meadow). It's your call. Either pick your way along the left bank (bushes, rotting logs), or wade Nivelle Creek and recross the by now turbulent creek just above the bend on a snow bridge.

Headwall You're going to be looking for signs of struggle with the vegetation. Start left of the lower cliff, wending left initially, then crawl straight up under menziesia bushes. Angle and bushes ease as you approach the middle cliff band. Here, turn right, following the rising base of the rock. It gets quite steep and when the cliff ends it's a straight-up thrutch to a terrace for a brief respite.

Resume climbing, wending left below a small crag and up to a strip of meadow running below the top cliff band. At a 'T-junction', traverse right on a trail halfway between the trees and the bottom of the cliff. This trail leads to the one place where you can break through the cliff at its lowest point, right at the angle of the north and west-facing facets. Climb a five metre-

high grungy groove, a bit difficult to start but handholds are good. Next up is the crux traverse high above the canyon. Just as the situation becomes airy, the trail turns uphill and dissipates on easy ground. I need hardly tell you it's essential you hit this traverse line on the descent. I mean, who wants to return via Cadorna Creek and the Elk River!

The final slope is easy going through forest, flats alternating with steps. The trail reappears at the top of the slope and heads slightly right and downhill through forest and meadow to Nivelle Creek, which is reached about 300 metres back from the lip of the canyon.

Just below the right-angled bend at GR327968 cross to the west bank and follow a trail alongside the river into larch and meadow country. Emanating from the upper canyon ahead is the thunder of waterfalls. The trail climbs above the first fall,

View from Coral Pass of Mt. Battisti, one of the three giants of Nyahe-ya-Nibi.

then heads off up the hillside. Level with a crag on the left, keep left in the open. Above the crag turn left onto a good traversing trail that peters out in meadow not far above the confluence at GR323967. This is a heavenly spot, bright green grass and flowers a startling contrast to the glitter of glacier, névé and rushing stream.

To Coral Pass (GR318956) Wade Nivelle Creek. As you climb out of meadows onto rock the lie of the land becomes clear. You're in a huge basin rimmed by a semicircle of ridges draped with permanent snow. To your right the Elk Glacier sticks out a white tongue between Mts. 'Gamelin', Nivelle and 'De Gaulle'. Farthest away, the low point in the ridge is Coral Pass.

Rock ribbons streaming towards you offer obvious ascent routes. However, crags immediately below the pass make a direct approach impossible. We gained the pass from the right and exited on the left via the scree ramp. Whatever route you decide on, you're sure to run into a huge fossil bed several kilometres square where horn coral is scattered all over the rock like grass seed.

Just a reminder not to pick. Just as exciting for me was the karst we encountered on our descent route, which extends across to the meadows and down into the trees. Dropping into one sinkhole and popping out another can give you hours of childish fun.

But I've got ahead of myself. At the pass you're looking into what George Pocaterra always referred to by its Stoney name 'Nyahe-ya-Nibi' meaning 'Go-up-into-the-mountains country': Cadorna Creek (the lake is out of sight) and the "three giants of Nyahe-ya-Nibi", Mts. Cadorna, Swiderski and Battisti. Beyond Mt. Cadorna is the fabled Pass in the Clouds which has retained its name all the years since Walter Wilcox's famous crossing in 1901. Pocaterra and Raymond Patterson's attempt was stymied by bad weather and it was only later that Patterson traversed the pass from the White River end in an incredible solo trek covering vast distances. Not only is the pass fabled, it's remote. Even from the Elk River and with the aid of bikes (there's a cutline up Cadorna and Abruzzi Creeks) it was for us, once again, a return trip in complete darkness. After viewing our photos, Donnie Gardner skied over the pass en route to Disneyland, which is not a route I would have taken myself.

Directly across Cadorna Creek is a grassy mountain with horizontal cliffs called Misty Mountain by old-timers. The day after crossing the pass, Walter Wilcox and Henry Bryant climbed to the summit and saw this gap. "Aha, a shortcut to the Kananaskis Lakes", they thought. They returned to camp and the whole packtrain moved down Abruzzi Creek and up Cadorna Creek to where the trail petered out. Wilcox carried on alone, climbing a hillside to view Cadorna Lake and with field glasses pressed to his eyes noted "no trail led up to the pass", so he assumed the valley was a cul-de-sac and the party retreated down to the Elk River. Just as well; they'd have had a terrible time lowering packhorses down the headwall.

Opposite: Upper Kananaskis Lake, east shore.

97 UPPER (KANANASKIS) LAKE CIRCUIT — map 16

Day hike
Official trail with signposts
Distance 16.5 km loop
Height gain 60 m
High point 1783 m
Map 82 J/11 Kananaskis Lakes

Access: Kananaskis Lakes Trail (Hwy.).
1. North Interlakes parking lot. Walk down to the trailhead at the signboard.
2. Upper Lake day-use area, a complicated collection of parking lots. Keep left (boat launch to right), keep right, turn next right into parking lots nearest the lake. For south shore trail, turn left and drive to the far end. For east shore trail turn right.
3. White Spruce parking lot. From the start of Canadian Mt. Everest Expedition interpretive trail (hereafter known as CMEEIT), a wide track climbs to the dam.
Also accessible from routes #98, 99 & 106.

"A revelation of beauty hardly equalled anywhere... has four large islands and several small islets, all densely wooded, which give an endless variety of views from various points", said Walter Wilcox in 1901. "A scene of wreckage to be shunned or hurriedly passed by en route to the Palliser", said Raymond Patterson post reservoir. "Nobody in their right mind would willingly visit the place now as an object of a trip".

He was wrong, but knowing nothing better we continue to come to the heart of K Country. Who can resist circumventing a lake? Each shore is totally different in character to the other and presents different views. This trail also serves as access to Rawson Lake, Aster Lake and as alternate access to Three Isle Lake trail.

The circuit is described anticlockwise from North Interlakes parking lot.

Lower Kananaskis Falls.

North Shore 4.7 km Follow Three Isle Lake trail along the isthmus and cross the intake pipe by bridge, noting North Interlakes Power Plant down below at Lower Kananaskis Lake. Swing left onto the fire road. Almost straightaway Indefatigable trail turns off to the right. In another half kilometre turn left off the fire road onto a soft forest trail running along the shoreline within sound of the slap of waves. Off shore is Hawke Island, its few scraggy larch trees a sad remnant of those "small islets, all densely wooded". In about 1.5 km the trail climbs into the blinding glare of a large boulder field where craftily constructed steps facilitate passage across its humps and hollows. If this doesn't appeal an escape trail climbs to the fire road at this point.

While still in the boulder field, now disguised by a sparse covering of vegetation and trees, the spur trail to North Point backcountry campground turns off to the left, servicing 20 sites scattered up and down the peninsula. The main trail continues past a stony basin of viridian green water so still and clear it looks like glass. A few minutes later you contour around the head of a deep inlet and turn up the east bank of the Kananaskis River, at this point a boisterous stream culminating in Lower Kananaskis Falls. Cross the river above the falls and in a couple of minutes reach the junction with Lyautey. Turn left.

West/South Shore 8 km Initially, the word 'shore' is a misnomer. The trail lies so deep in forest you're without views unless you count cliffs glimpsed from time to time above the treetops. Begin with an uphill and two kilometres later hit the Hidden Lake turnoff (no signpost). Keep left.

The trail drops to the lakeshore at an islet and stays there for the rest of the way to Upper Lake parking lots. It's a quite boring plod below strangely menacing spruce forest, which to the imaginative harbours a grizzly behind every tree. In 1883 the fledgling Eau Claire and Bow River Lumber Company hungered after these trees, but stayed only long enough to name the lake Ingram after C. H. Ingram Associates, who'd advanced capital for the trip from Wisconsin. Luckily, the name didn't catch on. Points of interest? Mt. Indefatigable across the lake, a rowan tree at the bottom of the avalanche gully, Rawson Lake trail, and Sarrail Creek waterfall. The final kilometre undulates in and out of every indent to the southernmost Upper Lake parking lot.

East Shore 3.6 km Walk through to the northernmost parking lot where the trail continues. Cross a bridge at interpretive signs, then cross the boat launch road onto Upper Lake Dam. I loathe walking along the dam. It reminds me of all the beautiful features I won't see, like Twin Falls instead of a pathetic little canal carrying seepage. At dam's end the track from White Spruce parking lot joins in from the right and you wend left across a grassy 'bay'. In the trees, a side trail to the left leads to the chimney on the point, all that's left of Geoffrey Gaherty's honeymoon cabin.

Finally you gain the east shore which is characterized by rocky headlands and the half-moon curve of bays. When strong west winds send waves racing across the lake to break with a thump on the shore, it's easy to imagine yourself by some inlet of the ocean. Heightening that impression are terraces of shingle shaped by someone hitting a computer key. Across the water Mt. Sarrail and the Mt. Lyautey massif fall in great precipices, while farther away the distinctive shape of Mt. Putnik is revealed through the gap of the Kananaskis River.

For all the fine scenery the east leg is a depressing section to walk. When the plug's out, the bones of the drowned forest are exposed and offshore islets seen once again as headlands of the former shoreline. The deeply indented bay next to the treed 'island' joined to the mainland by a causeway of stumps was once a lake. Near here archaeologists recovered a few prehistoric flakes. The biggest find was in Lower Kananaskis Lake, across the isthmus at Interlakes campground. Unfortunately, at high water the artifacts are covered to a depth of 16 metres.

At the halfway point the trail comes close to the highway (old road connection), then continues around what's left of a promontory, a splendid viewpoint 50 years ago for a half dozen islands that crowded this half of the lake. Schooner lay about half a kilometre out, a boat-shaped island whose few trees were so arranged to resemble the masts of a sailing ship. On windy days, the dash of spray against the rocks gave the illusion it was the island itself that was moving.

All that remains is to turn into a large artificial bay, completing the loop when you reach Three Isle Lake trailhead. Turn right for North Interlakes parking lot.

98 LYAUTEY — map 16

Day hike, backpack
Official trail
Distance 2.2 km
Height gain/loss 31 m
High point 1750 m
Map 82 J/11 Kananaskis Lakes

Access:
1. Via Upper Lake trail (#97).
2. Via Three Isle Lake trail (#99).

A connector, which can be coupled with Upper Lake trail (north shore section) to provide an alternate start to Three Isle Lake trail (#99). The distance isn't much greater, the scenery incomparably finer.

From access 1 Upstream of the junction the Kananaskis River is very much quieter, welling over its banks into the forest and necessitating the use of boardwalks and bridges. A drier area with sandbars and low-lying willow bushes allows you to enjoy the view. The trail then moves away from the river and climbs across an avalanche slope, up and over a forested ridge to the junction with Three Isle Lake trail.

99 THREE ISLE LAKE & SOUTH KANANASKIS PASS — maps 16 & 15

Long day hike, backpack
Official trail
Distance 6.7 km to forks, 10.2 km to
lake, 13 km to pass
Height gain to lake 490 m,
to pass 626 m
High point near lake 2200 m
High point at pass 2306 m
Map 82 J/11 Kananaskis Lakes

*Below: Three Isle Lake, looking
southeast towards peak GR228087.*

Access: Kananaskis Lakes Trail (Hwy.) at North Interlakes parking lot. Walk down to the trailhead (signboard).
Also accessible from #100, #101 & #107.

Three Isle Lake is the most popular destination of all the trails radiating out from Upper Kananaskis Lake. Although you can hike there and back in one long day, it is far, far better to backpack in for a long weekend and spend time looking around some fantastic high country. Despite 'improvements', the headwall still exacts its pound of sweat. Consider biking the fire road section to Invincible Creek.

To Forks Head north across the isthmus and cross the intake pipe by bridge. Swing left onto the fire road which is a boring stony track and gives you sore feet. If someone were to start a ferry service across Upper Kananaskis Lake, I'd be the first to get in line. But since that hasn't happened, keep left at Indefatigable trail junction, and in half a kilometre keep right again unless you elect to follow the Upper Lake/Lyautey combo which is nearly two kilometres longer. In case you change your mind there's a cutoff at km 2.2. This occurs at the Palliser Slide where a big chunk of Mt. Indefatigable collapsed and rolled to the north shore.

Turning your back to the lake, plod stonily on to Invincible Creek, which is where you leave the fire road. Turn left and cross the creek. After what's gone before, walking a soft forest trail under the cool canopy of climax forest is heaven. Somewhere among the spruce is a stand of Alberta's oldest lodgepole pines which sprang from seed after a fire in 1586. To put it into perspective, this occurred during the reign of England's Elizabeth I, just a year before Mary Queen of Scots was executed.

Cross the Kananaskis River by a fine log bridge just upstream of Upper Kananaskis Falls. A few minutes later the T-junction with Lyautey is reached at the 5 km mark. Turn right.

The trail stays within earshot of the noisy river, at one point crossing the bottom of a talus slope with a view of Mt. Putnik, and a more distant one of the headwall below Three Isle Lake with Mt. Worthington peeping over the top. On your left you pass a bewildering array of cliffs and towering peaks that are all part and parcel of Mt. Lyautey. A wonderfully clear spring bridged by the trail is the best place to fill up the water bottles, because the next creek (Three Isle) is milky from glaciers and so is the Kananaskis River. In the shadow of Mt. Putnik the two rivers meet and the trail splits. Forks backcountry campground, located in the angle, is a logical place for refueling, attending to blisters, etc.

To Three Isle Lake Turn left at the trail division and climb steadily along the north bank of Three Isle Creek through monster Engelmann spruce. At GR236097 the valley turns a right-angle, aiming for the glaciers of Mt. Northover. The trail, however, continues due west towards a lacy waterfall, the resurgence of Three Isle Lake. It's here where you start up the headwall, a bushy avalanche slope turning to scree as you near the first rock band. Rather disappointingly, the scramble has been replaced by tiers of wooden steps not quite up to the standard of Lawrence Grassi who would have built a staircase out of rocks. Thereafter, the trail threads an ingenious path between rock

bands: a long traverse to the right, eight short zigs straight up, a long traverse left, another to the right and you're at the top.

Drop 30 vertical metres down a draw to the lake. At a split go left for the lakeshore and right for Three Isle Lake backcountry campground. A little farther on you cross a creek and climb to Three Isle Creek backcountry campground which has lake view lots available.

The headwall below Three Isle Lake.

I have a confession to make. I don't find Three Isle Lake beautiful. The shoreline reminds me too much of a reservoir. And I have yet to find the third isle! The setting is undeniably grand, though, with Mt. Worthington presiding at the head.

You're settled in the campsite and looking for places to go. Three suggestions for all level of hikers follow in the next few pages. Another possibility is route #107, a stroll up the side valley or a scree scrabble to the col at GR221065 for a fabulous view of the Royal Group framed between Mts. Defender and Onslow.

South Kananaskis Pass 2306 m

Distance 2.8 km, height gain 125 m. An easy stroll to a pass of no historic significance.

From the campgrounds the official trail continues along the north side of Three Isle Lake, at times following the shoreline of bays. Ahead is the bulwark of Mt. Worthington and to its right the little scree summit climbed as an option from the pass. Looking across the lake, ridge walkers will be motivated by an end-to-end view of Northover Ridge showing its glaciated aspect

From the west end of the lake the trail turns right, the lake quickly lost to view as you climb steadily through trees to South Kananaskis Pass at the demarcation of meadow. A signpost marks the Great Divide.

Nearing South Kananaskis Pass from the B.C. side. The mountain trimmed with glaciers is Northover Ridge.

OPTIONS FROM THE PASS

Beatty Lake add 2 km one way from pass, height loss 122 m.

From South Kananaskis Pass an unofficial trail carries on into B.C., making a gradual descent through meadows to a gem of a lake—much nicer than Three Isle. As you can see by the photo on page 223, it's rimmed by spruce and larch, and enclosed on the south side by a high craggy wall.

Climb grassy slopes to the east for the classic view of the lake backdropped by pointy Mt. Prince Edward and glacial Mt. Queen Mary. If you have time I recommend the col at GR201137 on the southwest ridge of Mt. Beatty, which is a superb vantage point for the pass and for LeRoy Creek seen flowing out of the Haig Icefield. Down below you can spot the trail to North Kananaskis Pass. In good conditions scramblers used to atrociously loose rock can descend the north slope to the trail. It may cut the corner off but it's no shortcut.

Royal Group Viewpoint 2798 m loop 6 km, traverse 9 km, height gain 497 m. Although the peak at GR193107 is a modest summit compared to everything else around, you'll be ecstatic at the views it reveals of the Royal Group. While the traverse to Beatty Lake can be done in a half day by starting before dawn, a full day is recommended if you don't want to return to the parking lot looking like a dropout from the Iron Man triathlon. The suggested loop is a ridge walk with some easy scrambling and mild exposure. Missing out the first part of the ridge does away with the exposure. Either way, you've got to be familiar with loose rubble and adept at routefinding.

To the col Head up steepening meadows on the west side of the pass. The aim is to gain the cirque north of Mt. Worthington, which means that at some point high up on the grass you're going to have to traverse left. When you hit a draw follow it up to the lip. The feeling is one of total astonishment at the scene in front of you. Once again the topo map is wildly wrong and any idea you may have of a simple scramble to the top of Worthington or McHarg is shattered by glaciers plastering the entire north face. Due west beyond a bewildering mess of moraines and bedrock your summit rises in an ungainly heap of scree. In between the two and presently out of sight, lurks the col at GR196095, your next objective.

When the draw you're in starts to go downhill, haul yourself out of it onto the moraine to its left (hoofprints) and head off in the direction of the col. Wend slightly left, keeping the draw to your right. When this particular pile of moraine ends tackle a low rock step to the right. Sidestep the step above by a weakness further to the right. Enter a second draw likely covered by nevé. Now if you want to forego the ridge walk, and this *is also the usual descent route* from peak GR193107, follow the draw to its end, then climb diagonally right, taking whatever line appeals between slabs, to gain the east ridge above steps. Finish up easy rubble.

If game for the ridge walk, climb the sharp-edged moraine to the left of the draw. It ends below a higher, steeper step, a scree-covered ramp offering the only way into the basin below the col. Traverse up left below a welter of slabs, watching for some nasty tottery boulders at the mid point that require the light touch. If you get mashed and have to be rescued by helicopter Kiwi will have my head, so be extra careful!

On gaining the basin, walk left. As the slope rises follow rock ribs, then low-angle nevé to the col. Perhaps you'll be thinking tuna salad sandwiches and a sit down and be totally unprepared for the stunning view. Unlike other Royal Group viewpoints, this lofty col is perfectly located for looking straight down the Palliser River. Bounded on the left by the great wall of the Divide and on the right by tier upon tier of cliffs capped by the superb Royal Group, is a view almost as sacred to view specialists as Mt. Assiniboine.

I have never understood why, when Walter Wilcox's party went down the Palliser River from Palliser Pass in 1901, he made no mention of the Royal Group. I can only assume they were so intent on finding the trail up to North Kananaskis Pass they never looked to see what was to the right. So it was left to George Pocaterra in 1911 to climb several hundred feet above South Kananaskis Pass and look across the Palliser River to "a country of burnt timber and hanging glaciers". So impressed was he, when he got back to Buffalo Head Ranch he contacted the Geographer General about his discovery and sent photos. In 1913 the Boundary Survey were sent into the area (Wheeler claiming first discovery) and on their return, the Geographer General wrote Pocaterra asking him to give the group an Indian name. Since he knew an "Indian name would be cruelly mutilated", he advised an English name. As luck would have it the number of peaks coincided with the members of Britain's Royal Family. Though if I'd been Prince George I'd have complained at being given a sub-standard peak you can walk up. Prince Albert, of course, became George VI on the

Above: A composite of three photos showing the sweeping view of the Palliser River valley from col GR196095. On the far left is the great wall of the Continental Divide. To right, the Royal Group rising above the Royal Valley.

Below: Photo taken from below the final pull up to peak GR193107. Looking back to col GR196095 (centre) above the nevé. To its left is glacier-hung Mt. McHarg. The route follows the ridge around from the col.

abdication of Edward who owned the EP Ranch near Longview for a staggering 43 years. Other tidbits: the first and second ascents of King George (V) took place 52 years apart and American climbing legend Fred Beckey was the first to climb the icy north face of Queen Mary.

Ridge traverse to peak GR193107 From the col the entire ridge to the unnamed summit is revealed. Nevé reaches almost to the ridgeline of the first section, which is occasionally scrambly, narrow and exposed. If necessary, cut it out by returning to the bottom of the basin and walking up a ramp the other side to rejoin the ridge beyond at GR195099. After this the going is easy, though the final approach to the summit is steeper than it appears and requires a harder effort up fine scree. Top out at two cairns.

Some of the new things you can see are the Royal Valley, Tipperary Lake, Mt. Assiniboine, Palliser Pass slung between Mt. King Albert and Mt. Sir Douglas, and farther to the right the pocket handkerchief of the Haig Icefield. Some might say the best view is of Three Isle Lake.

Descend the rubble of the east ridge to a saddle above the first step, then pick your way down right into the upper draw where you join the ascent route to the col. Don't try and follow the east ridge all the way.

The traverse to Beatty Lake is not quite as straightforward as you might think. To avoid steep nevé head down the east ridge a short distance before cutting left onto the broad north ridge. Lower down, curve right with the strata into the bottom of a basin. Three hundred vertical metres above the lake and you're stymied by cliffs! Traverse right until stopped by another line of cliffs rising to the east ridge! The first time we did this route we were a little worried by this point. But all is well. A ridge drops towards the lake, unravelling beautifully in little rock steps and grassy platforms. Low down, drop off into the small valley on the right (meadows, larches) and head north on game trail into the spruce to—another drop-off. Far below is a glimpse of blue water. By walking right you'll find obstacle-free grassy slopes descending to the east shore. Now for a swim!

100 SOUTH KANANASKIS PASS TO NORTH KANANASKIS PASS VIA LEROY CREEK — map 15

Backpack
Unofficial trails, creek crossings
Distance 10.5 km
Height gain S-N 738 m
Height loss S-N 655 m
High point 2368 m
Map 82 J/11 Kananaskis Lakes

Access:
South Via Three Isle Lake trail at South Kananaskis Pass (#99).
North Via Lawson Lake trail at North Kananaskis Pass (#101).

On the B.C. side it's possible to traverse from one Kananaskis Pass to the other without dropping all the way to the Palliser River. Except for one section, the old Indian trails are in fairly good shape. Nevertheless, this is still a strenuous trip, in parts rocky, bushy and steep, with a humongous height gain coming at the end of the day.

To LeRoy Creek From South Kananaskis Pass a trail continues through meadows to Beatty Lake, spectacularly located near the edge of a drop-off. Cross the outlet and turn right with the creek, shortly entering a *dry* canyon bed, Beatty Creek having sunk underground in the meantime. The nice, safe canyon ends cold turkey above a steep rockslide down which the trail picks a tenuous line into the wild middle reaches of Beatty Creek. Here, rockfall has created a miniature 'valley of rocks', a cataclysmic mix of trees, boulders, sinks and tiny blue tarns. Amongst the chaos Beatty Creek resurges into the light of day.

Drop-off number two is supposedly unassailable, although I did hear of a mad mountain biker downclimbing the route with the bike wrapped around his neck. The trail gets around this impasse by *ascending* the hillside to your right onto the flat shoulder (GR177133) of the mountain above Beatty Lake. The terrain funnels you

to the escarpment edge for useful views of Palliser Pass and your objective.

The descent to LeRoy Creek is the worst part of the trip. You're almost certain to lose the trail in some horrible over-the-head willow bush. Not surprisingly, another trail has developed over the years, one that traverses right (northeast) to an avalanche slope offering a more reasonable descent to the creek. Either way, cross LeRoy Creek and pick up an excellent trail on the northwest bank. Turn right.

To North Kananaskis Pass At bend GR188148 is a trail junction. Turn right, recross the creek to the east bank and begin a gradual climb away from the river. As soon as you've crossed the tributary arising from the pass, the trail steepens dramatically and climbs straight up the tributary's left bank on a grass and talus mix. The situation grows in magnificence and no excuse is needed for stops to admire the Royal Group framed between the canyon-like walls of LeRoy Creek. Near the top the trail crosses to the right bank. Nowadays the creekbed carries hardly more than a trickle, but before landslides blocked Maude Lake's exit to the west, the white rushing water and waterfalls must have been a fine sight.

Unlike the south pass, North Kananaskis Pass is a bleak ridge of tundra slung between Mts. Beatty and Maude. With the view behind past its best you may as well head down a line of cairns towards Maude Lake and pick up route #101. As you descend, you're treated to a fabulous view of the Beatty Glacier as shown on pages 4 and 5.

Bottom: View from the shoulder of Palliser Pass bounded by Mt. Queen Elizabeth (left) and pointy Mt. Williams to right.

Top: Beatty Lake backdropped by the Royal Group. Left to right: Prince Edward, Prince Henry, Prince John and Queen Mary. Photo Alf Skrastins.

101 LAWSON LAKE & NORTH KANANASKIS PASS — maps 15 & 10

Backpack
Official trail
15.2 km to Turbine Canyon campground from trailhead, 17 km to pass
Height gain from trailhead to campground 530 m, to pass 670 m
High point at campground 2240 m, at pass 2368 m
Map 82 J/11 Kananaskis Lakes

Access: Kananaskis Lakes Trail (Hwy.) at North Interlakes parking lot. Via Three Isle Lake trail (#99) at the forks.
Also accessible from #100.

In October 1854 some 100 men, women and children urged on by James Sinclair were struggling over 'Mackipictoon's secret pass', walking their horses and stumbling over boulders made treacherous by a heavy fall of snow. This new route for Red River immigrants under the Oregon Emigrating Scheme elicited such comments as "our rascally guide took us by a pass over the mountains (known only by himself) which he represented as the best and the shortest (30 days instead of the usual 10)", and "altogether it is the worst road I ever travelled".

Mackipictoon (or Mas-ke-pe-toon), known as Broken Arm because of a conspicuous infirmity, was a very great Cree warrior of ungovernable temper. Miffed because Hudson's Bay boss Sir George Simpson had not engaged him to lead his party over Simpson Pass, he inveigled chief trader James Sinclair into trying a new route over the Rockies, faster even than the White Man Pass he had shown him a few years earlier. Unfortunately, when they got to Kananaskis Lakes the Cree admitted he was lost and Sinclair was forced to take over the role of guide as well as leader, so who knows where they really went?

Incidentally, if any filmmaker is reading this, Sinclair (Brad Pitt) was "brave, restless, ambitious", and constantly at odds with the rather pompous Simpson (An-

thony Hopkins). Only two years later, in the Columbia River valley, he was killed while trying to save a party of American settlers besieged by Snake Indians. The survivors were about to take a boat into the rapids and perish together rather than under the cruel hand of the Indians when, like in all good westerns, help arrived in the nick of time. Too late for Sinclair, of course, who was finally thinking of settling down with his family to farm.

You know, if it hadn't been for this trip it's unlikely the Palliser Expedition would ever have travelled up the Kananaskis Valley and it would be called something completely different like Eau Claire, Thorpe or Ingram (now there's a thought). Anyway, in 1858 Cptn. John Palliser and party apparently crossed the pass in search of a southern trade route across the Rockies. I say 'apparently' because there's a move afoot, spearheaded by Longview's Larry Boyd, to show that Palliser took another route. Actually the description fits reasonably well apart from a few strange discrepancies like the summit lake flowing to the Pacific and the omission of Lawson Lake. They apparently camped at the forks, at the "foot of a cone-shaped mountain, the northerly one of a pair of conspicuous mountains flanking the height of land they were to cross". If this means Mt. Putnik and the equally shapely outlier of Mt. Lyautey, then they went up South Kananaskis Pass which is neither easy nor above treeline. On the other hand, his altimeter reading of 5,985 feet correlates closely to the height of Elk Pass. Strangely, the John Jones Overlanders intended going

Lawson Lake backdropped by the twin summits of Mt. Maude (left), the Haig Glacier and Mt. Jellicoe. Photo Clive Cordery.

over North Kananaskis Pass in 1859 using the sketchmap given them by James Hector, but most people are agreed they went over the Elk (although, as mentioned previously, I think it was the Highwood).

If only all these people had taken an artist along!

In 1901 Walter Wilcox couldn't even find the pass from the Palliser River end and finally arrived at Kananaskis Lakes via Pass in the Clouds and Elk Pass. He decided to pay the missed pass a one day flying visit and fell prey to one of Palliser's discrepancies, as you'll read. In July 1916 the Boundary Commission's Richard Cautley, alone and on snowshoes, reached the pass after many attempts and determined once and for all that it was absolutely useless as a route through the mountains. Since then the old Indian trail has seen spasmodic use, a faint revival occurring in the 1960s and '70s with the growth of a new breed called backpackers.

When K Country took over the trail was upgraded and realigned at the avalanche slope, destined to be trodden by a torrent of grateful hikers and skiers clad in GoreTex and Spandex. You can make the pass every time. Don't emulate Wilcox, though. A long weekend is recommended for seeing the sights. And it's still a tedious pull to treeline but astonishingly easy after that.

To Turbine Canyon Head up the right-hand fork for about 20 minutes of riverside walking. Just after the waterfall, start a tedious climb up and across wide, steep avalanche slopes covered in head-high willows and alders that have a permanent downhill lean from the weight of the winter snowpack. Reenter forest and climb some more to the stream exiting the cirque between Mt. Putnik and 'Razor Flakes'. Cross and drag yourself up a final set of switchbacks to treeline.

The payoff for all the hard work is kilometres of joyous wandering along an almost level bench through meadows and larches. The Haig Glacier comes into view ahead, enclosed by mountains shaped like battleships. A tarn is where Walter Wilcox and packer Jim Wood lunched in 1901 and where Wilcox went on alone and on foot, telling Wood he'd be back in an hour. Wood probably said, "Oh sure". A little farther on, the trail descends slightly to beautiful Lawson Lake, named by Wilcox who thought at first it was the lake at the pass.

The trail follows the west shore, then descends past the ranger cabin to Maude Brook. Cross to a T-junction on the north bank. Back at Lawson Lake in 1901, a perplexed Wilcox, though realizing his hour was up, was determined to find the wretched pass and after divesting himself of his field glasses, and later on his jacket,

then his camera on various "scrubby spruces", broke into a run down the hill "splashing through an icy stream" with no time to see what lay downstream. Nowadays, a right turn leads past Turbine Canyon backcountry campground to the dizzying brink of Turbine Canyon, where Maude Brook and a stream from Haig Glacier moraines join and drop into an abyss. Supposedly it can be jumped across in one or two places as it twists its way down 330 m of hillside to the Upper Kananaskis River.

North Kananaskis Pass 2368 m

2.2 km from campground, height gain 128 m. An easy walk from the campground on official trail.

Head west from the T-junction on the north bank of Maude Brook. The trail gains height slowly through alternating meadow and forest, passing to the right of huge morainal mounds hiding South Maude Lake. What's left of Beatty Glacier is still a thrilling sight below the shapely peak of Mt. Beatty. A steeper pull up a forested knoll reveals the classic view of Maude Lake and North Kananaskis Pass backdropped by Mts. LeRoy and Monro, "a desolate lake surrounded by bare cliffs and the awful solitude of that halfway belt which has neither the beauty of the green valleys nor the grandeur of the great snowfields", said Wilcox. Palliser called it "our little tea-kettle lake".

The trail follows the west shore to the northwest corner, where a line of cairns leads you into the windswept passage between Mts. Beatty and Maude. Back in 1901 Wilcox was still running, along the muddy shore and over snowbanks, finally gaining the pass at the mind-boggling hour of 4 pm! I bet he rued not bringing his camera.

Left: Turbine Canyon.

Opposite: The classic view of Maude Lake and North Kananaskis Pass. Through the gap are Mts. LeRoy and Monro.

OPTION

Haig Glacier trail 5 km from campground, height gain 533 m, high point 2728 m. The skier's trail to Haig Glacier is a fairly strenuous slog across moraines.

Walk down to Turbine Canyon and find the new trail on the *east* bank of the creek issuing from Haig Glacier moraines. Unlike the old west bank trail, this one climbs some distance from the creek in trees, reaching the moraines via a grassy draw. Look behind. Already there's a pretty good view of Lawson Lake and Mt. Beatty.

Follow cairns across smooth mounds of white bedrock to Haig Creek. Unlike what is shown on the topo map, the glacier has retreated and is now locked behind high rock walls penetrated by a gorge cut by the glacial stream. Below the gorge the waters slow down and make plaited patterns across an alluvial flat, then gathering together and picking up speed, pass under a rock arch and shoot out into space above a 300 m-high cliff.

Eclipsing this wonder of nature is the improbable sight of two huts, five minutes walk away across the bridge and up the broad ridge opposite. This is not a teahouse, but a CODA training facility for X-C ski racers.

In the footsteps of skiers who have stomped out the trail, continue up the ridge above the huts, then turn left and traverse a lateral moraine under Mt. Jellicoe. The way is undulating but trending uphill. One hour from the huts, the trail drops to the Haig Glacier at about GR205189. While the Haig appears safe compared to such crevassed horrors as the Athabasca, casual wandering can be dangerous. I know of someone who almost disappeared down a moulin. Also, don't try following ski tracks as you're liable to be set upon by irate skiers wielding ski sticks. I recommend ending the walk on the moraines. This higher vantage point gives you astonishing views back to Lawson Lake on the bench and ahead to Mts. Sir Douglas, Robertson and French towering over the Haig Icefield.

102 INVINCIBLE LAKE — map 15

Long day hike
Unofficial trails & route, creek crossings
Distance 6.8 km from trailhead
Height gain 707 m from trailhead
Height loss 106 m
High point 2362 m at ridge
Map 82 J/11 Kananaskis Lakes

Access: Kananaskis Lakes Trail (Hwy.) at North Interlakes parking lot. Via Three Isle Lake trail #99 at Invincible Creek crossing.

This is a strenuous haul over a ridge into the secluded valley west of Mt. Invincible, which has no easy way in. If you can't navigate without signposts, don't go. Leave it for the connoisseurs!

To the ridge At Invincible Creek stay on the fire road which crosses the creek slightly upstream of the official trail. Just after the first left-hand bend keep left (steep shortcut to right). At the next left-hander, turn right onto a rougher road (shortcut comes in from the right) and follow it uphill. Cross a horizontal road. Just after your road bends left and becomes impassable take to the hillside above.

Climb straight up. Consider the alternative: a messy traverse above Invincible canyon with slabs, deadfall, dense trees and dense undergrowth to contend with. So up the slope it is, with no grumbling please. Pick your way through the ruin of a forest extending all across the hillside to the left (hence the fire road). Tree skeletons contrast strangely with lush green grass. Even stranger is the eerie flute music made by wind blowing among the dead white branches. After a solitary crag is passed, the slope tapers to a ridge and curves around to the west, levelling off. The dead trees end at a grassy notch with cairn (about GR270128).

The ridge is a very fine vantage point for Upper Kananaskis Lake and the mountains to the south. Best of all, you can look into Invincible valley. Unfortunately, without climbing higher, the lake remains hidden by Mt. Nomad—the mountain that stands alone in the angle of the two forks.

To Invincible Lake As long as you're going the same way as they are, animals generally pick the best line. After all, they've had thousands of years to get it right. So it is here. From the cairn, elk have made a pretty good trail down the steep north slope of the ridge into the west fork. It takes a diagonal line from right to left, lower down crossing a shale slope, then a wider scree slope before fading out on grass near valley bottom. Jump the creek and walk up easy-angled grass to the lake.

Long and bluish, Invincible is bounded on the west by scree and a line of sombre cliffs, and on the east side by a grassy terrace under little Mt. Nomad (2536 m), an easy scree bash. It was named as recently as 1995 by 'The Grand Fleet Expedition' (alias Calgary's 144th Lake Bonavista Sea Venturer Company), which in 1991 climbed a few of the ship mountains to commemorate the 75th anniversary of the Battle of Jutland. It is, of course, named after a destroyer sunk in the battle. In fact, the whole valley is enclosed by mountains named after ships that sank. To save you hours of research, two sunken ships are still available for future nominations: HMS Defence and HMS Ardent (discounting HMS Queen Mary, there already being a peak named after the Queen, after whom the Battle Cruiser was named).

The alternative to Mt. Nomad is to cross the low ridge beyond the lake into the head of the north fork for hours of pleasurable wandering in the meadows below Mts. Warspite and Invincible.

Bottom: #103, Upper Kananaskis River Viewpoint. Upper Kananaskis Lake backdropped by the Elk Range and Elk Pass.

Top: #102, Invincible Lake and unnamed ridge.

103 UPPER KANANASKIS RIVER VIEWPOINT — map 15

Day hike
Unofficial trail & route, creek crossing
Distance 7.5 km from trailhead
Height gain 500 m from trailhead
High point 2225 m
Map 82 J/11 Kananaskis Lakes

Access: Kananaskis Lakes Trail (Hwy.) at North Interlakes parking lot. Via Three Isle Lake trail (#99) at Invincible Creek.

The promontory overlooking the forks of Upper Kananaskis River is one of the very best vantage points in the park, discovered back in 1916 by the Boundary Survey who set up a camera station called Lyautey N on the point. Getting there requires careful routefinding over rough and complicated terrain, a challenge to anyone who's just completed Map Reading Level 1. If you've the energy it can be combined with the ridge section of #102. Bring binoculars.

At Invincible Creek stay on the fire road that crosses the creek slightly upstream of the official trail. Continue along the fire road, keeping left everywhere, to its end at the bottom of a firebreak zooming up the hillside.

Climb the break to a small meadow. From a cairn at its top left-hand corner, a trail heads left to the edge of a steep bank—cairn and blazes—then turns uphill and ends near treeline on an avalanche slope. Memorize this spot for the return journey. Has anyone built a cairn yet?

Using fragmented game trails, traverse left across a rough mix of talus, grass and shrub until you are able to drop a little into the head of a tiny creek. The promontory's complexity of knolls and sinks is best handled by heading west up the draw of the creek, aiming for the low point between the promontory and the slopes of the mountain to the right. Only then head south along a ridge to the camera station cairn at GR256114 on the point.

To anyone plodding along Three Isle Lake trail Mt. Lyautey appears a hugely complicated massif, but from this viewpoint you're finally able to sort out what's going on, such as which top is the true summit. Another highlight is a rare view of Upper Kananaskis Lake backdropped by Elk Pass and the Elk Range. Best of all, you can follow route #101 from start to finish as it climbs onto the bench to Lawson Lake, then slips through the gap between Mts. Beatty and Maude to North Kananaskis Pass. With binoculars you can even follow the route onto the Haig Glacier. To the right of Mt. Jellicoe is a tantalizing glimpse of the glacier between Mts. French and Smith-Dorrien where the Upper Kananaskis River plummets from its source in strings of waterfalls.

All this and larches, too.

Cairn on the point built by the Boundary Survey in 1916.

104 INDEFATIGABLE — map 16

Day hikes
Official & unofficial trails
Distance 2.5 km to end of official trail
Height gain 503 m
High point 2225 m
Map 82 J/11 Kananaskis Lakes

Access: Kananaskis Lakes Trail (Hwy.) at North Interlakes parking lot. Via Three Isle Lake trail (#99).
Also accessible from #88, Gypsum Quarry.

If you had to choose only one trail in Peter Lougheed Provincial Park, this should be the one; the views of both Kananaskis Lakes will have you reaching for your camera at every twist and turn. Naturally, the most spectacular views are from Mt. Indefatigable, though, in my opinion, the alpine meadows of Indefatigable Outlier are no less thrilling. Wherever you go, payment is exacted in the shape of demanding climbs.

Official trail Head north across the isthmus on Three Isle Lake trail. Shortly after the fire road swings left turn right onto Indefatigable trail. After easy preliminaries through pine forest, the trail climbs up the left side of a ridge, a dry, dusty treadmill up rocks and shales. Only when sufficient sweat has been wrung from your brow does the trail swing right onto a promontory with bench for a well-earned rest. This is the superb Wendy Elekes Viewpoint.

Continue more easily up the ridge between a gully on the left and the eastern escarpment. As Upper Kananaskis Lake falls astern, Lower Kananaskis Lake comes into prominence and the whole of the Opal Range. On your left rises the south summit of Mt. Indefatigable which is mainly of interest to summiters who can pick out the route. Where the trail levels two narrow trails take off up the hill, the second at a sign urging you to stay on the official trail. Both lead to Indefatigable Outlier. But why not bag another viewpoint? Continue on the official trail to its end at a bench.

Upper Kananaskis Lake from Elekes Viewpoint.

GOING FARTHER
Mt. Indefatigable South 2646 m add 1.3 km, height gain 933 m from trailhead. Did you know Walter Wilcox made the first ascent in 1901 after lunch? The fact is Indefatigable's south summit is nothing more than a strenuous walk up steep slopes. There's nothing to be scared of unless you count the final two hundred metres, which are slightly exposed and entirely optional.

The starting point is Indefatigable trail at the top of the ridge. As soon as the official trail levels, turn first left onto a narrower trail trending uphill through spruce, larch and heather. At a flat stretch an arrow made of branches laid on the ground points you up an even narrower trail to the left. Follow it through a glade to flagging, then either follow flagging or the trail to its left that the flagging joins higher up. This gets you started up a broad grassy ridge.

231

Initially the trail veers right (view of Indefatigable Outlier), but after the gully on the left dies out, swings left across grass to another broad ridge. Look for it crossing patches of shale.

Toil up the new ridge on grass. When the ridge steepens, becoming rocky, the trail enters a shallow scoop on the left and splits, the easier option climbing diagonally right to left across the scoop on good firm rubble. Top out on the south ridge at a cairn.

Ahead is a view to die for: Upper Kananaskis Lake with a backdrop of blue mountain shapes receding into the distance. When the sun is west of south it puts a glitter on the water and a shine on the icefields and nevés about Mt. Joffre. Farther to the right you can pick out the routes to Aster Lake, Three Isle Lake and Invincible Lake, and identify such notable peaks as the Royal Group and Sir Douglas.

The view doesn't change much as you plod up a low-angle scree ridge to the repeater station (boxes and aerial). Either call it a day or carry on to the true summit across Wilcox's "several hundred yards of knife edge". It certainly gives you a taste of the moderately difficult scramble between the two peaks: a dramatic narrowing, a drop on the right, scree and slabs on the left, a sudden feeling of exposure. After setting up his tripod Wilcox found no room to stand behind his camera and "had to focus and expose plates by a method adapted to such emergencies".

Opposite:
Top: One of K Country's greatest views: Upper Kananaskis Lake from the easy south ridge of Mt. Indefatigable South. Prominent among the mountain shapes are Mt. Sarrail and Mt. Joffre (far right).

Bottom: The trail to Indefatigable Outlier at the seasonal pond. Note the grizzly diggings. In the background is Indefatigable Outlier (right) and to its left the col accessing Gypsum Tarns.

Indefatigable Outlier 2484 m add 1.8 km, height gain 762 m from trailhead. A less strenuous option is Indefatigable's eastern outlier at GR298132, a good choice if you love flowery meadows. This is also the cross country route to Gypsum Quarry.

From behind the bench a trail sneaks up the hillside into the larch and glacier lily belt. Turn right at the next two T-junctions.

The trail traverses steep hillside to a meadow crammed with Valerians and Indian Paintbrushes all the colours of nail varnish. On the right is a useful side trail leading to a spring. Continue past a seasonal pond and up a draw as if making for the col between the outlier (on the right) and the north summit of Mt. Indefatigable (a moderately difficult scramble with a lot of loose rubble). A faint trail does, indeed, climb to the col at GR297329 which is the route to Gypsum Tarns and Gypsum Quarry (#88). The main trail, however, heads right, making for the south ridge of the outlier. It's here you'll find long-stemmed fleabanes that blur to a purple haze on hillsides dropping away to the escarpment edge—a wonderful sight never forgotten.

The trail peters out and the ridge, now covered by scree, rises more sharply above the drop-off and features dozens of unnecessary cairns constructed either by people with energy to spare or by a Scout group. The final summit cairn occupies an airy spot on the edge of the escarpment which here attains its greatest height. Added to Lower Kananaskis Lake and the Opal Range is a new view up the Smith-Dorrien Valley. Remarkably, the whole of route #88 can be traced from Gypsum Quarry through to Gypsum Tarns and up to the col below you.

Descent variations Walk down to the col. Turn left and descend a faint trail on the west side of the shaley gully to join your upgoing route. Another variation occurs after the traverse. Instead of turning left, go straight. Keep left (Mt. Indefatigable trail to right) and arrive back on the official trail at the sign.

105 RAWSON LAKE — map 16

Day hike
Official trail
Distance 3.9 km to lake
Height gain 305 m
High point 2025 m
Map 82 J/11 Kananaskis Lakes

Access: Kananaskis Lakes Trail (Hwy.) at Upper Lake parking lots. Via Upper Lake trail (#97) south shore section.

Since the second edition an official trail has been built to the beautiful jade lake under Mt. Sarrail. While grovelling in mud and moss is a thing of the past, the climb is still steep enough to make you sweat. No camping.

Turn off Upper Lake trail just west of Sarrail Creek waterfall. Almost straightaway you're into zigzags, climbing through musty old spruce forest. The angle eases for the last kilometre to the outlet and it's here, preferably from the other side of the creek, where you should push through to the shore for the classic view of the lake backdropped by Mt. Sarrail. The trail continues around the southeast shore below a wall of cliffs and ends in a thin strip of meadow. In

the shadow of the cliffs snowbanks linger until mid July, giving walkers the bonus of late blooming Alpine buttercups that appear to have been dipped in glossy yellow paint. More meadows at the head of the lake are reached by a faint trail across steeper side slopes.

OPTION
Ridge GR301064, 2392 m It doesn't look much from down below…. Start from the far end of the lake and climb 365 vertical metres at the forest edge. Above treeline is a spectacular piece of grassy ridge sandwiched between rock towers, so you can't walk too far in either direction. What you've come for is the fantastic view of Upper Kananaskis Lake.

Not the classic view. Looking back from the west end. Photo Alf Skrastins.

106 ASTER LAKE — map 15

Aster Lake. View from the east shore looking northwest.

Long day scramble, backpack
Unofficial trail
Distance 11 km from trailhead
Height gain 570 m from trailhead
High point 2292
Map 82 J/11 Kananaskis Lake

Access: Kananaskis Lakes Trail (Hwy.) at Upper Lake parking lots. Via Upper Lake trail (#97). Follow the south shore of Upper Kananaskis Lake for 5.3 km.

Aster Lake and the high glacial valleys under Mt. Joffre are not easy to get into. If you're hoping for an easy park trail with lots of zigs up the woody slopes of Aster Creek's west bank, you're out of luck, though I've known people who've given the slope a go, usually on the descent, like Henry Bryant in 1901.

Unaccountably, the trail takes a thrilling line up the east bank, crossing scree slopes poised above cliffs that aren't for anyone whose legs turn to jelly in such places. To steep slopes and narrow trails add navigational problems.

To Hidden Lake Follow the south shore of Upper Lake trail to the Hidden Lake turn-off marked by a directional sign indicating Upper Lake trail. Before Joe Kovach cut the trail in 1945 (October 12th to be precise), access from the shoreline to Hidden Lake was described by Walter Wilcox as "an hour of the most difficult bush work I have ever seen". Of course, he started from the shore of the original lake, which was a lot lower down in 1901. He noted that Aster Creek, which travels underground east of the lake, burst forth in a spring quite close to where the Kananaskis River also emptied into the lake. Unfortunately, all this interesting stuff is now under water. So you turn left on Kovach's trail, cross a meadow and follow the overflow channel to a mess of driftwood at the shore.

Hidden belongs to the bathtub class of lakes. When full to the brim a bushwhack is required to reach the extreme south end. When empty (in the fall usually), you can slop across mud flats blotchy with scarlet cepepods. In such conditions, Aster Creek splays across the flat to a tiny holding pool from which a tail of water escapes and swirls counterclockwise down a mud hole to the underground. Interesting!

To Fossil Falls viewpoint A good steep trail starts between blazed trees and climbs the first forested step. From the top at GR282065 is a view back to Hidden Lake and forward to Fossil Falls, still a kilometre away across rough ground. Should you go there, don't emulate Wilcox and Bryant by trying to rejoin the 'goat' trail from the falls. The gully, sadly, was the scene of a recent fatality.

The headwall At GR282065 the trail turns left uphill, then crosses low-angle scree to a gully with water. Tighten boot laces, adjust packs and stagger up the right bank of the gully below thin waterfalls coursing down the slabs and cliffs of Mt. Sarrail. Cut right to below a rock island. Endure a few metres of powder scree, then head diagonally left up a ramp to reach the top of the island. A right turn up a corner gets you onto the proper traverse line. (If you want, continue flailing up scree and join the traverse to the right of the island hours later.)

Traverse much steeper scree (and one slab), then climb onto the first of those hanging scree slopes. Another climb leads to hanging scree slope number 2 with cliff bands peeling off immediately below the trail. It's here, going down, where the exposure grabs you by the throat.

The trail continues its amazing line, descending to much less vertiginous ground at a boulder field. Cross a creek, climb up the right bank, then traverse below a waterfall. A short scramble gains you a grassy terrace. Climb the cliff above via the dirty black gully. From the top (a talus slope) is a remarkable last view of Fossil Falls and the headwall and a first view of Warrior Mountain and Waka Nambé up ahead.

To Aster Lake The trail dips into the trees. The contrast is astonishing, the savagery of the headwall replaced by the beauty of alpine meadows with flowers, larch and spruce; a hugely complicated terrain of miniature ribs and valleys all sloping in a southeast to northwest direction. People getting lost have made a surfeit of trails.

The first feature you come to is a seasonal pond with a dazzling glacial backdrop. Follow a trail along the right bank and across a meadow down the centre of which dribbles Foch Creek, a tiddly little thing you can step over. Climb over a rib. Cairns on the left side precede a T-junction. Turn right (trail to left blocked by branches). Almost immediately turn off left down a miniature rock band—two trails to choose from—and cross a miniature creek running through one of the miniature valleys. Wend slightly left into a parallel valley, dry at this point (though just upstream a small waterfall is available for filling water bottles). At two cairns turn right and descend the dry draw towards Aster Creek. At three cairns turn uphill.

This final climb up the left bank of Aster Creek is alternately flat and scrambly. If you're a sucker for pools and waterfalls like me, you'll be continually rushing over to the creek to see what it's doing. In 1916 the Boundary Survey made a blunder compounded ever since by every edition of the topo map. They named lower Aster Creek after a trifling tributary.

Aster Lake's surroundings are spectacular. Nearly all the mountains you can see: Sarrail, Foch, Lyautey and Warrior were first climbed in July 1930 by a woman, Katie Gardiner, with guide Walter Feuz. Disappointingly, the lake is an unattractive grey colour from glacial silt deposited by the braided streams of the gravel flat. Another surprise is the lack of available campsites unless you've come equipped with a

Opposite: The headwall. These photos should help you decide whether this trail is for you.

Simmons Beautyrest mattress. Add to this katabatic winds blowing nightly off the Mangin Glacier, shaking the tent like a worrying terrier and you'll agree you've had better campsites.

But back to Walter Wilcox. While Wilcox was getting off a few photos of Fossil Falls, Bryant wandered off and climbed a gully to join today's access. Wilcox followed later and independently of each other they wandered all over the meadows, although only Wilcox ventured up to the lake "half a mile long at the base of a long glacier". So Wilcox was the first discoverer.

HALF DAY OPTIONS

Route #107 Stop off at the twin tarns or climb to the viewpoint for Waka Nambé.

Option A Ninety years after Wilcox was here, the Mangin Glacier has retreated, leaving the upper valley a barren place of gravel flats and braided streams, glacier-scoured rock and interminable moraines. Not too much here for the walker, but the view of Mt. Northover is spectacular.

The alpine meadows below Aster Lake. The seasonal pond backdropped by Mt. Marlborough. Photo Alf Skrastins.

Option B The valley upstream of two cairns yields an unexpected windfall: a bright blue moraine lake under Mt. Marlborough. En route pass a ranger cabin which is good to know about in case of accident, though I can't guarantee it will be manned.

Option C Combine the tarn under the great combed cliffs of Mt. Lyautey (at about GR270057) with a tour of Aster Creek to the ultimate drop-off at Fossil Falls. This is karst country where exciting things happen. For instance, stand on the pebbles shelving into the pool where the dry draw intersects Aster Creek at GR274047 and listen! Under your feet is the loud rumble of a subterranean waterfall, presumably the waters of the draw charging through an underground labyrinth and passing *below* Aster Creek to emerge who knows where?

Opposite: #107. Climbing the scree scoop to Northover col. Below are the twin tarns and pass GR252041 (centre left), which make a good half-day trip from Aster Lake. The white fang of Mt. Joffre (3450 m) is the highest peak between Mt. Assiniboine and the U.S. border. To its left the glacier is a climber's route to the Pétain Glacier. Photo Alf Skrastins.

107 NORTHOVER RIDGE — map 15 (ASTER LAKE TO THREE ISLE LAKE)

Backpack, scramble
Unofficial trails & route, creek crossings
Distance 10.5 km
Height gain 620 m from Aster Lake
Height loss 666 m
High point 2845 m
Map 82 J/11 Kananaskis Lakes

Access:
From the south via terminus of Aster Lake trail #106 at Aster Lake.
From the north via Three Isle Lake trail #99 at Three Isle Lake.

Waka Nambé.
Photo Alf Skrastins.

Northover Ridge is to Jasper's celebrated Skyline Trail what Smirnoff is to any other vodka, or so the ad goes. It is magnificent! Don't thank me for telling you about it; thank Alf Skrastins who first traversed the ridge in 1979 and brought it to everyone's attention in the much lamented Foothills Wilderness Journal. (As far as I can ascertain, the Boundary Survey in 1916 just visited the northwest tip to set up a camera station.) Combine it with route #99 (or routes #100 and #101) to make the best backpacking trip in K Country.

Between editions a trail has developed. So is it easier? Only in some places. The trouble is, there's no actual scrambling where you can cling to comforting rocks. The ridge is as narrow and as airy as it ever was. Don't go if you're a klutz with two left feet or are bothered by heights. Know how to read grid references—your life depends on it. Wait for good conditions and pick a relatively calm day.

To Northover col Wade Aster Creek (usually at the outlet), and follow the north shore trail onto a grassy bench offering a first view of Mt. Joffre. At talus return to the flat and cross the creek issuing from the glaciated pass to the east of Mt. Northover. Ahead is a knoll with trees, stepping off point for the grassy slope above. Climb the slope from right to left, aiming for a scree gully at GR256037, where cairns mark the start of a good trail up the right bank. From this high vantage point you can see beyond all those interminable moraines to the glacier snaking through a gap into the wild country of the Elk.

> **DETOUR to Waka Nambé viewpoint**
> Follow the main gully all the way to the high col northwest of Warrior Mountain, or better still, clamber up the ridge to the south for a close-in view of the curious peak Waka Nambé, which translated means Great Spirit Thumb or Hand of God. Shaped like a clenched fist, it overhangs Joffre Creek 1200 m below.

A short way up the gully the trail turns right up a more confined draw towards the pass at GR252041. High up, the trail traverses some horrible slab and cement shale, all of which can be avoided by a simple walk up the draw bottom on scree, then snow to the pass. A sign reads "Height of the Rockies", here represented by a hanging valley with two tarns. A pass implies you can travel through to Joffre Creek and while I know someone's who's done it, I can guarantee you'll be petrified.

Bottom: Northover Ridge. Descending from the high point to the northwest tip. Down below at lower right is col GR221065. The Royal Group is framed between Onslow Mtn. (left) and Defender Mtn. Photo Clive Cordery.

Top: Northover Ridge. Easy section behind them, the climbers are starting towards the high point. Photo Clive Cordery.

DETOUR to the twin tarns
It's an easy downhill stroll on scree and grass to two tarns backdropped by the Royal Group and Onslow Mountain. A few metres from the lower tarn the ground drops giddily away to the valley bottom where George Pocaterra did some gold panning. Streaked black and yellow and erupting here and there in crags, the Morder-like screes of Northover Ridge repulse. In the opposite direction the black rocks of Warrior Mountain and Waka Nambé are equally unattractive.

The northwest end of the ridge, looking back to the high point.

Continue along the upper trail (easily regained from the pass) that traverses the west face of Mt. Northover on scree. Keep high above an outcrop and enter a scree scoop with permanent snow patches at about half height. Plod up to the col immediately west of Mt. Northover at GR242054 and glory in the view shown on page 239.

Northover Ridge Gain the ridge to the west. At the top a narrow 10 metre stretch is a taste of the ridge to come: a three kilometre-long tightrope of scree and shattered rock poised between the cliffs and nevé of Northover Glacier, and scree slopes plunging over 1200 m (for you imperialists, that's nearly 5,000 ft.) into Joffre Creek. At first, though, the rolling rounded ridge and the thickness of the ice buffer the drops on either side.

The easy stretch ends at GR232062. WARNING! Don't think for one minute you can exit the ridge before the col at GR221065. Presumably unable to read grid references, enticed by a first view of Three Isle Lake or perhaps intimidated by the ridge ahead, some people have rushed off down the alluring side ridge at GR232062, which traps you in its fatal embrace. Slips on ice lower down have resulted in injuries and one fatality. I don't want this to happen to you. So ignoring the false trail, *keep left at GR232062, following a line of cairns* built in 1994. As you pass add a rock.

The ridge narrows, rising elegantly to the high point. Where nevé is replaced by cliffs you run into 'bad steps', vertigo-inducing places where careful footing is required or a bum shuffle if the pack is heavy. The excitement continues all the way down the other side to the northwest tip. Look out if you dare across the gulf of the Palliser River valley to the Royal Group framed between Mts. Onslow and Defender (Battle of Jutland destroyers nicknamed 'the Cripple and the Paralytic' by Rudyard Kipling). To the north, Sir Douglas rises above Three Isle Lake. To the south, the spectacular wall of the Great Divide is seen continuing past Mt. Joffre to the White River. Now there's a beautiful valley!

To Three Isle Lake All too soon the glorious ridge comes to an end and you drop about 150 metres down a well-beaten path to the col at GR221065. Turn right (north) and on glissadable scree, descend to meadows and finally to the flat valley floor of an unnamed stream arising from the glaciers of Northover Ridge. Follow it out to Three Isle Lake, reached halfway along the south shore.

Turn right for the campground, en route passing the ranger's tent.

108 KING CREEK RIDGE — map 12

Day hike
Unofficial trail & route
Distance 2.5 km to summit
Height gain 731 m
High point 2423 m
Map 82 J/11 Kananaskis Lakes

Access: Kananaskis Trail (Hwy. 40) at King Creek day-use area.

The grassy ridge north of King Creek, also called Kiska tha Iyarhe 'Goat Mountain' by the Stoneys, offers a relatively easy climb to a fantastic viewpoint.

Looking up King Creek Ridge to the shapely second summit (right).

Start from the segment of old road on the north bank of King Creek, which means either hopping across King Creek or using the highway bridge. To the left of the cliffs lining the creek, a steep trail and variants wind up a messy slope of scree, rocks and trees—definitely the worse part of the whole route. Best to get it over with right at the start. On grassy hillside above, small cairns take over when the trail peters out and guide you onto the south end of the ridge. Across the gulf of King Creek canyon the mountain shaped like soft whipped ice cream is Mt. Wintour, named after the captain of the ill-fated HMS Tipperary that sank during the Battle of Jutland in 1916. Strangely, the ship is commemorated miles away across the other side of the Divide in B.C.

Turn north and follow a trail up the wide, reasonably-angled ridge of grass and spruce over a lower top to the summit cairn. Five minutes on there's a second summit with drop-offs on three sides, not a place to drop your apple.

All the way up you've been ogling the Opals' hacksawed ridge. Virtually all the first ascents were made during the 1950s, one of the last to fall being The Blade, that impressive gendarme on the south ridge of Blane. The best view, though, is reserved for the summit. Now you can trace route #109 up King Creek, and can look without obstruction to the west where an immense ocean of conifers extends past Kananaskis Lakes to the mountains of the Elk.

Optional King Creek return From between the two summits a sheep trail plummets down a grassy gully on the east side of the ridge into the north fork of King Creek. Follow the creek out to the forks and return via #109 to the parking lot.

243

109 KING CREEK, ABOVE AND BEYOND — maps 12 & 16

Short to long day hikes
Official & unofficial trails, routes,
creek crossings
Distance 1.6 km to forks,
12 km whole traverse
Height gain to forks 122 m,
N-S traverse 1006 m
High point at Gap/Elpoca col 2414 m
Map 82 J/11 Kananaskis Lakes

Access:
1. Kananaskis Trail (Hwy. 40) at King Creek day-use area.
2. Valley View Trail at Elpoca day-use area.
3. Valley View Trail at the bridge over Elpoca Creek. Use a parking area on the north side.
4. Valley View Trail at Little Highwood Pass day-use area.
NOTE: Valley View Trail and Hwy. 40 south of Kananaskis Lakes Trail are closed between December 1st and June 15th.

Though spectacular, King Creek canyon leads to better things a world away from interpretive trails: that wild country hidden behind the outliers of the Opal Range. With two vehicles, experienced mountain addicts can cross three passes between accesses 1 and 4 (the traverse), or cut off down

either Opal or Elpoca Creek to accesses 2 or 3. Or with one vehicle make a loop with Elpoca and Opal Creeks. Although I've indicated a few useful game trails, it's up to you to plan your own route through rough terrain where there's little possibility of meeting other hikers.

To the forks In the company of tourists head up King Creek canyon on interpretive trail. Right from the start the trail is forced back and forth across the creek via bridges for the first 800 metres. At the sign 'Above and Beyond' leave all this behind. Stream hopping becomes the norm to the forks where the canyon ends. After tantalizing glimpses of Mt. Blane between canyon walls, you're treated to a full Opal panorama from Mt. Hood through to Mt. Jerram.

GOING FARTHER
The traverse

The first objective is King/Opal pass (2332 m) at GR369171, which is gained by a miserable 4 km-long forest trek up the south fork. Follow the creek, crossing and recrossing where necessary. The final stretch is clear of trees and on rising over the top you're greeted by a remarkable view of Elpoca Mountain as shown on page 246.

Look into the 'Kananaskis Ram' country of Opal Creek. It's satisfying to know the progeny of Ernst Hanisch's three-legged ram are still following the old trails. If you haven't read this true story dating back to 1943 when the author was a POW at Camp 130, and which contains a heart-wrenching revelation and a hint of mysticism, run to your nearest bookstore while stocks last!

An option here is the grassy ridge to the west, worth climbing for the view. You can actually get quite high on Wintour before running into insuperable obstacles. If doing the traverse, descend easily into the head of Opal Creek valley, then round the head of it, aiming for the narrow gap of Opal/Elpoca Pass (2362 m) at GR378159.

About seven contours down the Elpoca side, traverse into the northeast fork under Elpoca's towering cliffs. Gain the low ridge to the right (west flank is meadow), then make a sometimes steep diagonal traverse across both heads of the southeast fork to Gap/Elpoca col at GR383129. Sensationally slung between Elpoca and Gap Mountains, it is, at 2414 m, the high point of the traverse. What a place to view Highwood Pass and Pocaterra Ridge!

The south side drop to Pocaterra Creek is steep. The usual route is the ridge poking out between shaley coal beds looked into by George Pocaterra and John Allan. There's even an adit somewhere. Make a beeline for Little Highwood Pass day-use area, seen between your feet, continuing on the same line when you run into spruce forest and the incline levels. As an aside, Pocaterra called Gap Mountain 'George' and Elpoca Mountain 'Paul' after his Stoney blood brother Paul Amos, but nothing ever came of this self indulgence.

Opal Creek descent The head of Opal Creek is a beautiful place of meadows, larches and spruce. Lower down, though, a shadow falls over the valley. Avalanche chutes follow one after the other all the way down to the drop-off place at Opal Falls. Where the right bank trail crosses the creek, either traverse south bank avalanche slopes about 30 metres up, or muddle through the valley bottom to the death place of the 'Kananaskis Ram' above the drop-off. Now what? Trust the sheep who have spent thousands of years perfecting routes around the impasse. Climb the sheep trail up the *east* bank avalanche slope.

The trail eventually cuts right to another avalanche slope. Descend, low down deking left through an unsuspected gap between cliffs into the head of a dry canyon, an awesome place of ruddy cliffs thrust vertically into columns. Still the trail continues, climbing up the edge of the left-hand cliff and around a slit to a tree blazed with a cross.

This marks the place where sheep and scramblers can slither down a stony gully to Elpoca day-use area. More safely, follow the scenic rim trail in a southerly direction, losing height gradually. Low down, beyond residual cliffs, circle left around a bog, then turn right and descend to Valley View Trail, reached about 300 metres north of Elpoca Creek at a place impossible to pinpoint.

Elpoca Creek descent Apart from the pass at GR378159, there's another of the same height, also reached by trail, at GR370155. From the first why not traverse the ridge to the second? The top (2493 m) is surprisingly narrow, being the apex of a rock band shaped like a hooped tent pole. Just west of the summit another alternative presents itself: the glorious, grassy, south ridge descending to the confluence at GR375146. From here a trail heads along the west bank to an open area overlooking the lower forks. Drop steeply, then turn west with the creek, traversing high grassy banks. When the grass ends drop to a creek level trail that can be followed out to access 3.

Top: #109. View from King/Opal Pass of the next
pass GR378159 and Mt. Elpoca. To the right of the
pass is the ridge 2493 m. Photo Ruth Oltmann.

Bottom: #110 Elbow Lake
and an outlier of Mt. Rae.

110 ELBOW LAKE & RAE GLACIER — map 17

Day hike
Official & unofficial trails
Distance 1.3 km to lake
Height gain 150 m to lake
High point 2105 m
Maps 82 J/11 Kananaskis Lakes,
82 J/10 Mt. Rae

Access: Kananaskis Trail (Hwy. 40) at Elbow Pass day-use area.
NOTE: this section of Hwy. 40 is closed between December 1st and June 15th.

WARNING! This gorgeous blue lake is incredibly popular. As you walk up the trail be alert for such dangers as fishing rods and tackle boxes, skis and poles, swinging Safeway bags, gung-ho mountain bikers and horse dung.

Lose the crowds by heading to the Rae Glacier or to other destinations off Big Elbow trail described in Volume 2. Tombstone Lakes, for instance, are usually accessed from Elbow Lake as a weekend trip with a night spent at Tombstone backcountry campground.

The trail (former OHV road, formerly historic trail) is smoothly gravelled for trainee walkers who are usually gasping by the time they reach the avalanche runout. Continue to the next left-hand bend. Almost unnoticed, the old forest trail—my preference—turns off to the right and heads straight to the campground on the south shore of Elbow Lake. Alternatively, follow the official trail over a forested rib to the southwest corner, the lake obscured at this point by sundry signs.

A circuit of the lake! Circling anticlockwise, wind through campsites to the forested east shore. Pass Rae Glacier turnoff and in meadow arrive at the provincial park boundary and Big Elbow trail where there's a view of Mt. Rae. Turn left, cross the infant Elbow on logs and return along the fabulous west shore below talus slopes shelving into translucent blue water.

A very foreshortened view of the Rae Glacier, showing the col between Mt. Rae and peak GR428089.

Rae Glacier

2.2 km from Elbow Lake, height gain 405 m. A visit to the easternmost glacier in K Country, located on the north face of Mt. Rae at GR423099 (and unmarked on the topo map), is a much more strenuous trip on unofficial trails.

With the skiers, you abandon the east shore trail about halfway along and on new trail head northeast to the creek issuing from Mt. Rae. Turn upstream. To avoid a mini canyon, the trail climbs the rib on the right to a viewpoint for Mts. Elpoca, Tombstone and Rae. Continue along the rib, then, crossing snow glades and tree ribbons, make a gradual descent to the creek. Walk up the right side on talus.

Where the creek turns left (the true source is nevé in the twin cirque to the east, another magnet for skiers), the trail climbs moraines straight ahead to the flat floor of the Rae Glacier. Likely, you'll bump into geology students from the University of Saskatchewan who have been gathering ice core and water samples from the Rae for nearly 20 years. Skiers will be making for higher slopes that steepen alarmingly below the col. This is not the route up Mt. Rae. OK?

111 LITTLE HIGHWOOD PASS — maps 17 & 16

Day hike
Unofficial trails & route, creek crossings
3.5 km to pass, 9 km right through
Height gain 396 m
Height loss 640 m
High point 2545 m
Maps 82 J/10 Mt. Rae,
282 J/11 Kananaskis Lakes

Above: Climbing the south side of Little Highwood Pass. See photo on page 251 for a view of the north slope.

Opposite: Tarn in Pocaterra Cirque. In the background is Mt. Arethusa and peak GR433073 climbed in Volume 2. Photo Alf Skrastins.

Inset: Pocaterra's cache.

Access:
1. Kananaskis Trail (Hwy. 40) at Highwood Pass parking lot.
2. Valley View Trail at Little Highwood Pass day-use area.
NOTE: This section of Hwy. 40 is closed between December 1st and June 15th.

The name is inaccurate and confusing, better applied to Grizzly Col surely, because Little Highwood Pass does not lie either within or on the boundary of the Highwood River drainage, but between the two forks of Pocaterra Creek! It separates Pocaterra Ridge from the backbone of the Elk Range.

Of course, if going right through, you'll need vehicles at both ends. Alternatively, make it a there and back trip from Highwood Pass, an easy ascent made more

difficult by taking in the 4th summit of Pocaterra Ridge. Or, combine with Pocaterra Ridge (#112) to make a loop from access 2 or a point to point to access 1. The least strenuous option is a ramble among the larches of Pocaterra Cirque. Know that snow lingers in the pass area until late July. Actually, snow is a bonus since it cuts out some of the scree slog.

South to north
To Pocaterra Cirque Set off along Highwood Pass Meadows interpretive trail. When it veers right, follow the meltwater channel in front of you to a large rock at the bottleneck. This marks the start of the trail that climbs over the forested ridge—go either way at a split—into Pocaterra Cirque at a picturesque tarn among the larches.

To the pass Walk up the edge of talus slopes (cairns) and pick up a trail heading right towards Pocaterra Creek. Cross and follow the creek to the left. When you stub your toes against the formidable east face of the Great Divide, turn right and slog up a stony draw with lingering snowbanks to the pass. Look back into Tyrwhitt Cirque. To the right of the very much steeper Grizzly Col, the east ridge of Tyrwhitt rises in profile, displaying a free-standing arch with an uncanny resemblance to a wishbone.

West fork of Pocaterra Creek Keeping right, descend into the west branch of Pocaterra Creek via the shallow gully at the demarcation of grey and brown rocks. Cross fans of nevé to the east bank of the stream where a ribbon of meadow provides fast, easy going among drifts of snowy anemones. Halfway down the valley is Rockfall Lake, formed when a large portion of the slope to the west slid and piled up in great mounds across the valley floor and halfway up Pocaterra Ridge opposite. Pick your way around the west shore and descend rubble into forest where the biggest boulders, bounding down the hillside, have landed. Scary thought.

Tiny blue pools mark the limit of easy travel and although less than a kilometre from home, why get enmeshed in some dreadful willow bush and deadfall surrounding the resurgent creek when you can have an easier time of it by traversing the more open slopes of Pocaterra Ridge to the right? Aim to cross Pocaterra Creek and Highway 40 opposite Valley View Trail.

DETOUR to George Pocaterra's Cache
About 500 metres west on Highway 40 at a yellow road sign, head into the bush towards Pocaterra Creek. Look for the 70 year-old cabin in a willowy clearing quite close to the creek.

112 POCATERRA RIDGE — map 16

Day hike
Unofficial trail & route, creek crossing
Distance 5 km to Little Highwood Pass,
10.5 km round trip
Height gain 1036 m N-S to pass
High point 2667 m
Map 82 J/11 Kananaskis Lakes

Access: Valley View Trail at Little Highwood Pass day-use area.
NOTE: Valley View Trail and this section of Hwy. 40 is closed between December 1st and June 15th.

The 'Kootenay Ridge', as Geologist John Allan called it in 1947, is a heavenly ridge walk where it's possible to pick off four tops named, even further back in time, 'the Pocaterra Peaks'. Scrambling is optional (the ridge is mostly grass), exposure is nil and you can escape from almost anywhere in the event of a thunderstorm. It is, though, a strenuous flog. Hike it in combination with #111 to make a loop. With two cars you can make it a one-way trip to Highwood Pass, also using #111.

North to south
Walk through to Hwy. 40. Cross and thrash through willow brush to Pocaterra Creek. It was named by a Dominion land surveyor who found a mining stake with George Pocaterra's name written on it on behalf of the MacKay & Dippie Coal Syndicate. The Stoneys were of the same mind; Wasiju Wachi tusin ta Waptan Ze means 'Crazy mischievous white man creek' or 'where this Easiju Wachi was taking a leak'.

But I digress. Cross, using fallen trees or the beaver dam if you're at the right place. Bearing right all the time, head up the ridge through menziesia bushes which gradually thin out as you climb higher into the coal

Peak 2 rising above the 1-2 gap.

belt. Emerge from trees onto a wide, grassy ridge with rocky outcrops bejewelled with clumps of alpine cinquefoil. Though beautiful and the sort of place one wishes could be transferred at a wave of the wand to the rock garden back home, it doesn't compare with the actual summit of peak 1 (cairn, surveyor's bench mark), whose west-facing slopes are packed with an incredible array of flowers. Having said that, you'll probably hit a bad flower year and I'll lose credibility.

Descend to the low point on the ridge where larch trees, spilling through the gap, make a soft carpet of yellow needles. At this point an intersecting game trail offers an escape route into the west fork of Pocaterra Creek. After one brief sortie above treeline, the ridge shakes off the last of the larches and climbs a steepening, narrowing ridge to peak 2 which is capped with an elegant cairn.

Drop to 2-3 gap. Peak 3 is, from either direction, a very easy walk that one is tempted to miss out altogether by traversing to the 3-4 gap. Should you, as a ridge walker, be guilty of such unnatural behav-

On second summit looking towards peaks 3 and 4. Above the figure is Little Highwood Pass and Mt. Tyrwhitt. In the background at extreme left is Highwood Ridge.

iour, pretend to be checking instruments that for a good many years have been measuring creep along the traverse line.

Peak 4 looks more difficult. Start off by walking along the east side of the horizontal section, then switch over to 'the sidewalk'. The cockscomb of rock can be bypassed on the east side by a narrow bench of scree and shale that, as is often the way in these mountains, slants up to the ridge beyond the rock. Alternatively, enjoy a mild scramble along the crest. A shale slope leads to the first of three tops. As you cross from one to another (scree), ultimately attaining the high point of Pocaterra Ridge, it becomes apparent that the formidable-looking rock bands seen from down below and that may have caused you some apprehension are merely north face facades.

At the summit a couple of descent routes present themselves. If making for Highwood Pass parking lot walk down the grassy, flowery south ridge into Pocaterra cirque. Otherwise, drop in on Little Highwood Pass by the rather steep west ridge and return by the west fork of Pocaterra Creek.

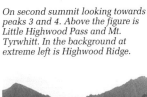

113 TYRWHITT MIX & MATCH — map 17

Day, long day hikes
Unofficial trails & routes, creek crossings
Maps 82 J/10 Mt. Rae,
82 J/11 Kananaskis Lakes

Access: Kananaskis Trail (Hwy. 40).
1. Highwood Pass parking lot, via #111.
2. Mt. Lipsett day-use area.
NOTE: this section of Hwy. 40 is closed between December 1st and June 15th.

Southwest of Highwood Pass is a compact group of ridges loosely connected to Mt. Tyrwhitt by a col. Geographically, their valleys are the headwaters of Storm Creek and should rightly belong in Volume 2, but here they are at the end of Volume 1. That's because the usual access is from Highwood Pass via route #111.

It's amazing the permutations that can be made with two ridges, two valleys, a pass and two vehicles. However you mix them up, be aware most options *are strenuous undertakings* with steep sections on grass, scree and snow.

113A Highwood Ridge 2708 m

GR422058, 1.3 km from access 1, height gain 498 m. Who can resist the summit looming over Highwood Pass parking lot? We know the Boundary Survey used it as a camera station called 'Highwood Ridge north' in 1916. And we know from an undated photo that George Pocaterra likely beat 'em to it.

Set off along Highwood Pass Meadows interpretive trail. When it veers right, follow the meltwater channel in front of you to a large rock at the bottleneck. This marks the start of the trail that climbs over the forested ridge into Pocaterra Cirque. From the high point strike up the ridge.

Above treeline, a craggy slope leads to the gently inclined mid section, where you can piece together bits of trail on meadows sloping down to the right. Follow the trail back to the crest for the final strenuous effort to—a rock band. The direct finish is

Highwood Ridge traverse. The southeast summit from the low point.

an exciting scramble. If it looks too intimidating, escape left to the broad southeast ridge, which offers an easy walk up grass to the summit cairn. Remember this traverse should you return this way.

OPTIONS FROM HIGHWOOD RIDGE
1. Highwood Ridge traverse add 5.3 km, extra height gain 152 m, height loss 850 m.

Head southeast along a remarkably straight grassy ridge, up and over two minor bumps, then up a longer rise to the other-end summit. Because your attention is not constantly on where to put your feet, you're free to admire the views. To the east you're treated to a parade of cirques, including Ptarmigan (showing the route up Mt. Rae) and Arethusa (showing the route over to Burns Lake), while ahead is the lovely country of the Highwood described in Volume 2. From the southeast summit look back at Highwood Pass. You, too, can take a photo *almost* identical to the one taken by Pocaterra, which archivists have unaccountably labelled 'looking down the Elk Valley'.

From the southeast summit Mt. Lipsett day-use area is in view. Either drop straight down or, easier on the quads, descend the south ridge to intersect option 2.

Top: Tyrwhitt Cirque as seen from the route to Little Highwood Pass. Grizzly Col at centre, Mt. Tyrwhitt to right, showing the arch.

Bottom: Grizzly Ridge, looking into Paradise Valley. Mt. Tyrwhitt at top left.

2. Paradise Valley add 5.7 km to access 2, height loss 712 m.

Head down the southeast ridge to the first dip, then descend a simple slope (grass, shale) into Paradise Valley, a local name in use pre-1947 but since forgotten. You'll be captivated by the astonishing green of the grass, short-cropped and watered by numerous riverlets. Lower down, where it grows as high as an elk's belly amid larch and spruce, cross to the west bank and find the game trail taking you out to Highway 40.

The trail deteriorates in the burnt-over area, but improves as it descends the rib between the two forks of Storm Creek to the confluence. Cross the left-hand creek into trees and traverse the lower slope of the ridge above. When trail and blazes peter out—maybe I missed something—head for the highway, aiming left of a pond and boggy meadow. Turn left and walk the asphalt a few metres to access 2.

113B Grizzly Col 2606 m

GR409050 3.2 km from access 1, height gain 472 m.

Set off along Highwood Pass Meadows interpretive trail. When it veers right, follow the meltwater channel in front of you to a large rock at the bottleneck. This marks the start of the trail that climbs over the forested ridge—go either way at a split—into Pocaterra Cirque at a picturesque tarn among the larches.

Walk up the edge of talus slopes (cairns). Instead of turning right as for Little Highwood Pass, round the ridge and turn left up a grassy draw into Tyrwhitt Cirque. As you pick your way among boulders, look up Mt. Tyrwhitt's east ridge to the wishbone arch which has also been likened to a vertebrae. Now for the col! Unless you're lucky enough to have snow, flounder up big rolling scree to the narrow gap between Tyrwhitt and its eastern outlier. While no one's yet met a grizzly face to face on the col, plenty of people see tracks in the snow leading down to Storm Creek.

OPTIONS FROM GRIZZLY COL

3. Grizzly Ridge add 400 m to ridge top, extra height gain 122 m.

Head east up mostly grass to the ridge top. With relatively little effort comes the reward of a view: Paradise Valley down below, and the full length of Highwood Ridge. Best of all you can pick out scramblers labouring up high-angle scree and slabs to the top of Mt. Tyrwhitt. Look for the elusive Alpine poppy before you retrace your steps. Alternatively....

Yearning for a ridge walk? No, I don't mean the connecting ridge over peak GR413055 to Highwood Ridge, which is for grade 2 scramblers with a taste for exposure. I'm talking about the comfortably broad, grassy, 3-km long southeast ridge that offers a high altitude alternative to option 4. Drop off the gable end into the west fork.

4. The west fork of Storm Creek add 6 km to access 2, height loss 610 m.

After the rigours of scree, it's heaven to step down what is normally easy-angled snow slopes into the valley between Grizzly Ridge and the immense barrier that is the Great Divide. In mid valley you run into krumholz ribbons *and larches,* and flowery meadows holding a tarn and tiny blue pond eyes, a lovely place presided over by Mt. Storelk (an ugly acronym that took 25 years to gain acceptance).

Below treeline keep left, hugging the bottom of Grizzly Ridge until you can see your way onto the rib between the two forks, where you can pick up option 2, taking you out to access 2.

5. Tyrwhitt Loop 11 km round trip, height gain 984 m, high point 2708 m at Highwood Ridge.

A convoluted route that allows you to visit almost everything in one trip. Follow option 5 down the west fork of Storm Creek. Round the southeast end of Grizzly Ridge into Paradise Valley and reversing option 2, drag yourself up Highwood Ridge to the summit, this climb coming late in the day when you're tired. Descend the north ridge (113A) to Highwood Pass parking lot.

Mt. Allan's Centennial Ridge. Looking across the north fork of Ribbon Creek to Ribbon Peak and Mt. Bogart.

THE MAPS

Key map

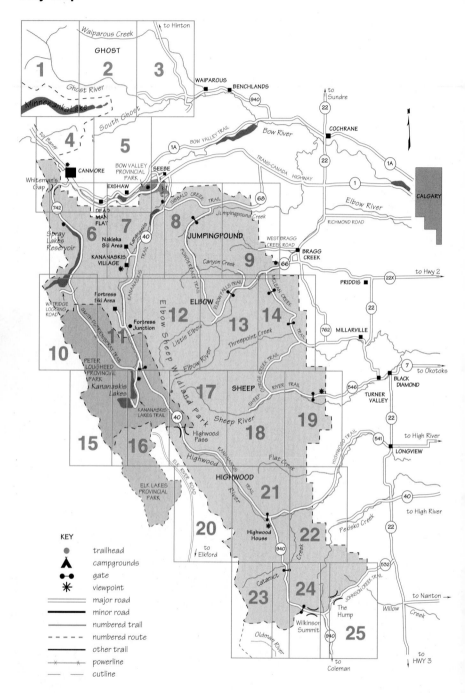

KEY

- trailhead
- ▲ campgrounds
- •▬• gate
- ✳ viewpoint
- ═══ major road
- ▬▬ minor road
- ──── numbered trail
- ------ numbered route
- ──── other trail
- ─✳─✳─ powerline
- ─ ─ ─ cutline

Map 1

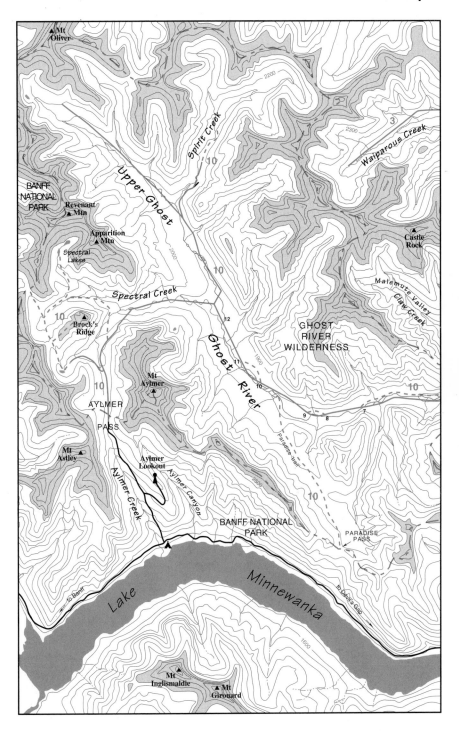

Map 2

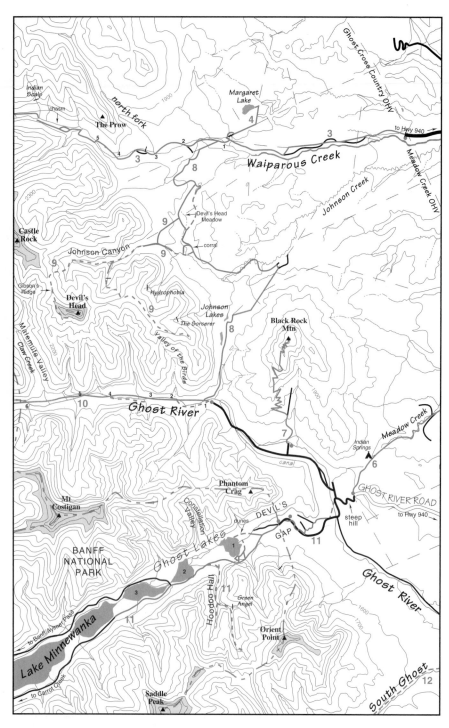

Map 3

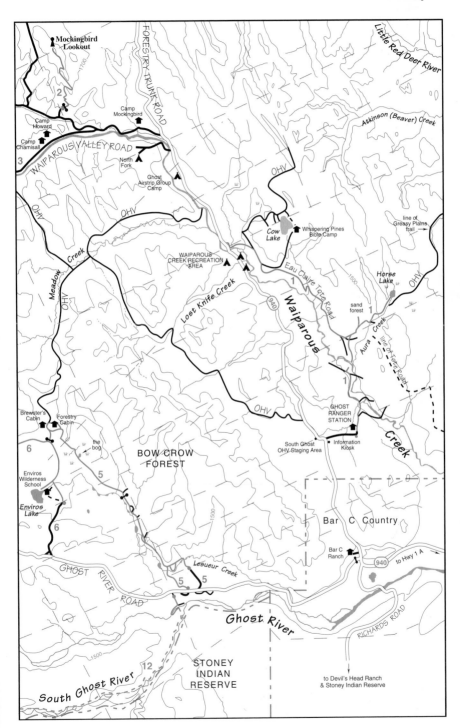

Map 4

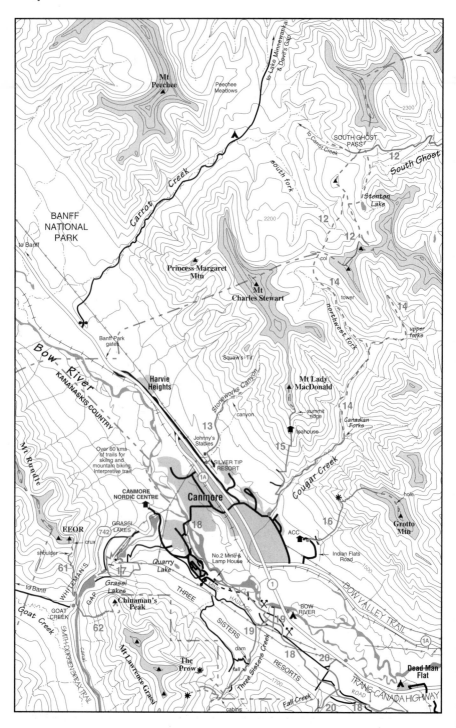

Map 5

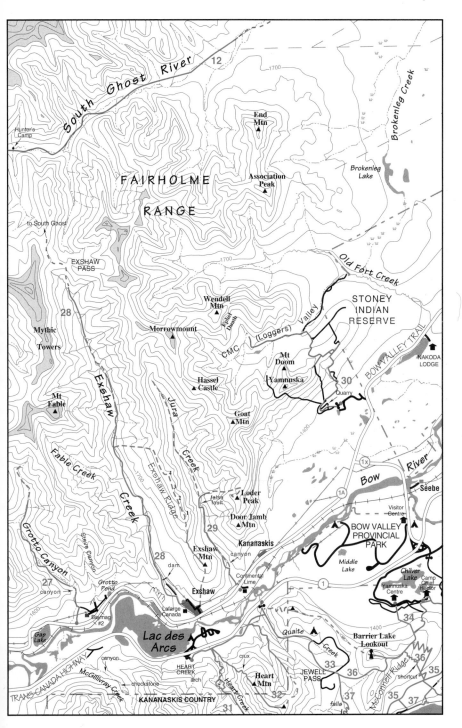

Map 6

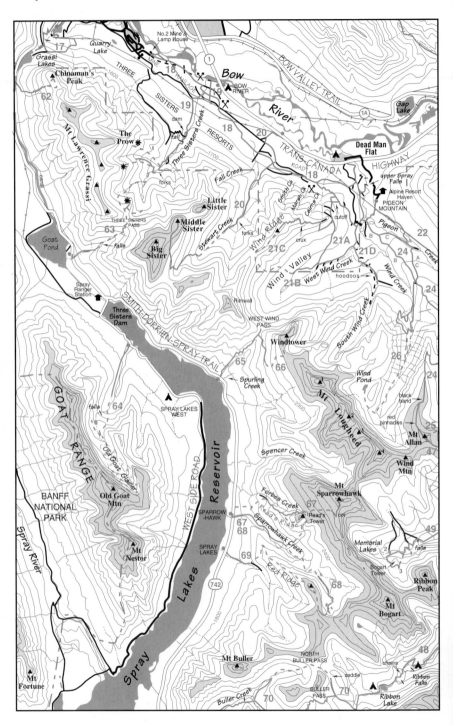

Map 7

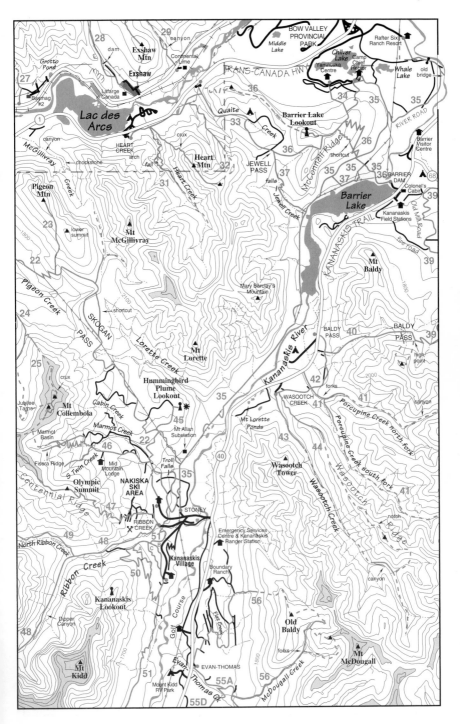

Map 8

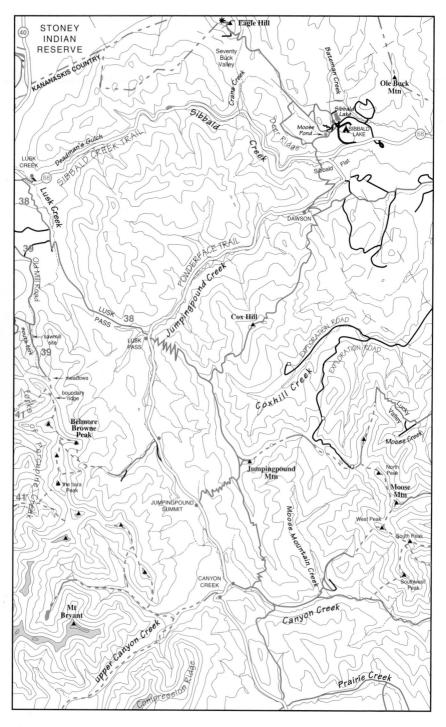

Map 10

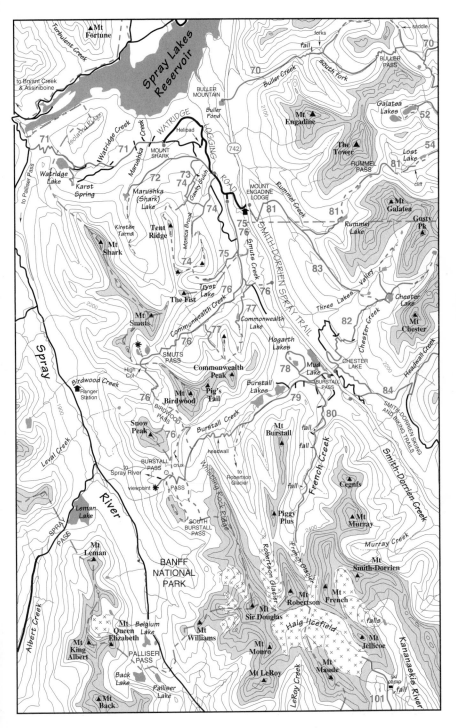

Map 11

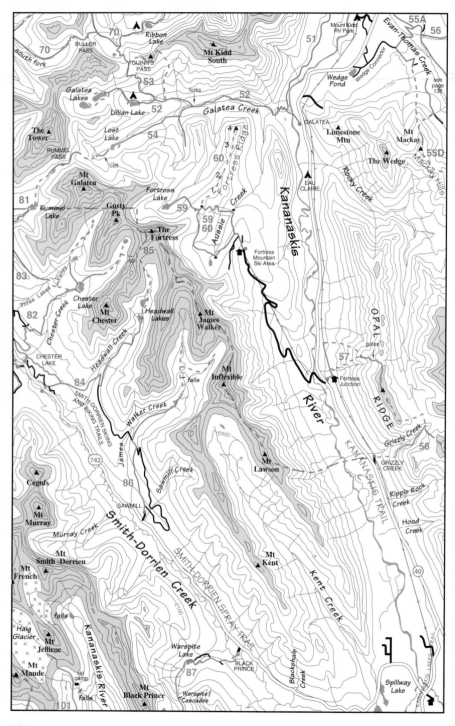

Map 12

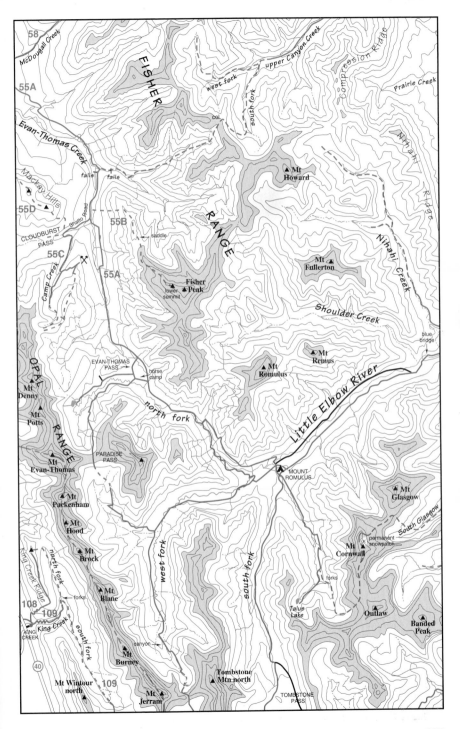

Map 15

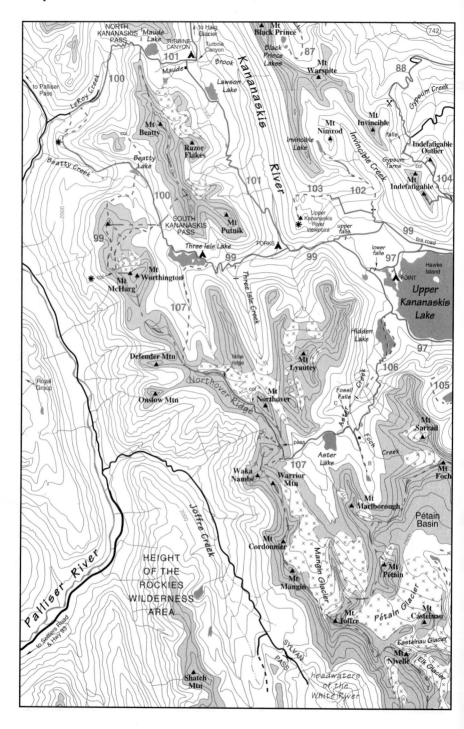

Map 16

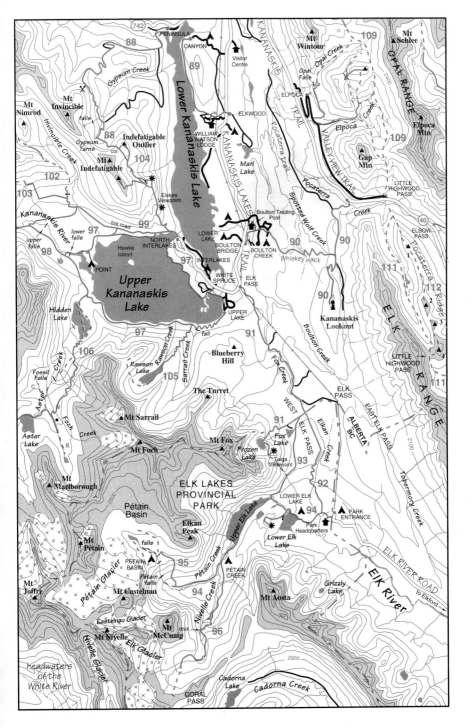

742
88
PENINSULA
CANYON
89
Visitor Centre
ELKWOOD
Mt Wintour
Opal Creek
109
Mt Schlee
109
OPAL RANGE
Gypsum Creek
Opal Falls
ELPOCA
Elpoca
Elpoca Mtn
Lower Kananaskis Lake
Mt Nimrod
Mt Invincible
falls
88
Indefatigable Outlier
col
104
Indefatigable Tarns
Mt Indefatigable
Gap Mtn
102
103
Elekes Viewpoint
Marl Lake
Pocaterra trail
VALLEY VIEW TRAIL
LITTLE HIGHWOOD PASS
Kananaskis River
fire road
99
Boulton Trading Post
Pocaterra
Spotted Wolf Creek
Creek
90
ELBOW PASS
40
lower falls
97
LOWER LAKE
BOULTON BRIDGE
NORTH INTERLAKES
Hawke Island
98
upper falls
KANANASKIS LAKES TRAIL
Lower Lake
BOULTON CREEK
90
Pocaterra Ridge
111
112
POINT
Upper Kananaskis Lake
97
INTERLAKES
WHITE SPRUCE
ELK PASS
Whiskey Jack
90
Kananaskis Lookout
Boulton Creek
Hidden Lake
UPPER LAKE
97
fall
491
Blueberry Hill
ELK PASS
ELK
106
Rawson Lake
Rawson Creek
Sarrail Creek
105
Fossil Falls
Aster Creek
The Turret
Fox Creek
WEST ELK PASS
RANGE
LITTLE HIGHWOOD PASS
111
Mt Sarrail
491
Fox Lake
ELK PASS
EAST ELK PASS
Foch Creek
Aster Lake
Mt Foch
Mt Fox
Frozen Lake
Taiga Viewpoint
93
ALBERTA
BC
Tobermory Creek
2100
Mt Marlborough
ELK LAKES PROVINCIAL PARK
Elkan Creek
92
Pétain Basin
Elkan Peak
Upper Elk Lake
LOWER ELK LAKE
94
Park Headquarters
PARK ENTRANCE
ELK RIVER ROAD
Mt Pétain
falls
95
Lower Elk Lake
Mt Joffre
Pétain Glacier
PÉTAIN BASIN
Pétain falls
Pétain Creek
94
PÉTAIN CREEK
Mt Aosta
Grizzly Lake
Elk River
to Elkford
Mt Castelnau
Niwelle Creek
96
Mt McCuaig
crux
Castelnau Glacier
Mt Niwelle
Elk Glacier
Niwelle Glacier
Headwaters of the White River
Cadorna Lake
Cadorna Creek
CORAL PASS
2000
2000

Map 17

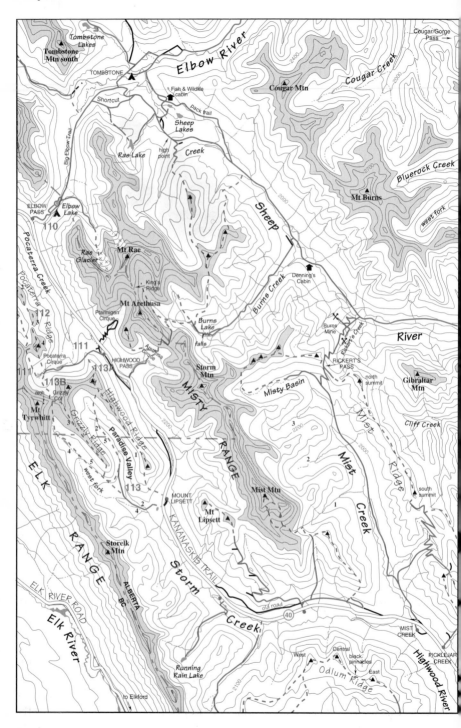

INDEX OF TRAILS

Index of trails